LAW'S HUMILITY

This book advances a philosophical account of a substantive, albeit less elaborated, variant of jurisprudential disagreement about which kinds of non-legal facts determine the content and the normative force of the law. At the most abstract level legal philosophers disagree about the proper methodology of jurisprudence. Opinions are divided as to whether the proper method of philosophical inquiry about law consists in refining our description of what a legal practice is or, conversely, in justifying the practice of law from a normative vantage point. Further downstream, the bulk of jurisprudential controversy centres on the concept or the nature of law. Debates in this domain are usually cast in modal or essentialist terms such that the main question becomes whether legal validity can be attributed to norms promulgated by morally wicked governments or whether by its essence law serves a moral aim.

Without suppressing the relevance of formal disputes about the methodology of jurisprudence or the nature of law, the content of the book focuses on what makes the grounds of facts about legal content and legal normativity philosophically contestable. For instance, two judges may converge in their interpretation of a particular statute or precedent but disagree about 'the content of the law' because they diverge in their beliefs about whether statutes and precedents are the sole determinants of legal content. Perhaps less commonly, disagreement may also erupt about the 'force of the law', namely, about what makes legal authority or a particular institutional arrangement practically compelling.

Philosophers of both a positivist and anti-positivist persuasion commonly refer to instances of this type of dispute about the grounding of a class of facts as 'theoretical disagreements'. Theoretical disagreement about the content and the force of the law is used as a term of art to be contrasted with empirical and doctrinal conceptions of legal disagreement commonly encountered in the context of legal advocacy, administrative and judicial practice about whether a legal rule applies to a particular circumstance. Whereas the latter type of disagreement is resolvable by consulting the appropriate legal materials (statutes, court rulings, executive decrees etc), the former type of disagreement invites us to inquire into what grounds the fact that a legal rule or principle is applicable in a given context or, respectively, what makes it the case that this rule or principle has a binding effect on its addressees.

Volume 11 in the series Law and Practical Reason

Law and Practical Reason

The intention of this series is that it should encompass monographs and collections of essays that address the fundamental issues in legal philosophy. The foci are conceptual and normative in character, not empirical. Studies addressing the idea of law as a species of practical reason are especially welcome. Recognising that there is no occasion sharply to distinguish analytic and systematic work in the field from historico-critical research, the editors also welcome studies in the history of legal philosophy. Contributions to the series, inevitably crossing disciplinary lines, will be of interest to students and professionals in moral, political, and legal philosophy.

Recent titles in the series

Volume 6: Law and Authority under the Guise of the Good
Veronica Rodriguez-Blanco

Volume 7: Shared Authority
Dimitrios Kyritsis

Volume 8: Private Law and the Value of Choice
Emmanuel Voyiakis

Volume 9: Freedom and Force: Essays on Kant's Legal Philosophy
Edited by *Sari Kisilevsky and Martin J Stone*

Volume 10: The Nature and Value of Vagueness in the Law
Hrafn Asgeirsson

Volume 11: Law's Humility: Enlarging the Scope of Jurisprudential Disagreement
Triantafyllos Gkouvas

Law's Humility

Enlarging the Scope of Jurisprudential Disagreement

by

Triantafyllos Gkouvas

•HART•

OXFORD • LONDON • NEW YORK • NEW DELHI • SYDNEY

HART PUBLISHING

Bloomsbury Publishing Plc

Kemp House, Chawley Park, Cumnor Hill, Oxford, OX2 9PH, UK

1385 Broadway, New York, NY 10018, USA

29 Earlsfort Terrace, Dublin 2, Ireland

HART PUBLISHING, the Hart/Stag logo, BLOOMSBURY and the Diana logo are trademarks of Bloomsbury Publishing Plc

First published in Great Britain 2021

A catalogue record for this book is available from the British Library.

Library of Congress Cataloging-in-Publication data

Names: Gkouvas, Triantafyllos, author.

Title: Law's humility : enlarging the scope of jurisprudential disagreement / by Triantafyllos Gkouvas.

Description: Oxford, UK ; New York, NY : Hart Publishing, an imprint of Bloomsbury Publishing, 2021. | Series: Law and practical reason ; volume 11 | Includes bibliographical references and index.

Identifiers: LCCN 2020052057 (print) | LCCN 2020052058 (ebook) | ISBN 9781509936502 (hardback) | ISBN 9781509945191 (paperback) | ISBN 9781509936526 (pdf) | ISBN 9781509936519 (Epub)

Subjects: LCSH: Law—Philosophy. | Jurisprudence. | Law—Interpretation and construction.

Classification: LCC K230.G59 A35 2021 (print) | LCC K230.G59 (ebook) | DDC 340/.1—dc23

LC record available at https://lccn.loc.gov/2020052057

LC ebook record available at https://lccn.loc.gov/2020052058

ISBN: HB: 978-1-50993-650-2
ePDF: 978-1-50993-652-6
ePub: 978-1-50993-651-9

Typeset by Compuscript Ltd, Shannon

To find out more about our authors and books visit www.hartpublishing.co.uk. Here you will find extracts, author information, details of forthcoming events and the option to sign up for our newsletters.

To Charlotte

Contents

Introduction

THERE IS NO royal way from semantics to ontology. Although in its generality this byword can be used as a term of censure against those of an anti-metaphysical sentiment, my aspiration is specifically geared to showing that law could be a fitting instance of this truism. Some would say that I am already assuming too much. There is no denial that language is law's primary vehicle of materialisation. Therefore, the semantic 'royalist' can argue, we shouldn't so readily dismiss the thought that language seems to point the way to law's reality. To what extent can the meaning of legal statements diverge from what their truthmakers are? At the same time, there is a long tradition of suspicion that law is not the kind of thing that can be distinctly normative in any robust sense. In the best case, a pessimist would retort, the fact that an action is legally required is verdictive[1] in the sense that it merely reports a conclusion as to what ought to be done, without being in itself a further reason in favour of that action. In the worst case, the same pessimist would lament that the normativity of legal requirements only piggybacks on moral reasons or values, but that there cannot exist a distinct source of legal reasons.

One can adduce numerous platitudes in support of both semantic royalism and normative pessimism. If there is anything self-evident about law, it is the fact that jurisprudential claims about what grounds legal facts always take on board predications of legal content. One need only accept the further premise that legal predications have propositional rather than expressivist content and there naturally emerges the metaphysical question of what in the world accounts for the truth of legal propositions. Moreover, it is the same propositional content expressed by legal claims that seems to premise its binding effect on further extra-legal conditions such as social acceptance, validation by external standards or a logical-pragmatic presupposition of bindingness.

My focus on cognitivist theories of law renders the treatment of legal disagreement across the semantic spectrum of legal discourse irredeemably partial. The sprawling expressivist theories of law, within and beyond the legal realist tradition, will be ostentatiously absent in the following exposition. On an expressivist understanding of legal statements, to understand what a legal utterance means is to understand what it is *to have* a peculiarly 'legal' thought.[2]

[1] To the best of my knowledge, Christopher Essert develops the most detailed account so far in this line of criticism; see Essert (2013).

[2] Kevin Toh provides the most semantically refined account of legal expressivism, which he further associates with HLA Hart's positivist project. According to Toh, an utterance of an (internal) legal statement is an expression of a conditional conative attitude by which the speaker displays

On this approach, it is the having or possession of the thought that calls for jurisprudential scrutiny rather than any extra-mental element that could serve as the object of legal representation. The exclusion of these views from the scope of my direct engagement is not an indication, on my part, of their irrelevance for regimenting deep disagreements in law, but a confession of their radical opposition to any robustly metaphysical account of the nature of such deep disagreements.[3]

The following chapters provide a gradual elaboration of the idea that jurisprudence is answerable to questions of ontological commitment both with respect to the truthmakers of legal propositions and the grounds of legal normativity. As it is commonly used, ontological commitment is a technical term, but this does not prevent philosophers from endowing it with potentially conflicting meanings. That being said, there is at least convergence in the acknowledgement of the Ockhamite flavour of this term. At this highest level of abstraction, ontological commitment is an achievement term in the sense that it can be associated with the score assigned to any metaphysical theory when judged for ontological parsimony.

The possibility of metajurisprudential inquiry into the grounds and normativity of law stands and falls with the existence of the object of such ontological commitments. This project is as frail as any project in lofty metaphysics and as resilient as any armchair or scientific confidence in a mind-independent reality.[4] Accordingly, this book lacks the resources but also the ambition to be a direct counter-argument to the possibility of dispensing with the existence of metaphysically secure truths at the fundamental level. This is still far away from arguing that legal entities are necessarily part of the world's layered fabric. There is room for arguing that legal categories are metaphysically shallow, yet the ultimate grounds of their truth-apt use are firmly grounded in hard facts about the existence of fundamental stuff, objects, structures or processes.

her willingness to act in a particular way on the assumption that others have similar or mirroring conditional commitments. See Toh (2005) and (2011).

[3] Assuming that expressivism is the most promising avenue to pursue in the semantics of legal discourse, there would be no further matter of *fact* about the grounds and the normativity of law than what is suggested by an account of what makes it the case that someone *thinks* that (or is in a mental state to the effect that) something is legally required (grounds) and that someone *thinks* that (or is in a mental state to the effect that) a legal requirement provides a reason to act accordingly (normativity). By sharp contrast, a cognitivist approach to the legal point of view treats the propositional contents of mental states about the existence and force of the law as the primary loci of metaphysical and metanormative inquiry. The latter contents are usually portrayed as truth-evaluable propositions whose identification makes essential appeal to *conceptual* representations.

[4] Karen Bennett provides a systemic overview of suspicious treatments of lofty metaphysics. She suggests that there are at least three varieties of anti-metaphysical theorising: *epistemicism*, *semanticism* and *anti-realism*. The epistemicist will concede that metaphysical verdicts can be informative, but will abstain from privileging any viewpoint over another. The semanticist will treat core instances of metaphysical discourse as merely verbal disputes centred on questions of description rather than existence. The most radical of all three variants is the anti-realist who will deny *tout court* any robust sense of truth-aptness for metaphysical discourse. See Bennett (2009: 39–42).

Behind the metaphysical centrality of predications of legal content, I plan to argue, lies an unarticulated but pervasive semanticist bias, namely that we can somehow draw conclusions about the structure of reality from the logical regimentation of its linguistic representation. What I intend to convey by using the term 'metaphysical centrality' is the misguided – as I intend to argue – assumption that the correspondence of legal truth to reality consists by logical fiat in its correspondence to legal facts, namely, facts about the existence of entities of a distinctly 'legal' kind (legal norms, legal rules, legal obligations, legal directives etc). If a legal philosopher wants to commit to more substantive metaphysical arguments about law, then she should ask what kind of non-legal facts ground legal facts. What remains available for lofty theorising can be either an exercise in descriptive sociology or modest conceptual analysis. There is no further question, the story goes, to be asked about the ontology of law that does not amount to espousing an immodest approach to metaphysics, at least from the perspective of general jurisprudence.

This will be the leitmotiv that will drive my argument in Chapters 1, 2 and 3. In Chapter 1, I will outline the virtues and inherent limitations of Dworkin's model of theoretical disagreement in law. This brief exposition is meant to smooth out the transition from the value-laden vocabulary of his argumentative prose to a more abstract articulation of the joints that connect legal thought and talk with the metaphysical impact of governance by law. In Chapter 2, I examine the relationship between legal facts and legal propositions from what I would like to refer to as the *verificans* point of view, namely, the point of view of what in the world makes legal propositions true. At first glance, this perspective appears to be nothing more than a theory of legal facts, namely, facts about the existence of legal norms or legal obligations and rights, the obtaining of which guarantees the truth of assertions of legal content. But this is precisely the assumption that I will try to challenge by replacing our familiar talk of legal facts with a more abstract talk about the truthmakers of legal propositions. I will defend this replacement by explaining how it allows jurisprudential theories with disparate ontological commitments but a common cognitivist ambition to account for the nature and grounds of legal truth.

In Chapter 3, I examine the relationship between legal facts and legal propositions from what I would like to refer to as the *verificandum* point of view, namely, the point of view of the shareable objects of the cognitive attitudes we hold vis-a-vis the content of the law of a particular legal system. This is perhaps a loftier way to talk about the propositional point of view or, less abstractly, the point of view of thinking about the law in truth-conditional terms. As I plan to show, truth-apt statements about what the law requires here or there need not be indexed to a normatively privileged point of view. In other words, instead of conveying practical information about what is obligatory or required from the point of view of the law, they convey metaphysical information about what counts as part of the content of the law of a given legal system. This constitutive (as I will call it) reading of legal statements offers a much more inclusive array of options with respect to how speakers carrying determinate jurisprudential commitments can articulate their understanding of what legal practices contribute to the content of the law.

The same story will have a counterpart in the discussion about the relation of law to practical normativity. Again, the origin of my objection is metatheoretical as the problem that I see arising stems from what I believe to be a metanormative bias in favour of measuring the eligibility of something as normatively compelling by testing it for its reason-giving capacity. Whereas I do not intend to question the close connection between practical normativity and guidance by reason-giving considerations, I do intend to scrutinise its scope of application and more specifically whether and how legal facts, if they exist, can be normatively relevant by means of being reason-giving. My suspicion is that at least part of what explains the association of legal normativity with reason-giving is the intuitive pull of a currently pervasive metanormative view of practical normativity. According to this view, a consideration or fact is a full-fledged *reason* for an agent to perform an action or adopt an attitude if this consideration or fact *influences* or bears upon the selection of a particular course of response, can serve as an *explanation* of those behavioural responses that exemplify this act- or attitude-type and, finally, can operate as a *standard of appraisal* of the agent's exercise of her rational capacity.

Chapters 5 and 6 concern the restrictive effect of this association of practical and, consequently, legal normativity with the influential-explanatory-evaluative function of reasons. In Chapter 5, I will take the liberty of venturing a digression in the broader discussion about the different roles that reason-giving considerations are assigned in different normative contexts (normative bearing or influence, evaluation and explanation). More precisely, I plan to use the space of this chapter to offer reasons to resist the thought that practical considerations operate at their highest normative capacity only when they perform all three functions (influential, evaluative, explanatory) at the same time. By enlisting the support of recent advances in the areas of rationality and the semantics of thick evaluative concepts, I will suggest that a much richer normative terrain exists where these three functions can be assigned to different types of consideration without there being any sort of normative or epistemic underperformance.

In Chapter 6, I will avail myself of this broader 'alliance' of 'normative dissidents' – social practices featuring the attribution of thick evaluative properties and rational requirements of coherence and consistency – in order to show how legal philosophers who are not willing to shoulder the metanormative commitments of full-fledged legal reasons for action can delineate the practical space within which the truthmakers of legal propositions become normatively relevant. In this regard, I will re-introduce Joseph Raz's theory of *Nexus* reasons as an advocacy of the co-performance of the influential, evaluative and explanatory roles by considerations that aspire to attract the status of a full-fledged reason for action. Accordingly, I shall argue that the *Nexus* model operates as standard of normative robustness for theories of law that enlist the normative concept of a reason for action in their metanormative inventory.

Chapters 4 and 7 have been assigned the task of illustrating how the reconfiguration of the site of jurisprudential disagreement about the metaphysics and normativity of law can result in an enlargement of the scope of first-order and second-order variants of ontological and practical disagreement respectively. In Chapter 4, I will put to use the arguments regarding the truth-conditional understanding of ontological commitment (legal propositionalism) and the constitutive structure of legal statements from Chapters 2 and 3 respectively by showing how their joint validity can accommodate two levels of metaphysical disagreement about law. In Chapter 7, I will take a similar step in treating the triple function of reason-giving considerations (influential, evaluative and explanatory) and the exemplary appeal of the *Nexus* model as guides for designing a counterpart two-layered model of normative disagreement about law.

In the service of enlarging the scope of jurisprudential disagreement about the metaphysics and normativity of law, I shall take the liberty of recruiting Ronald Dworkin's integrity theory of law,[5] Joseph Raz's service conception of legal authority,[6] Scott Shapiro's planning theory of law[7] and Mark Greenberg's moral impact theory[8] as the four exemplary illustrations of the potential impact of metajurisprudential scrutiny. These four theories of law will serve as the diagnostic material of the alternative model of jurisprudential disagreement I will try to develop and defend in this book. As I purport to demonstrate, this sampling is anything but random. Cumulatively, they represent an ideal amalgamation of analytic jurisprudence's gradual descent from the modal terms in which the relationship between law and morality has been examined. Driven by different visions, all four model theories converge in their rejection of crude supervenience accounts of the co-variation between descriptive and legal facts, and instead offer valuable insights in the relevance of grounding explanations in law.

[5] Although the argument from integrity first appeared in Dworkin's seminal paper 'Hard Cases' (Dworkin (1975)), *Law's Empire* (Dworkin (1986)) remains the *locus classicus* for the theory of integrity. Ancillary sources will include Dworkin's more unified treatment of the concept of interpretation in *Justice for Hedgehogs* (Dworkin (2001)) as well as his extensive elaboration of the 'stages' in thinking about law (semantic, jurisprudential, doctrinal and adjudicative) and the concomitant different concepts of law (taxonomic, sociological, aspirational and doctrinal) in the collection of essays entitled *Justice in Robes* (Dworkin (2006)).

[6] Even though Raz's development of his idea about the nature of legal authority is evenly spread across his prolific scholarship, I will attempt to single out as reference material the seminal moments in the deployment of his theory. These moments primarily include the following works: Raz (1986), (1994), (1999b) (2006) and (2011).

[7] My main source of reference will be *Legality* (Shapiro (2011)). Two instructive precursors of Shapiro's theory of law are Shapiro (2002) and (2007).

[8] Mark Greenberg's Moral Impact Theory of Law remains a work in progress; consequently, currently there is no definitive source covering all the implications of his argument. The most autonomous elaboration so far is Greenberg (2014). I will also rely on further essays that demarcate the periphery but also the ambition of his theory: Greenberg (2004), (2011) and (2017).

The aim of this book is to demonstrate that to their detriment, our local jurisprudential disagreements are oblivious to the formative impact of their unpronounced metaontological and metanormative commitments. What motivates my characterisation of this oblivious stance as detrimental is my concern that the dominant parlance in which we frame our disagreement about the grounds and force of the law makes it too parochial or even too cryptic to be charitably understood by 'non-legal' (so to speak) philosophers working in general metaphysics and metaethics. To see why the potential fault lies more on our side and less on theirs, one need only observe the frequency with which we blame ourselves for talking past each other when we argue about the scope and plausibility of a normative versus descriptive jurisprudence.

1

From Legalese to Ontologese

THIS IS NOT the place to review the voluminous secondary literature spawned by Chapter 1 of Ronald Dworkin's *Law's Empire*. Nevertheless, one particular point remains relevant, namely, that this event remains an unsurpassed peak in our disagreement about the nature of law precisely because it illustrated how close towards existential denial legal philosophy has marched. The self-denying argument that this famous chapter raised is the idea that the scope of meaningful disagreement among competent legal practitioners and theorists meets its farthest radius at the intersection of empirical and theoretical disputes. That said, a proper vindication of the possibility of theoretical disagreement about the grounds of law remains a desideratum, as a sizeable cohort of legal philosophers voice sonorous objections against either the centrality or the very possibility of theoretical disagreement in law.

For the sake of my argument, I will single out three instances of the type of objection I just described as being particularly poignant. Each case features a different attempt at retranslating the phenomenon of legal theoretical disagreement in non-theoretical terms, be they empirical, (meta)pragmatic or (meta) semantic. The first has been forcefully articulated by Brian Leiter and purports to disprove the pervasiveness of theoretical disagreement about the grounds of law on *empirical* grounds.[1] On Leiter's account, what is theoretically informative is the existence of massive agreement about law in the sense that the existence of this agreement points the way to exploring positivism's unpronounced explanatory virtues. His line of attack bifurcates into mutually supportive theses. According to the *Disingenuity Thesis*, disputants about the grounds of law are consciously or unconsciously driven by the urge to mould the law into what they believe to be an ideal version of legality. According to the *Error Thesis*, parties to the purported disagreement about the grounds of law are literally mistaken precisely because what makes the matter about the grounds of law a non-issue is simply the fact that there is no convergent practice among legal officials with regard to what is valid law in this particular case.

The second objection is rather recent and draws its impetus from the impressive progress in philosophy of language in relation to the modelling of our semantic and pragmatic disagreements. Philosophers like David Plunkett and Timothy Sundell argue that what at first glance looks like an instance

[1] Leiter (2009); see also Leiter (2019).

of theoretical disagreement about the grounds of law is more likely to be explained as an instance of *metalinguistic* disagreement where the grounds of the relevant dispute are *pragmatic* rather than theoretical – or, more specifically, jurisprudential.[2] On their view, disagreement about whether legal content is determined solely by social facts or also by normative facts can be construed as an instance of what they describe as metalinguistic negotiation concerning the normative issue of which of a range of competing *concepts of law* should be used in a given conversational circumstance.

The third objection comes from recent advances in truth-relativist semantics.[3] Persistent disagreements about matters of taste or prudential value, the relativists hold, are less puzzling or urgent than empirical disagreements about the earth's rotation or the current weather in Chicago. The former point to situations in which it seems that neither of the two opposing parties is at fault in terms of upholding their respective positions. In a recent article, Andrej Kristan and Massimiliano Vignolo provide a novel legal realist response to the possibility of the existence of two incompatible yet faultless interpretations of the same set of legal provisions. In their view, there are cases where both interpretations are legally correct and justified by virtue of their being in agreement with the sources of law, but inasmuch as they are incompatible, they constitute a disagreement. Accordingly, episodes of faultless disagreement involve 'two agents having attitudes or performing speech acts that cannot both be accurate and yet with neither agent being responsible for violating constitutive norms concerning belief/assertion'.[4] Moving beyond the case of formally contradictory legal

[2] Plunkett and Sundell (2013).

[3] In the philosophy of language, arguments from faultless disagreement are advanced as defences of truth- or assessment-relativism over minimalism and as indexical and non-indexical variants of contextualism in certain areas of discourse (predicates of personal taste, epistemic modals, knowledge attributions, future contingents, gradable adjectives and indicative conditionals). The current state of art on this topic makes little if any reference to the metanormative and metaphysical commitments of proponents of faultless disagreement. In this regard, it is quite difficult to engage head-on in a charitable extrapolation of the implications that such views would have on the question of what it means to faultlessly disagree about the explanation of the existence of legal facts and their normative force. An authoritative locus of argument about the possibility of faultless disagreement is Kölbel (2004).

[4] Kristan and Vignolo (2018: 399). To this very apt formulation, I would dare to emphatically qualify 'being responsible' as 'being individually responsible'. Despite its pleonastic allure, this addition highlights what I take to be a pivotal yet underexplored, metanormative commitment of friends of faultless disagreement, namely, that an episode of faultless disagreement between A and B has *no individual normative impact* on either A or B in the sense that by having their respective attitudes or by performing their respective speech acts, A and B do not *commit themselves* to respond to certain questions and criticisms addressed by each other – namely, those questions or criticisms that would be answered by the considerations that bear on the question of whether p is part of the content of the law or whether the fact that p is part of the content of the law provides a reason to φ. The absolution from a 'duty of response to further questions', so to speak, is an intuitive way to frame my line of counter-argument to the relevance of appeals to faultless disagreement in debates about legal metaphysics and legal metanormativity. The idea I have in mind is that the justification of this 'absolution' presupposes a controversial view of the rationality of cognitive states and/or attitudes that draws an arbitrary wedge between the reasons that bear on their *formation* and the reasons that

statements, Vittorio Villa goes a step further to suggest that the quintessentially faultless interpretive disagreements in law are substantial and thickly evaluative, and hence they cannot be formally resolved.[5]

As already evidenced by my way of framing the dispute, I purport to argue that, despite the independent plausibility of their non-jurisprudential (ie, empirical, linguistic and epistemological) grounds, these anti-theoretical conceptions of the ambit of our disagreement about law do not exhaust the material out of which jurisprudential disagreements take shape in the minds of philosophically inclined interlocutors. However, the source of my resistance to taking these objections as direct refutations of the possibility of theoretical disagreement in law is not Dworkin's insistence that the argumentative character of legal interpretation points both to the existence of such disagreement as well as to its resolvability by appealing to the best set of practice-sensitive principles.

As I am about to argue, Dworkin's rendition of the nature and object of theoretical disagreement is part of the problem I am bent on addressing in this book. Likewise, his imperial avenue for adjudicating episodes of theoretical disagreement on the basis of the best political argument is too narrow and, perhaps, too demanding to be diversely populated. The respect in which Dworkin's model of theoretical disagreement in law will be found lacking is not its depth or elegance, but its scope of application. What drives my resistance to these potent objections to imperial disagreements in law is that it remains, I dare to believe, an open question just what the precise *object* of theoretical disagreement in law is. My contention will be that this object is real and its reality is primarily metaphysical rather than linguistic, conceptual or psychological. Accordingly, the broader the scope of our theoretical disagreements about the reality and force of the law is proven to be, the humbler our aspiration to guess the profile of a potential winner in these debates should be.

That said, the idea that jurisprudential disagreement is at its core an instance of theoretical disagreement has yet to earn its pride of place in metaphysical debates about law, despite promising evidence that almost 30 years after the onset of this controversy, prominent recent contributions – positivist and antipositivist alike – to legal philosophy appear to be unhooked from the task of (dis)proving the possibility of theoretical disagreement in law, and are more perspicuously oriented towards offering victorious arguments against a commonly acknowledged background of meaningful theoretical disagreement. Even though I will try to convey my optimism that the acknowledgement of the possibility of theoretical disagreement about law tends to acquire the shell of a mainstream view, I caution against thinking that this is a certain victory precisely because this trend has only gained ascendancy recently and is still widely challenged. Keeping this caveat in mind, this book aspires to make good the finite ambition

bear on their 'public', so to speak, *evaluation*. For an account of commitment-constituted attitudes, see Hieronymi (2005).

[5] Villa (2016).

to scale a particular peak in the hope that it can lend additional support to the reality of theoretical disagreement about law by expanding its scope to what I will dare to term *metajurisprudential* questions.

The line of defence I intend to adopt will not focus on addressing the critiques advanced against Dworkin's initial argument from theoretical disagreement head-on, but, perhaps surprisingly, on developing a critique of Dworkin's chosen route to defending the prominence of theoretical disagreement about law. As it stands, Dworkin's deployment of the argument from theoretical disagreement is aimed at debunking legal positivism rather than re-inviting legal positivists to deploy their own arguments after having reshuffled the vocabulary of their dispute with legal antipositivists. The idea behind this unorthodox effort to take sides in this debate is that Dworkin's way of presenting jurisprudential disagreement as an instance of first-order normative disagreement is precisely what makes the whole project of theoretical disagreement vulnerable to multilateral criticism. More precisely, I purport to argue that by restrictively associating theoretical disagreement with the question of what grounds *legal facts* instead of what grounds the *truthmakers* of legal propositions, we already assume too much about the relationship between the semantics and the metaphysics of legal discourse.

I. DWORKIN'S VISION OF JURISPRUDENTIAL DISAGREEMENT

By proceeding as if legal facts are the trivial truthmakers of legal propositions, we also grant that the concept of law, whatever that is, is an instructive guide to our ontological commitments. By putting the 'semantic cart' before the 'ontological horse', if I may use this metaphor, we first and foremost condition the subject matter and scope of the ensuing metaphysical disagreement on our verdicts regarding the truth-conditional form of assertions of legal content. If this is how the route to disagreement about the grounds of law is paved, then it should come as no surprise that arguments targeted against the possibility of theoretical disagreement are preponderantly semantic rather than metaphysical in nature. This confusion among varieties of disagreement has been compounded rather than dispelled by the fact that Dworkin set out to defend the possibility of theoretical disagreement about the *grounds* of law by arguing that law is an interpretive *concept*.[6] Before explaining why Dworkin's way of defending the centrality of theoretical disagreement about law prematurely excludes from consideration positivist variants of this type of disagreement, it is useful to briefly recount his argumentative route from law being an interpretive concept to making theoretical disagreement about the grounds of law intelligible and

[6] Note that Dworkin's claim that law is an interpretive concept should be distinguished from the particular interpretive theory he offers, which he labels 'law as integrity'.

ultimately to identifying this disagreement as a type of normative political disagreement about the responsibilities of government.

Dworkin does not begin by drawing law's essential profile, but by attributing to legal practice the essential property of being argumentative. Thus, he claims that: 'Every actor in the practice understands that what it permits or requires depends on the truth of certain propositions that are given sense only by and within the practice; the practice consists in large part in deploying and arguing about these propositions.'[7] He then makes a first step to regiment the structure of this argumentative practice by drawing a distinction between what he calls 'propositions of law' and the 'grounds of law'. The former are statements about what the law requires, permits, prohibits or empowers one to do, whereas the latter, he argues, are the determinants of the truth or falsity of those propositions. Provided that the most prominent occasion on which legal practitioners argue about propositions of law and their grounds is that of disagreement, making sense of the latter acquires special importance.

Equipped with this first distinction, he proceeds to distinguish between two ways in which legal practitioners may disagree about the determinants of the truth of propositions of law. The first type of disagreement that he identifies as a kind of empirical disagreement is not about the grounds of law, but about whether those grounds hold in a particular case. The second type of disagreement which he calls theoretical is the most interesting one as it directly regards the grounds of legal truths. The rest of the story is too familiar to be rehearsed in exegetical detail here. Dworkin's conclusion is that theoretical disagreement is a real phenomenon and that available theories of law fall short of accounting for the pervasiveness of this type of disagreement. His solution is to suggest that law itself is an interpretive concept that already encodes in its conditions of application the possibility of disagreement about when it is applicable.

The preceding narration gives me the opportunity to make a couple of critical remarks. First, given Dworkin's own distinction between the grounds of law and propositions of law, it seems that he would regard the notion of legal truthmakers as a complication that elevates the locus of disagreement to an unnecessarily higher level of abstraction. On his account, legal facts are, on pain of banality, the truthmakers of propositions of law, and what is available for scrutiny are the grounds of legal facts. Second, he projects the reality of a metaphysical type of disagreement (about the grounding of legal facts) onto the application conditions of the concept of law. More precisely, he suggests that what could be a promising start in making sense of theoretical disagreement about law is to entertain the thought that it is the concept of law that is first and foremost argumentative or interpretive. As a result, a proper regimentation of legal talk (legal judgments) and thought (concepts of law) becomes the vehicle that will drive us to law's contested realm (the grounds of law).

[7] Dworkin (1986: 13).

As I am about to argue further below, a preliminary step in defending the possibility of theoretical disagreement about law is to challenge the assumption that the spectrum of our disagreement about the grounds of law is adumbrated or even partly adjudicated by the way we disagree about the application conditions of the concept of law. On the picture under review, the concept of law as well as other interpretive concepts – for instance, democracy – is such that it heralds the type of disagreement that we should anticipate when we argue about particular legal cases. It does so because the non-evaluative and embedded evaluative aspects of interpretive concepts underdetermine their extensions relative to a particular context.[8] The rest of the argument that leads to the conclusion that the kind of theoretical disagreement at stake is normative disagreement is a typical instance of an inference to the best explanation. The argumentative character of interpretive concepts is such that their non-evaluative and embedded evaluative constituents underdetermine their extensions. In other words, one can know what law means without knowing which features of a legal practice trigger the best total justification of that practice. Assuming that a concept's criteria of application impose constraints on what any literal use of it stands for in a given context, what else could best explain what determines the extension of the concept than a general set of principles of political morality? On the emerging picture, it turns out that theoretical disagreement about law is full-fledged normative disagreement because in disagreeing about the grounds of law, we disagree about which principles of political morality justify the totality of legal practices.

This lengthy digression into Dworkin's argumentative route from the argumentative nature of legal practice to the normative character of theoretical disagreement about the grounds of law is not meant as a preparative step preceding a reconstruction of Dworkin's interpretivist theory. What it is meant to highlight is the slippery slope character of its course to sparking a misguiding and potentially damaging confrontation with deniers of theoretical disagreement. The crucial moment at which this unnecessary confrontation becomes inevitable is when Dworkin chooses to *encode* the archetypal scene of disagreement about the grounds of law *into* the concept of law. We are already familiar with the two sides of this dispute: positivists claim that legal practices determine their own jurisgenerative relevance, whereas antipositivists claim that normative arguments are necessary in order to make this determination intelligible or

[8] In the legal case, the salient context will be that of a particular legal system, institution or jurisdiction. I owe the argument from underdetermination to Daniel Elstein's and Thomas Hurka's ingenious defence of 'thinning' the shell of contested thick concepts like 'distributively just', 'selfish' and 'courageous'. With respect to these concepts, they remark that they lie 'in a middle position between purely thin ones and fully thick ones such as "Kraut". In so doing it explains why anti-reductivists like McDowell have to assume that any reductive analysis of these concepts will have a descriptively determinate two-part form. It is only if the descriptive part of the analysis fully determines a concept's extension that there is no room for evaluations to help do so. Given an only partly determinate descriptive part, however, that room is clearly available' (Elstein and Hurka 2009: 524).

possible. Dworkin tries to conceptualise this controversy by treating law as a moderately thick concept featuring legal practices as its non-evaluative component and their justification as its evaluative component. Inevitably, however, thick normative concepts are such that they allow evaluation to determine their extension by locating the relevant disagreement in the question of what the right-making features of legal practices in fact are.

The result is that those who are suspicious of the pervasiveness of theoretical disagreement about law have a legitimate reason to complain that Dworkin tries to steer the debate towards his antipositvist way of making sense of this type of disagreement by taking things for granted. The empiricist, pragmaticist and truth-relativist objectors mentioned earlier are reasonably alarmed by the fact that for Dworkin, the strongest evidence for the ubiquity of theoretical disagreement about the grounds of law lies not in the world, but in our thought. In other words, instead of documenting the possibility of theoretical disagreement by locating it at a level where the controversy between legal positivists and antipositivists is not yet fully articulated and thus more malleable,[9] Dworkin tries to pre-empt the discussion by positing that the reality of legal facts and in part the reality of their grounds are already mirrored in the way we think about law in its most focal manifestations. Besides the fact that this is a tacit metaontological position that remains unargued in Dworkin's work, his view remains vulnerable to competing thoughts or conceptualisations of law precisely because it is grounded in what he takes to be an explanatorily privileged conception of law.[10]

II. THE SITE AND SCOPE OF JURISPRUDENTIAL DISAGREEMENT

Despite my critical remarks on why Dworkin's way of defending the possibility of theoretical disagreement potentially serves as a weapon in the hands of his opponents, I do not believe that their criticisms are fatal, nor do I think that the vulnerability of theoretical disagreement *thus construed* poses a serious objection to Dworkin's own interpretivist theory of law. What I do believe instead is that some amendments must be made and that this task would turn

[9] For instance, a way to begin one's argument in favour of the possibility of theoretical disagreement would be to remark that it is an open question as to whether legal philosophers should be ontologically committed to the obtaining of legal facts.

[10] In this regard, Dworkin invites us to 'recognize that we share some of our concepts, including the political concepts, in a different way: they function for us as *interpretive* concepts. We share them because we share social practices and experiences in which these concepts figure. We take the concepts to describe values, but we disagree, sometimes to a marked degree, about what these values are and how they should be expressed. We disagree because we interpret the practices we share rather differently: we hold somewhat different theories about which values best justify what we accept as central or paradigm features of that practice. That structure makes our conceptual disagreements about liberty, equality, and the rest genuine' (Dworkin 2011: 6).

into a vicious circle if it were directly aimed at discrediting Dworkin's opponents on that matter. After all, their arguments have so far served more as a targeted response to Dworkin's own argumentative strategy than as an independent and full-fledged attempt to categorically reject once and for all the possibility of theoretical disagreement about the grounds of law. As previously noted, my way of bringing the argument from theoretical disagreement back on track is to begin by questioning the way in which its subject matter has been configured thanks to Dworkin's seminal introduction of the idea. This critical appraisal will deliver a reconfiguration of what I will call the 'site' of theoretical disagreement in a way that allows the expansion of its scope at a level where the traditional dispute between legal positivists and antipositivists has not yet arisen. The resulting picture will endow theoretical disagreement with a more fine-grained structure gradually descending from a domain of what I will call metajurisprudential questions to more familiar, substantive questions pertaining to the grounding of facts about legal content.

An immediate advantage of this reconfiguration will be a less committing semantics for legal propositions (see Chapter 3). In the spirit of keeping the 'semantic cart' behind the 'ontological horse', I will argue that it is not only possible but also strongly advisable to refrain from packing into the meaning of legality, in whichever semantic form it figures in assertions of legal content, substantive information about the relevance of descriptive or normative facts as well as their relationship. In this vein, I believe that it is possible to withhold the emergence of these aspects until the time becomes ripe to ask what grounds the truthmakers of legal propositions. This will, at least, slow down the pace of those who will remain unconvinced about the prospect of theoretical disagreement until the conclusion of my argument. By elevating the apex of theoretical disagreement to a higher level of abstraction, its possibility can be welcomed without the qualms inevitably associated with premature attempts to narrow the scope of the dispute between positivist and antipositivist philosophers.

The project animating this argument for the possibility of metajurisprudence is fuelled by its analogical affinity with metaethics and, ideally, it aims to emulate the formative impact of the latter on our understanding of moral thought, talk and practice. Given that both law and ethics share membership of the domain of practical philosophy, it is at least conceivable to submit that the domain of metajurisprudence can be subject to similar subdivisions with those pertaining to the structure of metaethical discourse. Consequently, metajurisprudential questions could in principle follow the pattern of division applied to metaethics such that one can plausibly declare a theoretical interest in understanding the metaphysical, epistemological, semantic and psychological/normative presuppositions of legal thought, talk and practice. The bulk of this exposition will be dedicated to exploring the metaphysical and normative commitments of jurisprudence. In this vein, I will treat some questions about the semantics of legal discourse as auxiliary to the elucidation of the controversy surrounding the relationship between language and ontology.

To forestall a forthcoming objection, there is no doubt that the value of metatheoretical arguments in law has been incrementally recognised by many scholars espousing radically different visions about how legal philosophy should proceed. Denying this reality would be an injustice to the remarkable progress owed to the masterful sophistication of jurisprudential prose and the gradual extrication of legal philosophy from the eliminativist contours of imperative or sanction-based theories of law that marked the early stages of what we now identify as analytic jurisprudence. What I do plan to take issue with is the methodological status which metatheoretical arguments are accorded in the adjudication of theoretical disputes about law or, as Dworkin further specifies it, in settling our disagreement 'about the grounds of law, about which other kinds of propositions, when true, make a particular proposition of law true'.[11]

The idea that I hope to make salient throughout this exposition is that the restrictive way in which the object of theoretical disagreement about law has been identified is the result of the peripheral or ad hoc role assigned to questions pertaining to the foundations of analytic jurisprudence vis-a-vis the questions associated with the foundations or grounds of law. In other words, it is potentially misleading for all participants in this debate to infer from its label that the ambit of theoretical disagreement about law cannot incur an expansion similar to the one brought into moral philosophy by the introduction of metaethics. On the alternative picture with which I intend to take issue, theoretical disagreement about law is akin to the type of disagreement witnessed between proponents of deontological ethical theories and virtue-ethicists or consequentialists.

Normative ethicists who remain suspicious of the relevance of metaethical arguments wish to block the ascension of their debates beyond the first-order question of whether, for instance, rightness is about the maximisation of utility or the realisation of autonomous agency. By contrast, metaethical theorising invites us to boldly examine the linguistic, metaphysical and epistemological commitments that underlie our ordinary moral convictions with a view to, at least partly, reshuffling the terms in which we disagree about matters of everyday morality. In a similar vein, as I intend to show, metajurisprudential theorising points towards the existence of a higher level of abstraction wherein we are licensed to ask not just whether legal positivism is a better theory of law than antipositivism or vice versa, but also whether and what justifies our ontological commitment to the thing called law. If this turns out to be a valid criticism, it could point the path towards reshuffling the terms of jurisprudential discourse in a way that also reconfigures the points at which the traditional participants actually diverge.

It is not a coincidence, I tend to believe, that the ambit of theoretical disagreement about law has so far remained vulnerable to Dworkin's potent argument in

[11] Dworkin (1986: 5).

favour of equating the foundations of jurisprudence with the foundations – or, more accurately, the grounds – of legal facts. The latter aspect of jurisprudential inquiry pertains to the kind of non-legal facts – descriptive, conceptual and normative – that ground legal facts as well as to the justification of the explanatory relevance of these non-legal facts vis-a-vis the grounding of legal facts. There is no denial that the long-term impact of Dworkin's argument from theoretical disagreement has been a valuable – though still faintly celebrated – leap towards bringing legal philosophy closer to its identity *qua* philosophy and farther from its reduction to legal theory. Nonetheless, as I am about to argue, what remains problematic is the reluctant if not sluggish way in which the literature on theoretical disagreement about law is willing not just to affirm but also to defend the relevance of metatheoretical arguments for law.

Along with the incremental acknowledgement of Dworkin's insistence in praising theory, there has been a parallel concern about the level of critical evaluation at which our theoretical disagreement about law should be staged. Whereas I do believe that Dworkin's argument in favour of welcoming theoretical disagreement in law has been victorious, I remain humbly reluctant to concur that the terms in which he purported to delineate the *scope* of this disagreement are correct. More precisely, I believe that his insistence on skipping levels of abstraction between the 'methodologically proper' internal judgements about the point of legal practice and the 'methodologically erred' external judgements about what identifies a legal practice as such has had a weakening effect on the strength of his opponents' defensive responses. To venture a possible interpretation, the allure of Dworkin's way of deflating the purpose of metatheoretical routes for illuminating the nature of law owes much of its potency to a dimly argued assumption that the *site* of theoretical disagreement about law also determines its *scope*. But the latter claim is not a platitude or a first-order evaluative claim, but rather a full-fledged metatheoretical claim, or so I shall argue.

Before fleshing out my objection, let me, first off, unpack the way in which I intend to apply this inherited distinction between the site and scope of theoretical disagreement about law. The former term should be understood as referring to the way in which we demarcate the *locus* of our disagreement about law. Being aware of the alluring comfort of hiding behind lofty words, I will immediately proceed to offer an example of what could qualify as the site of theoretical disagreement about law. Given the standard definition dating back to Dworkin's own initial proposal, the site of theoretical disagreement about law would turn out to be identical to the problem of the *grounds of legal facts*, that is, the question of what kind of non-legal facts are the proper grounds of legal facts. On this restrictive (as I purport to argue) understanding of the site of theoretical disagreement, the reality of legal facts is taken for granted and what remains available for discovery is the nature of non-legal facts that operate as the grounds of legal facts.

By sharp contrast, the extension of the term 'scope' purports to cover the *range of questions* that can be meaningfully asked about law. On the available restrictive understanding of the site of theoretical disagreement, it would be accurate enough to say that the scope of legal disagreement would be analogically co-extensive with the scope of disagreement in normative ethics. This is not to say that legal disagreement *just is* a variant of normative disagreement, even though this is precisely how Dworkin purports to understand theoretical disagreement about law. Recall that this restrictive understanding of theoretical disagreement is meant to be equally available for the legal positivist. As a result, there should also be a positivist reading of the same story available such that theoretical disagreement about law can turn out to be a kind of descriptive disagreement about where to draw the boundary between what the law is and what the law should be. What remains critical is that on either reading, if theoretical disagreement is possible, it is about the *law* and not about the *foundations* of law, much in the same way that theoretical disagreement in normative ethics is about, say, what constitutively defines the right and the good and not about their metaphysical and semantic properties.

As it stands, Dworkin's dismissal of the utility of distinguishing the foundations of jurisprudence from the grounds of legal facts retains a strong argumentative background.[12] Its strength resides in the idea that because the grounds of *legal facts* are the primary site of theoretical disagreement about law, our disagreement can remain intelligible only insofar as we limit its *scope* to the range of questions for which *law* as a concept and a practice is a proper target.[13] In order to see how this idea purports to deflate the value of metatheoretical arguments in law, I will provide two alternative templates of theoretical disagreement about law, one normative and one descriptive, which nevertheless share their identity as *first-order* theoretical disputes.

First, I will try to exemplify Dworkin's own understanding of theoretical disagreement about law as a type of first-order *normative* disagreement.[14] On this approach, legal philosophy moves a step closer to occupying a position within the broader domain of political philosophy that deals specifically with the normative relevance of historical facts about the activities of government officials for the determination of the rights and obligations of members of a political community. Second, I will venture to exemplify the same conception of theoretical disagreement as a type of first-order *descriptive* disagreement. On this alternative approach, when legal philosophers disagree about whether

[12] I deliberately avoid the qualification of first-order theoretical disagreement about law as normative or descriptive precisely because I believe that Dworkin's argument against the possibility of metajurisprudence remains equally strong, regardless of whether he also succeeds at demonstrating that our first-order disputes about law are normative all the way down.

[13] I do not intend to convey the idea that any eligible type of ground for legal facts must be capable of *conceptually* entailing a particular type of question to which it counts as a plausible answer. For Dworkin to ask what type of questions can be answered by recourse to the grounds of legal facts is itself a substantive, normative question.

[14] For Dworkin's rejection of metaphysical or second-order claims about morality and law, see Dworkin (1996) and (2011: 40–68).

moral facts jointly with social facts ground legal facts, they disagree about what makes *de dicto* or perspectival normative statements about law true.

According to Dworkin's own interpretivist theory, legal facts are grounded in interpretive facts about what best justifies the coercive impact of past political practice. By sharp contrast, according to Joseph Raz's famous 'sources thesis', legal facts are grounded in facts about the existence of authoritative directives that communicate the legal officials' views on how those subject to their authority are to behave. Given this contrastive depiction, we could ask which types of question are amenable to the invocation of interpretive facts or facts about the existence of authoritative directives as the grounds of legal facts. Assuming, again, that the scope of disagreement is determined by its site, it makes sense to respond that to posit facts about how an authority believes its subjects should behave or facts about how state coercion is limited by reference to past political practice *just is* to answer the question of what the proper responsibilities of government vis-a-vis its citizens are.[15] On the one hand, the pronouncement of authoritative directives as the proper ground of legal facts is or entails the endorsement of an instrumental value of legal authority in helping its subjects comply with antecedent – or law-independent – reasons by way of replacing them with its say-so. On the other hand, to seek out those aspects of the practices of legal officials that 'depend on a single and comprehensive vision of justice'[16] amounts more or less to upholding the value of equally distributing the burdens and benefits of political arrangements backed up with coercive force or, in Dworkin's own terminology, the value of integrity.

The alternative construal of theoretical disagreement as a kind of descriptive first-order discourse provides, as expected, the only format that can accommodate the legal positivist's terms for participating in this discourse. To unpack this idea a bit further, take the assertion that from the point of view of legal system S, A ought to φ and suppose that in the actual legal system S, the legal point of view of its officials *is just* the point of view of rule consequentialism. Is it then a valid step to infer from the assertion 'from the point of view of legal system S, A ought to φ' that the point of view of rule consequentialism requires A to φ within the jurisdiction of legal system S? If the answer is in the affirmative, assertions of legal obligation are true *de re*, as they directly allow a privileged set of standards to operate as a source of normative requirements for law subjects. But if the answer is negative, as most legal positivists would expect, the same assertion will be true *de dicto*, as its truth does not entail the truth of a proposition directly featuring a concrete normative theory.

[15] Any theory of grounds for legal facts operates as an answer to the question of what the political relevance of legal facts is. On this normative construal of theoretical disagreement, to ask for the non-legal grounds of legal facts is to ask about the normative grounds that make political history relevant for the determination of obligations and rights in a political community.

[16] Dworkin (1986: 134).

Consequently, theoretical disagreement about *de dicto* normative truths about legal content could most probably revolve around what is entailed by a proper description of the legal point of view of a given system. It thereby follows that on a positivist understanding, theoretical disagreement could mean at least two things: disagreement about what makes a description of the legal point of view proper and disagreement about what is entailed by a proper description. On this view, what theoretical disagreement is *not* about is the *truth* of what the legal point of view properly described refers to. For instance, a relevant and rather popular description would take the legal point of view to be the point of view of a legal authority. This is the normative viewpoint of legal officials who claim to possess legitimate authority. If our theoretical disagreement about whether this description is correct is settled, a further theoretical disagreement may erupt with regard to what qualifies as the object of an authoritative intention.[17] Alternatively, on Shapiro's planning theory of law, the correct description of the legal point of view is taken to be the normative point of view of a legal system's master plan such that theoretical disagreement about law boils down to disagreement about what purposes those assigned with the design and revision of the master plan have, as well as about which interpretive methodology best fits with those purposes.[18]

Returning to my critical appraisal of Dworkin's praise of theory in law,[19] I will proceed to state my objection, which actually animates and informs the entire exposition. My opposition to this restrictive understanding of legal disagreement derives its strength from the plausibility of engaging in theoretical disagreement about law by first asking metatheoretical or, more concisely, metajurisprudential questions. As soon as we grant that it makes sense to enlarge the scope of legal disagreement beyond empirical and into theoretical territories, I am inclined to believe that the scope of questions about law should be wide enough to include foundational questions about, for instance, whether legal truth requires the existence of legal facts or whether law can be normative by virtue of its being reason-giving. The expansion I am envisaging aims to leave

[17] Raz seems to allow for some limited theoretical disagreement about law when he remarks that facts about the nature of law are relevant for determining which interpretative theory is correct. Tellingly, he notes that his Authoritative Intention Thesis 'turns on our understanding of the notion of authority and its conceivable justifications' (Raz 1999a: 259).

[18] Shapiro's move towards making room for descriptive theoretical disagreement about law is licensed by his core idea that legal practice is not conventional in any robust sense. He notes that: '[At] first glance, conventionalism appears to be a positivistic conception of law, for both privilege social facts in the determination of legal content … It is crucial to see, however, that conventionalism is not a positivistic theory at all. For while both theories privilege social facts, only positivism does so at the ultimate level. According to the legal positivist, the grounds of law are *ultimately* determined by social facts. By contrast, conventionalism privileges conventions at the nonultimate level: conventions determine the content of the law only by virtue of the fact that morality requires that they do so. Conventionalists, in other words, are natural lawyers who believe that political morality requires them to act as though they were exclusive legal positivists' (Shapiro 2011: 297).

[19] See especially Dworkin (1997).

intact the lower level array of questions – in both their normative or descriptive versions – even though it becomes an open question as to whether and how the description of the object of our first-order theoretical disagreement about law can be affected by acknowledging a higher level of metajurisprudential discourse.

The possibility of metajurisprudential disagreement is heavily premised on how we are to understand the relationship between the site of jurisprudential or first-order disagreement and its scope. What has been blocking the emergence of a higher level of abstract theorising about law is the fact that the 'scope determined by site' thesis is silently treated by Dworkin as a kind of normative truth in the sense that somehow the site of our disagreement is supposed to determine its scope. But it is not, or so I shall argue. The only case in which the site of an idea necessarily determines its scope is when the site itself is an existence condition for the idea.[20] But settling controversies over the existence conditions of Xs is not the type of mental exercise one would identify as internal to the practice of proceeding as if Xs existed. In other words, only arguments external to the practice of proceeding as if Xs existed can qualify as favouring or disfavouring the existence of Xs. The upshot is that in order to show that the scope of legal disagreement is limited to first-order questions about the political relevance of legal facts, it should also be demonstrated that the site of disagreement about law cannot be meaningful if there are no grounds for legal facts.

III. LEGAL FACTS AND LEGAL PROPOSITIONS

At this point, it would make sense to ask whether the existence of legal facts is indeed an existence condition for the very possibility of theoretical disagreement. If it is, then Dworkin keeps a trump up his sleeve that allows him to insist in his claim that theoretical disagreement about law is a first-order normative disagreement. If it is not, it will remain an open question as to whether the scope of legal disagreement needs to be limited to first-order – normative or descriptive – questions about the nature of law. But could it be the case that the site of theoretical disagreement about law is not the grounding of legal facts? Or, equivalently, would our first-order legal disagreement remain meaningful if there were no facts that featured distinctly legal entities like legal norms, legal obligations and statutory provisions? And if so, would the scope of our disagreement be more permissive vis-a-vis the use of metatheoretical arguments?

[20] I owe this line of reasoning to Arash Abizadeh's site/scope thesis; see Abizadeh (2007). He develops a critical account of the idea that justice requires a basic structure as its site, which in its turn directly determines its scope, and remarks that the meaning of 'requires' is ambiguous between an existential, constitutive and instrumental reading. Of these, only the first meaning implies a limitation on the scope of justice by its site. On the existential interpretation of 'requires', justice '*presupposes* the existence of a basic structure before its demands *arise*' and consequently '[it] limits the scope of justice to where a basic structure already exists' (2007: 324).

My response is in the affirmative if there is room for arguing that facts about the existence of legal norms need not be the only plausible truthmakers of legal propositions, much in the same sense in which it is not a priori true that facts featuring a distinct ontological category of artefactual or ordinary objects like statues or chairs are the truthmakers of claims about the existence of statues or chairs.

This is precisely the moment that I identify as crucial for allowing metatheoretical questions to extend the scope of legal disagreement. If, for the sake of argument, we could allow that the site of theoretical disagreement about law is not the grounding of *legal facts*, but the grounding of the *truthmakers of legal propositions*, the scope of our theoretical disagreement about law glibly incorporates two metajurisprudential questions – namely, whether legal facts are ontologically fit to make legal propositions true and whether legal facts are normatively fit to explain the way in which legal content can assume the role of a guiding premise in our practical reasoning.[21] At this level of abstraction that Dworkin's 'anti-Archimedean' strategy seems to ignore, I have chosen to single out two interrelated metajurisprudential puzzles.[22] The first is about the relation of legal truth to the world, and it lies amidst a substantive discourse about the political or institutional difference legal practices make and a foundational discourse about the truth-aptness of propositions in general. The second is about the direction of fit between true representations of legal content and the world, and it lies amidst a substantive discourse about the practical difference legal practices make and a foundational discourse about which normative concepts are primitive.

On the one hand, the envisaged reconfiguration of the site of jurisprudential disagreement enables some revisionary thinking about the ontological indispensability of legal facts. For as long as our discourse is premised on the idea that true legal propositions purport to report distinctly legal facts, the available manoeuvring space remains restricted by the degree of flexibility of our linguistic representations. Thus, given this restrictive premise, the only two cognitivist alternatives to a blunt non-reductive realism about legal facts are no less semantically biased: either we should paraphrase talk about legal facts to a talk about a type of 'non-offending' entities and derive our truthmakers from the latter,

[21] To paraphrase a similar point made by Kenneth Ehrenberg with regard to Dworkin's suspicion against metaethics, he seems to have neglected the level at which the 'sceptic' can be dubious about whether legal facts in general are an appropriate category for use in claims about what makes legal propositions true. See Ehrenberg (2008: 513).

[22] My selection is not meant as a prioritisation of questions that matter from a metajurisprudential point of view. By virtue of the reconfiguration of the site of jurisprudential disagreement, further questions can be also classified as metajurisprudential. For instance, in *Legality*, Shapiro addresses the question of which epistemological theory is most appropriate for the purposes of legal philosophy. Tellingly, he describes the question as a 'metainterpretive' problem and identifies the metainterpreter as 'someone who evaluates interpretive methodology in the first stage of legal interpretation. An interpreter, on the other hand, is someone who uses a particular interpretive methodology to interpret a legal text in the second stage of legal interpretation' (Shapiro 2011: 305).

or we should eliminate our legal talk *tout court* as literally false and seek the origins of law outside the realm of analytic jurisprudence as narrowly construed. By contrast, if we elevate the level of abstraction by replacing legal facts with the truthmakers of legal propositions, it will become more natural to say that there may be a way of preserving the veridicality of our legal discourse without pledging any ontological commitment to ontologically frivolous entities.[23]

On the other hand, the same reconfiguration will allow a revisionary approach to the question of whether legal facts are normatively indispensable. On the standard picture, if we refuse to take on board legal facts as normatively relevant considerations, the price we are called to pay may be too sour for the taste of many. We will either have to conclude that legal normativity is reducible to the normativity of another domain of discourse, for instance, morality or rationality, or we will be led to declare that law is not normative in any robust sense either because legal facts do not exist or because legal facts are only derivatively normative. As I will aim to demonstrate in Chapter 5, the non-reductive, reductive and eliminativist accounts of legal normativity can be grouped together as silent entailments of a broader understanding of the site of jurisprudential disagreement as pertaining to the grounds of truthmakers of legal propositions. All accounts converge in their assumption that law's normative capacity is measured by the degree to which the truthmakers of legal propositions can emulate the reason-guiding capacity of other kinds of fact. As soon as we switch to a level of abstraction featuring the truthmakers of legal propositions, we may be in a better position to preserve the mind-to-world direction of fit of our true representations of legal content without assuming that the truthmakers of these propositions can be normatively impactful only by virtue of their operating as full-fledged normative reasons.

If there is a leitmotiv in the backstory I have been trying to sketch, it is the idea that the questions pertaining to the foundations of legal philosophy are not necessarily reducible to the questions pertaining to the grounding of legal

[23] Heather Dyke (2008) proposes a quadripartite division of ontological theories that rely on the same fallacious (as she argues) metaontological position, namely, the claim that our ontological commitments should be responsive to the formal structure of our linguistic representations. She invites us to witness the re-enactment of a dispute between four philosophers. Philosopher A is a non-reductive realist about lurches. In support of her argument, she says that one merely has to recognise that there are many true sentences that include the term 'lurch'. Philosopher B is a reductionist-realist. She retorts that there are no real lurches, even though sentences featuring this term are literally true. But she also denies that the truth of these sentences commits her to accepting the reality of lurches because these sentences can be paraphrased into sentences that make no reference to lurches and also reveal our true ontological commitments. Philosopher C is an error theorist. She interjects by saying that she denies both the reality of lurches and the fruitfulness of the paraphrasing strategy because the paraphrasing sentences do not have the same meaning with the paraphrased sentences. Whereas the sentence purports to refer to lurches, it is simply false because lurches do not exist. Finally, Philosopher D advances an expressivist argument. She remarks that A, B and C are wrong in their assumption that the use of these sentences is descriptive; while they appear to describe a thing, they actually perform another linguistic function (2008: 2–4). In what follows, I shall concentrate on the first three cognitivist positions, leaving the expressivist option aside.

facts construed as facts about the existence of distinctly legal entities. That said, although I will be no less interested in questions of legal grounding, their relevance will emerge as soon as the reconfiguration of the site and scope of theoretical disagreement about law will qualify as a template for the production of a new metajurisprudential taxonomy. This alternative map is not meant to subvert the diagnostic utility of our most familiar terms, like 'exclusive or inclusive positivism', 'natural law', 'interpretivism', 'legal realism', 'exclusionary reasons' or 'content-independent reasons', but to supplement it by enlarging the domain of informative contrasts and affinities between theories of law whose first-order commitments vis-a-vis the grounds of legal facts would not allow any 'rapprochement'.

2

Relating Legal Propositions to Legal Facts

DESPITE THE FACT that in most cases reference to pure metaphysical argument remains rather insular in the contemporary literature on the nature of law, it is my aspiration to show that the unfamiliarity of using a robust metaphysical language in jurisprudential debates is not an accurate depiction of what is actually being presupposed by the participants in these debates. It is my firm impression that despite the limited appeal of unmediated applications of metaphysical notions (such as properties, universals, tropes, states of affairs, relations and *de re* modality) to the domain of jurisprudence, there is an incremental allusion to questions of existence or fundamentality that cannot be dispensed with without downplaying the intricacies of ongoing disputes about the relationship of law to morality and the determination of legal content.

As I aim to demonstrate, my categorisation of positions in legal metaphysics does not adhere to the stringency of demarcations in metaphysics proper precisely because I do not intend to ascribe any robust ontological commitment to proponents of different accounts of the nature of law. Given the uneven and sparse deployment of ontological argument in law, I shall confine myself to venturing a rather loose and metaphysically inaccurate classification of prominent contributions to the debate on the nature and grounds of legal truth. If my understanding is roughly correct, a peak moment in the relevant dispute as it has been commonly framed can be identified by the almost exclusively modal terms in which the debate about the grounding of legal facts ended up being conducted. What was thought to qualify as a winning argument should be framed as a defence or rebuttal of the proposition that, *necessarily*, legal facts are connected to moral facts in a particular respect. This was perhaps the peak of the conceptual turn in analytic jurisprudence that culminated in HLA Hart's avidly contested *Separation Thesis*. This thesis, as an argument about the separation of law and morals, was subject to at least three angles of interpretation and dispute: an analytic question about the nature of law; a substantive question about the moral import of law; and a metanormative question about whether settling the analytic dispute by itself entails a set of substantive propositions about the value of law.[1]

In the light of this modalised articulation of the divide between legal positivists and antipositivists, my invitation to consider the value of re-assigning the 'the battle positions' in this debate purports to convey the thought that, perhaps, the relationship between legal facts and moral facts is not part of the question that divides legal philosophers, but a part of the answer to a more foundational question that could tow our quest towards the vicinity of debates in metaontology. As will become evident in greater detail later on in my exposition, I will try to question the methodological value of framing the controversy between friends and foes of legal positivism in terms of the necessity or not of the contribution of moral or, more broadly, normative facts to the grounding of legal facts. My emphasis on the methodological import of appeals to the role of morality in the determination of legal content is meant to leave intact the substantive aspect of it, as I will not try to downplay the importance of explaining why morality is or is not relevant for the determination of legal content.

What I aim to achieve instead is to relocate the moment at which the task of settling the relevance of morality for law assumes its urgency.[2] Given the standard method of staging the debate between legal positivists and antipositivists, morality or, more generally, practical reason enters the picture too early – or so I shall argue – by serving as a criterion for the identification of a position as positivist or antipositivist. Leaving the details for later on, the rough idea I intend to take issue with is that explaining – affirmatively or dismissively – the role of morality in the determination of legal content is *the* task to be accomplished by legal philosophers precisely because what is at stake for legal philosophy is whether the legal positivist or the antipositivist should win the argument at the end of the day.[3] The thought I aim to convey as a reaction to how these two 'camps' are deployed is that both sides prematurely assume that, irrespective of the issue of this battle, moral facts metaphysically piggyback on *legal facts* in the sense that if and however they have a role to play, they do so by operating as complementary – along with social facts – grounds of *legal facts*.

In other words, in the order of explanation from legal truths (legal propositions) to non-legal grounding facts (moral and social facts), legal facts occupy the mediating role of making legal propositions true *and* of being, in turn, grounded in non-legal facts. In Chapter 3, I will address a question regarding

[1] For this division, see Morauta (2004). For a comprehensive overview of the modality of the relation between law and morality, see Moore (2012).

[2] Mark Greenberg pursues the halfway avenue of taking the relationship between morality and law to remain the primary task of jurisprudential inquiry, whilst replacing the modal terms of their association with metaphysical vocabulary; see Greenberg (2017: 284).

[3] That said, I do not dismiss the importance of qualifying a victorious jurisprudential argument by appeal to how concisely it vindicates its positivist or antipositivist orientation.

the way in which the logical structure of legal propositions is sensitive to verdicts about the nature of legal facts. This is mainly a metalinguistic question that paves the way for suggesting an alternative regimentation of legal propositions that does not depend on any robust understanding of the normative or descriptive nature of legal facts as their proper truthmakers. In this chapter, the object of my concern is the reverse relationship between legal propositions and legal facts, namely, the ontological commitments that utterances of legal content carry with respect to the distinctly legal nature of their truthmakers – that is, legal facts. This is mainly a metaontological question which will pave the way for a looser conception of the legal character of the truthmakers of legal propositions. This is the last and necessary step before detailing in Chapter 4 the way in which competing jurisprudential theories can be meaningfully juxtaposed for critical appraisal without facing the obstacles of prematurely 'linguisticised' metaphysical verdicts about the nature of legal truthmakers.

Being aware that I may already be giving the impression of flirting with platitudes, I set out to disclose the precise nature of my objection to this picture. As briefly hinted at above, my objection is methodological, not substantive. In other words, I do not purport to question the value of asking if and how morality is relevant for law, nor do I intend to begin, at least, by questioning the existence of legal facts. What I aim to question is the accuracy of the shared position that morality enters the picture by the route of what *grounds legal facts*. In this sense, the relevance of morality is derivative of the main problem for legal philosophy, which is the *grounding of legal facts*. Put differently, even if most legal philosophers would be eager to welcome into their stratified ontology a category of *legal* facts superseding more basic social and/or normative facts, the worry I am expressing would be as poignant as ever precisely because their convergence in treating the relevant dispute as one about the grounding of *legal facts* serves to obfuscate the divergent paths leading to this conclusion.

In defence of my timid departure from the use of morality as a modally robust criterion of division among competing theories of law, I will try to show that the association of legal propositions with an account of truthmaking is a fairly common assumption among legal philosophers advocating remarkably different approaches to the question of what makes legal content true. In addition, I will argue that those who begin their ontological quest by inquiring into what makes legal propositions true are already exposed to the 'virus of metaontology' without allowing themselves the receiving of proper treatment. To put it in a less graphical way, the postulation of truth-evaluable legal content would be a perfectly legitimate task as long as one would be willing to dedicate a considerable amount of arguing space for questions pertaining to the logical structure of the propositions amenable to truth-evaluation and the ensuing problems regarding the translatability of this logical structure into proper 'ontologese'. By talking of the translatability of 'legalese' into 'ontologese' – instead of translation or, in proper truth-theoretic language, equivalence – I intend to convey the thought that the metaphysical quest (modest or immodest) of the legal philosopher starts way ahead of the quest for the ultimate grounds of the truthmakers of legal propositions.

By jostling, so to speak, our quest backwards, I purport to relocate the site of theoretical disagreement about law a few crucial steps before the postulation of legal facts. Recalling the distinction noted in Chapter 1 between the site and the scope of legal disagreement, it is important to note that insofar as it can be shown that the possibility of theoretical disagreement about law is existentially dependent on its site, the latter can also determine its scope, namely, the range of questions (theoretical and metatheoretical) that one can plausibly ask with regard to the problem figuring in the site of our disagreement. In this vein, I shall argue that whereas the possibility of *legal facts* is not an existential condition for the possibility of theoretical disagreement about law, the possibility of *truthmakers* for legal propositions is an indispensable premise if we want to make sense of our disagreement in cognitivist terms.[4]

By commencing our inquiry from the truthmakers of legal propositions instead of facts featuring distinctly legal entities (legal facts), that is, by ascending from the level of a determinate property to the level of a determinable property, the scope of our disagreement is expanded to the realm of metajurisprudence. More precisely, this ascension legitimises the metajurisprudential question of how to make sense of the relationship between legal truth and the legal philosopher's corresponding ontological commitments. This is a metatheoretical question precisely because its object is not directly about the grounds of law, but the ontological counterpart of truth in legal philosophy. By allowing this ascension to a higher level of abstraction, I will make a reconstructive move towards associating contemporary theories of law – positivist and antipositivist – with a metaontological position which I have chosen to call *legal propositionalism*. In very broad terms, this is the view that the truthmakers of legal propositions must be structurally isomorphic to the truth-conditional content of the latter. As I intend to argue, this is precisely the kind of metajurisprudential premise that lies behind the ubiquitous postulation of legal facts as the obvious or trivial truthmakers of legal propositions.

The primary objection I intend to put forward with regard to what I will opt to describe as the propositionalist methodology in legal metaphysics is that this approach takes for granted that there can be an easy transition from talk about legal propositions of whichever logical structure to talk about legal facts as their truthmakers and, consequently, to talk about the non-legal descriptive and/or normative facts that ultimately ground legal facts. My worry is that behind the seemingly trivial assumption that legal propositions are made true

[4] By announcing my intention to disprove the ontological indispensability of *legal* facts as the truthmakers of legal propositions, I do not aim to convey the impression that I also intend to do without facts as an ontological category. What I purport to show is that the type of facts that can serve as truthmakers for legal propositions need not feature any distinctly legal entity as one of their constituents.

by legal facts – and that, henceforth, the main question is that of the grounds of legal facts *themselves* – lurks a metaontological controversy which, if properly articulated, can significantly re-assign the 'battle positions' in the perennial dispute between legal positivism and legal antipositivism.

The strategy I will pursue in this chapter will be considerably less flamboyant than the chapter title suggests. Its structure will consist of four steps. First, I will try to show that the association of legal propositions with an account of truthmaking is a widely shared premise among legal philosophers whose jurisprudential allegiances are nonetheless irreconcilable. Second, I shall very briefly explain how a theory of legal truthmakers maps onto a definitional theory of legal truth. Third, I shall try to explain how dominant cognitivist accounts of legal content (positivist and antipositivist alike) are tacitly approving of a 'linguistic' understanding of ontological commitment in the sense that they are inclined to infer the existence of legal facts as the *truthmakers* of legal propositions from the *truth conditions* of legal propositions. As already disclosed, the jurisprudential application of this thesis will be termed 'legal propositionalism'. Fourth, I shall briefly sketch a conceptualist or anti-metaphysical, so to speak, variant of legal propositionalism that dispenses with the implications of treating legal facts as extra-propositional entities.

I. LEGAL TRUTHMAKERS

In this section, I shall argue that the first-order counterpart of a metaontological commitment to the derivation of legal facts from the representational content of legal statements is a fairly thin account of legal truthmakers. In the present context, a legal truthmaker will stand for whichever fact a jurisprudential theory treats as eligible for making a legal proposition true. Making my talk of a legal truthmaker more explicit is the first substantive task that this exposition aspires to deliver. This will require more space than what may have been implied by the ease of my association of legal metaphysics with topics in general metaphysics. As a first remark, I should repeat that my allusion to the possibility of demarcating a *distinct* domain of purely metaphysical questions about law is far from being a common assumption among legal philosophers. To be frank, it is a bulky premise to begin with! Consequently, bringing my methodological proposal to fruition will have to wait until I have adduced enough evidence in support of the idea that notions like propositions, truthmakers and grounds are already inscribed in our jurisprudential vocabulary.

In what follows, I want to suggest that we may plausibly track the conceptual origins of familiar jurisprudential arguments about the relation of legal truth to reality in a general theory of truthmaking. Truthmaking is an explanatory variant of ontological dependence that is actually more of a family of *non-causal* relations between entities. Being unable to adjudicate the fervent debate on how to demarcate the truthmaking relation vis-a-vis other types of relations of ontological dependence – for instance, the relations of constitution, determination and realisation – I will take on board Jonathan Schaffer's modest account of how propositions enter into relations of ontological dependence to their truthmakers.[5] Schaffer regards truthmaking as an instance of the broader ontological relation of grounding, whilst avoiding the pitfalls of modalised approaches to truthmaking explanations.[6] In informal language, the understanding of truthmaking in terms of grounding is formulated by the following proposition:

> *For entities a, b, c ... to make P true is for the truth of P to be grounded in the existence of a, b, c ...*

But what kind of ontological dependence is grounding? A particular trait of this relation is that it is widely taken to hold only between propositions, facts or states of affairs, so it is particularly well suited for legal content, provided that we accept the premise that the bearers of legal content are propositions and, say, not mental states expressing approval or acceptance. Moreover, grounding like any relation of ontological dependence is irreflexive (that is, nothing is allowed to be grounded in itself) and asymmetric (that is, if x makes y true, then it is not the case that y makes x true). Another feature of grounding relations is their hyperintensionality such that the mere fact that every world where there is H_20 is a world where 2 + 2=4 is true does entail that the latter truth is grounded in the existence of H_20. In other words, hyperintensional relations are such that they hold asymmetrically between their relata, both of which necessitate each other.

One need not subscribe to the arguments put forward by proponents of legal realism in order to be entitled to feel suspicious about the cogency of adopting the vocabulary of truthmaking for the purpose of describing the controversy between positivist and antipositivist accounts of legal content. Joseph Raz has been an optimist about the prospects of gaining insight into the concept(s) of law as it is being used within parochial societal contexts, but he has been rather reluctant to extend his faith to the possibility of discovering law's essential or transworld properties over and above our mundane understanding of past or extant legal systems. It would be no exaggeration to say that the popularity of conceptual analysis as a methodological tool for dealing with foundational questions about law at least partly reflects a tacit aversion to engaging in 'immodest metaphysics'. Even though it is a matter of debate as to whether conceptual analysis in law amounts at least to a modest metaphysics or conversely supplants any metaphysical quest, I am willing to recognise that talk

[5] On Schaffer's account, 'truthmaking is the claim that the truth of propositions is not a fundamental feature of reality, and as such requires *grounding* in what is fundamental' (Schaffer 2008: 10, emphasis added).

[6] In the contemporary literature, the modal understanding of truthmakers is usually dubbed 'truthmaker necessitarianism', according to which the existence of a truthmaker necessitates the truth of the proposition it makes true; for an overview of the debate, see Cameron (2008).

of legal metaphysics is far from being an established element of the common jurisprudential parlance.

Without downplaying the dearth of direct appeals to the notion truthmaking, I would like to offer some evidence in support of my intuition that irrespective of the overtness of one's engagement in metaphysical arguments in law, the postulation of legal facts as the truthmakers of legal propositions is premised on a metaphysically nuanced conception of the relationship of legal propositions to the world. For instance, standard defences of legal positivism – both in its exclusivist and its inclusivist parsing – readily confirm the propositional nature of legal content.

On Scott Shapiro's plan positivism, there is no hesitation to admit that there is such a thing as true propositions of law such as that the US Constitution determines the authority structure of the federal government and is legally binding on all officials, and instead of challenging the propositional nature of this statement, he declares that his 'aim will be to figure out why this proposition is true: What makes it the case that the United States Constitution is law in the United States?'.[7] In the antipositivist camp, Ronald Dworkin's seminal distinction between propositions of law and the grounds of law is presumably the most original depiction of the centrality of legal propositions and their grounding. Likewise, Mark Greenberg's antipositivist metaphysical task regards 'the full metaphysical explanation of the content of the law (of why certain legal propositions are true)',[8] which is to say that the claim that 'there is a substantial body of determinate legal content [means that] there are many true legal propositions (in the particular legal system)'.[9]

What elevates an apparently impenetrable wall between positivist and antipositivist theories of law is not their questioning of the possibility of legal facts as the truthmakers of legal propositions, but their starkly opposing conception of what grounds legal facts themselves. In other words, among legal philosophers of a cognitivist conviction, there seems to be ample room for convergence on the 'fact' that there is such a thing as legal propositions or truth-evaluable legal content and that the best way to capture the relation of legal propositions to their truth status is by appeal to the notion of legal facts. The rest follows as a sequel to a story already known, namely, that the onerous task for the legal philosopher begins at the moment when legal facts call for their grounding.

II. FROM A THEORY OF TRUTH TO A THEORY OF TRUTHMAKING

Fairness in argument obliges me to be more precise with regard to which implications a theory of legal truthmakers has for a theory of legal truth. Whereas the

[7] Shapiro (2002: 387).
[8] Greenberg (2004: 159).
[9] ibid 162.

two projects are far from being exactly overlapping they certainly stand in alignment with each other. In what follows I would like to suggest that treating legal facts as the truthmakers of legal propositions need not be more committing than what is entailed by an *Equivalence Principle* of the form:

⌜⌜P⌝ is true if and only if P⌝

The above principle is stronger than a material Tarskian biconditional in the sense that it postulates the identity of its two sides either in terms of their meanings or in terms of the speech acts performed with them. In the spirit of preserving the relation of legal truthmakers to legal propositions, I shall adopt a *propositionalist* version of deflationism about truth[10] such that instances of the equivalence schema are about propositions rather than sentences. On this deflationist variant, P and the proposition [that P is true] trivially, necessarily and a priori entail each other.[11] Hopefully I do not believe that I have to adduce extensive evidence in support of my first substantive premise, as it is plausible enough to assume that I can have the majority of legal philosophers of a cognitivist persuasion on my side, *at least* with regard to the espousal of an equivalence principle of the form <P> is true *iff* P. It will be a further question whether the Tarskian metalanguage can be *ontologese* – that is, an ontologically authoritative metalanguage whose terms all carve perfectly at the world's joints – or simply a logical regimentation of English.

In the light of these minimal commitments, it is important to notice that we should not infer from this that truthmaking theories are not a priori compatible with more robust accounts of truth such as the family of views described as correspondence theories. The only substantive exclusion that this minimal

[10] It is a further question whether the endorsement of a deflationist account of legal truth is compatible with a truth-conditional account of the *meaning* of legal utterances. There are loud objections to combining a deflationist theory of truth with a truth-conditional account of meaning on the grounds that, instead of remaining silent about the deflationary character of meaning, deflationists are engaged in a circular attempt to explain truth in terms of meaning. For instance, on the propositionalist version of deflationism, the proposition that snow is white is true if and only if this proposition means that snow is white. This statement is patently trivial as both sides of the equivalence schema feature propositions. Accordingly, deflationism cannot be combined with truth-conditional theories of meaning that invoke the notion of truth to explain meaning. A truth-conditional theory of meaning will be an account of what makes it the case that sentences of a natural language express particular propositions, but, given that according to the propositionalist version of deflationism, the equivalence schema features propositions on both its sides, it is implausible to say that deflationism also has legitimate semantic aspirations. This is not a problem for someone who holds a propositionalist view of meaning precisely because in this case, the meaning of a sentence is not exhausted by its truth conditions.

[11] For this interpretation of the propositional truth predicate, see Soames (2003). Soames remarks that on a deflationary account of truth, defining the truth predicate is not an indispensable task. As he notes: 'It is no part of deflationism that the truth predicate must be definable. Consequently, it would be expecting too much to demand that deflationists provide a synonym for the truth predicate, or identified the proposition expressed by the sentence the proposition that S is true with the proposition expressed by some other sentence in which the word true doesn't occur. Some deflationists may think that truth can be defined, but not all do, and it is not an essential part of the deflationary position' (ibid 372).

account of truth supports regards any version of the identity theory of truth according to which the truth of truth-bearers (e.g. propositions) is identical to a truthmaker (e.g. facts or states of affairs). An identity theory of legal truth is an available specification of one's legitimate espousal of an identity theory of truth *simpliciter* such that the truth of a legal proposition consists in its *identity* with a legal fact. On this approach, true legal propositions and legal facts are *one and the same* kind of entity![12] Whereas this is a substantive constraint on what individuates a theory as a first-order theory of legal truthmaking, it imposes no constraints on what individuates a metaontological theory as an instance of legal propositionalism. As I plan to explain further below (see section IV), there is conceptual space for accommodating a variant of legal propositionalism that does not treat legal facts as the extra-propositional entities performing the task of making legal propositions true.

III. LEGAL PROPOSITIONALISM

I will use the term 'legal propositionalism' in order to refer to what I take to be an accurate reconstruction of a latent metajurisprudential view on what follows from the admission of the possibility of truthmakers for legal propositions. At first approximation, a legal propositionalist perceives her foundational work as a task that involves the derivation of the truthmakers of legal propositions from the logical regimentation of assertions of legal content. This is roughly the view that the truthmakers of legal propositions must be structurally isomorphic to the truth-conditional content of the propositions.[13] The legal propositionalist's foundational work is a composition of a semantic and an ontological task. The semantic task corresponds to the process of refining the logical structure of assertions of legal content. In section II of Chapter 3, I will venture such a refinement by modelling legal propositions on the logical structure of claims of abstract constitution. The ontological task that is the focus of this chapter purports to provide a concrete verdict on the veridicality of the propositional content expressed by ordinary legal claims.

As I hope to be able to demonstrate, venturing to describe such a comprehensive position in legal metaphysics as propositionalist is not driven by the

[12] For the view that truthmaking theories are compatible with a deflationist account of truth, see Lewis (2001: 603–05); and Assay (2014). For an overview of the ramifications entailed by combining truthmaking with a correspondence theory of truth, see David (2009).

[13] DH Mellor eloquently describes this distinction, noting that 'a theory of truthmakers is no more a theory of *meaning* than it is of truth. In particular, therefore, the truth*makers* of propositions must not be identified with their metalinguistic truth *conditions* … The idea that truth conditions link meaning and ontology derives from an ambiguity in the expression "giving a sentence's truth conditions". The ambiguity is between saying what would *make* the sentence true and using a Tarskian metalanguage to say when it is true, which need tell us nothing about what, if anything, makes it true' (Mellor 2009: 279).

ambition to add more complexity to the extant jurisprudential jargon. At this point, I would even dare to claim that part, at least, of what explains the reluctance of non-legal philosophers to enlist current debates about the nature of law as a source of potentially formative contributions to the broader metaphysical discourse is precisely the fact that the debate in legal metaphysics is heavily dependent on an unnecessarily constraining terminology that either has no direct semantic counterparts in other fields of philosophical inquiry or has a radically different meaning than what is standardly associated with the use of similar terms in other domains. In light of this caveat about inventing new terms, my line of defence will be that despite the lack of a direct terminological counterpart in other philosophical domains, the use of the term 'legal propositionalism' aims to highlight the neglected affinity of debates in legal metaphysics with contemporary issues in general metaphysics.

By its very essence as a (reconstructed) metajurisprudential view of how to argue about the type of ontological commitment a cognitivist legal philosopher should be willing to shoulder, legal propositionalism is, strictly speaking, an applied version of what is known in metaontology as the Quinean or quantificational account of ontological commitment. In other words, legal propositionalism will be presented as a second-order thesis about how the reality of law – as an abstract object, property or relation – is related to the truth-conditional content of legal utterances. One way of adding some concreteness to this claim is to say that a theory's success is measured by how much ontological baggage it can unload by way of reducing or paraphrasing sentences quantifying over obscure entities into sentences free of 'offending' entities. In this regard, a theory's ontological commitment will be those quantified entities that the theory's reduced sentences cannot do without if they aspire to merit the label of being true. This approach has been traditionally associated with Quine's quantificational argument[14] that a discourse's ontological commitments must be read off its sentences' truth-conditions or, to put it another way, that we are entitled to accept those entities over which the sentences of our best theory quantify.[15] As soon as we track the truth-conditions of a given theory's sentences and succeed at regimenting sentential content in a proper metalanguage, our sole remaining task, according to this view, is to see which objects in the world are eligible for satisfying the variables figuring in the truth-conditional rendition of the sentence(s).

To illustrate the methodological impact of this approach, suppose that the locution 'there is a statue' is part of the inventory of sentences composing the theory T of what a specific room contains, call it T_{room}. This sentence can be aptly regimented into first-order classical logic as $(\exists x)\ x = a$ where 'a' stands for the sortal term 'statue'. Consequently, according to this picture, the metalinguistic

[14] See Quine (1948).

[15] This is a more canonical rendition of the Quinean dictum that 'to be is to be the value of a variable' or, in its unpacked version, '[w]hat entities there are, from the point of view of a given language, depends on what positions are accessible to variables in that language' (Quine 1976: 201).

translation $(\exists x)\ x = a$ can only be true relative to a domain that contains a statue such that the truth of our theory about the room's content is *ontologically committed* to the existence of a statue. The picture described above allows us to build ontology into semantics in the sense that a sentence's truth-conditional meaning is at least indicative, if not dispositive, of what extra-linguistic entities are to be treated as part of a theory's ontological commitments. As one may reasonably expect, there has been an array of objections to different varieties of the same endeavour of linguisticising ontology or, as John Heil describes it, the attempt 'to construe linguistic categories as legislating, rather than roughly reflecting, boundaries and divisions of the world'.[16] Labelling this position as metaontological is a result of its non-committal stance towards *what kind of entities* should figure as the content of our best theory's ontological commitments. All that it claims is that *irrespective of* what these entities – or properties, states of affairs, relations etc – turn out to be as a result of our best available explanations, they must be somehow *represented* or reflected in the logical regimentation of the sentences we use in constructing a theory.

Before articulating the basic components of alternative propositionalist approaches in legal metaphysics, there remain two further issues I should flag up at this stage. Both pertain to the methodology of legal propositionalism rather than its substantive content and, as such, they are conceptually linked to the possibility of making sense of the process of deriving legal truthmakers from legal truth conditions. Both issues regard the modal profile of legal propositions. First, we should ask whether legal propositions can be true as a matter of *metaphysical* necessity. This possibility could seriously compromise the propositionalist project as it is notoriously perplexing to make a plausible case for the claim that necessary propositions are literally made true by extra-propositional entities. Second, we should ask whether legal propositions can be true as a matter of *conceptual* necessity.

With regard to the first question, I should note that legal propositionalism becomes intelligible only if we agree that predications of legal content are contingent. Contingent predications like 'Socrates is wise' are usually contrasted with predications of essential properties (or relations) such as 'Socrates is human'. Whereas in the latter case the existence of Socrates as a concrete particular grounds the truth of the proposition that Socrates is human, in the former case Socrates cannot be regarded as the truthmaker of 'Socrates is wise'.[17] There are possible worlds in which the individual 'Socrates' might have existed and still not possessed wisdom. For friends of truthmakers, contingent predications are made true either by instantiated universals or by exemplifiables (tropes). Hence, in our example, the proposition that Socrates is wise is made true either by *the fact that* Socrates bears the property of wisdom or by the *trope*

[16] Heil (2007: 12).
[17] I have borrowed this illuminating example from Bergmann and Brower (2006: 80).

'Socrates' wisdom'. My corresponding intuition is that legal propositionalists also perceive predications of legal content as contingent predications. Mark Greenberg accurately depicts this intuition when he says that 'no legal-content facts are plausibly metaphysically basic or ultimate facts about the universe … like facts about the meaning of words or facts about international exchange rates … [they] hold in virtue of more basic facts'.[18]

With regard to the second question, one could begin by noting that conceptual truths cannot *be made true*. Any invocation of truthmakers points to an explanatory relation *in virtue of* which a proposition is true. However, there is a duality in the use of phrases such as 'being true in virtue of' depicting the two sides of the analytic/synthetic divide. Analytic or conceptual truths are true as a matter of a relation of *conceptual dependence* between their constitutive concepts. In such cases, as David Liggins explains, 'what depends on what would be mirrored in the complexity of the concepts we use to think about these things'.[19] In light of the present suggestion, then, pure analyticities are not literally *made true* by their constitutive concepts; hence, it is inaccurate to speak about conceptual facts *qua* truthmakers.[20] Locutions such as 'being true in virtue of meaning' can be legitimate as long as they are positioned within the context of sentential meaning, to the exclusion of any ontological posits whatsoever.

Provided that pure analyticities are not strictly speaking suitable candidates for truthmaking explanations, it becomes questionable whether we may intelligibly subsume theories of law that rely heavily on conceptual analysis under the label of 'legal propositionalism'. For instance, Joseph Raz's view on de facto authority and its relation to the claim to legitimate authority as well as his conception of the Sources Thesis as a claim about the identification of legal content are clearly endowed with conceptual arguments. Likewise, Scott Shapiro's understanding of the determination of legal content is premised on the conceptual argument that 'given that the law aims to solve moral problems through social planning, it cannot do what it is supposed to do when the logic of planning is violated'.[21] My understanding is that assigning a pivotal role to conceptual arguments is not enough to render unintelligible the relevance of genuine truthmaking explanations in law. The reason is that to the best of my knowledge, most if not all conceptual arguments employed by analytic legal philosophers do not take the form of fundamental analyticities, or even less logical truths.

[18] Greenberg (2004: 158).

[19] Liggins (2011: 262).

[20] At least since Wittgenstein's elaborate argumentation in his *Tractatus*, it has become almost uncontroversial that for pure analytical truths, there is no condition that the world must satisfy in order for them to become true.

[21] Shapiro (2011: 348).

To see how we can accommodate some conceptual fluctuations within the standard confines of truthmaking, I will briefly examine the impact of Raz's 'strong conceptual moment' as it unfolds in his conceptual account of legal authority. His pivotal conceptual claim is captured by the proposition that law necessarily claims to possess authority. As it stands, it is not directly evident how it is implicated in the question of what makes legal propositions true. However, its impact can become more manifest through its conceptual entailments. The latter claim entails the conceptual claim that law must be capable of possessing authority which further entails that '[first], a directive can be authoritatively binding only if it is, or at least presented as, someone's view of how its subjects ought to behave. Second, it must be possible to identify the directive as being issued by the alleged authority without relying on reasons or considerations on which the directive purports to adjudicate'.[22] Setting aside the familiar objections to this conceptual chain, I will focus on the question of whether these conceptual remarks about the properties of authoritative directives can deprive legal facts of their metaphysically robust status as truthmakers of legal propositions.

Bearing in mind that one of the targets of this exposition is to restrict the logical looseness in our assertions of legal content, I suggest we test the impact of Raz's conceptual argument by provisionally relying on a truth-conditional analysis of legal statements. So, let us assume, for the sake of this argument, that the proposition that *an authoritative directive X constitutes a legal norm Y* is a truth-conditional statement that can accommodate Raz's understanding of the structure of legal propositions.[23] Taking this assumption on board, the question that emerges is whether this proposition is amenable to truthmaking, that is, whether this proposition is literally *made* true by a legal fact about the existence of a legal norm. The part of Raz's argument that makes this question prima facie relevant is the purported conceptual truth that for it to be the case that X is an authoritative directive, X must exist independently of the reasons that make this directive morally intelligible.

What could possibly make our talk of grounding the truth of legal propositions spurious? Suppose that the fact that the proposition that an authoritative directive X constitutes a legal norm Y is true is grounded in *the fact that* Y *exists*. This is our default position as it seems unobjectionable that if Y exists, X exists. In other words, if a legal norm Y with content C exists, then there exists an authoritative directive X with the same content C. The next step is to see whether the obtaining of this fact can be fully accounted for in terms of more basic conceptual facts. On Raz's view, it is a conceptual truth that an authoritative directive X is not existentially dependent on the reasons that make this directive morally intelligible. Consequently, Raz takes this conceptual truth to entail the further conceptual truth that an authoritative directive

[22] Raz (1994: 215).

[23] In section II in ch 3, I provide a detailed account of how to parse legal statements in constitutive terms.

X is existentially dependent on facts about the actual sayings and doings of legal officials (the Social Fact Thesis). In light of his theory's basic assumptions, the latter facts are taken to be the grounds of legal facts, namely, facts about the existence of legal norms. As a result, we get the following chain of propositions:

(1) The truth [an authoritative directive X constitutes a legal norm Y] is grounded in the fact that legal norm Y exists.
(2) The authoritative directive X is not existentially dependent on the reasons that make it morally intelligible [conceptual truth].
(3) Point (2) conceptually entails (the proposition) that the authoritative directive X is existentially dependent on social facts about the sayings and doings of legal officials [conceptual truth].
(4) Legal norm Y is existentially dependent on authoritative directive X [metaphysical truth].
(5) Points (3) and (4) entail (the proposition) that legal norm Y is existentially dependent on social facts about the sayings and doings of legal officials. [conceptual truth].
(6) Points (1) and (5) entail (the proposition) that the truth [an authoritative directive X constitutes a legal norm Y] ultimately depends on social facts about the sayings and doings of legal officials [conceptual truth].

Keeping the analysis in focus, I will forgo the question of whether point (2) conceptually entails point (3) – which is what Raz argues for – and ask whether the conclusion (6), namely, the *conceptual fact that the truth of [an authoritative directive X constitutes a legal norm Y] ultimately depends on social facts about the sayings and doings of legal officials*, makes the claim that the fact that legal norm Y exists is the immediate ground of the truth that X constitutes Y metaphysically spurious. In other words, the question is whether the conceptual truth at which the previous syllogism arrives makes it the case that facts about the existence of legal norms cannot serve as genuine, extra-propositional truthmakers for claims of legal constitution *precisely because* the truth of the latter depends on social facts *as a matter of conceptual necessity.*

My response will be negative because as the syllogism stands, it is falsely committed to the transitivity of the relation of truthmaking. More specifically, the problem arises as soon as we take on board the idea that truthmaking can be fully captured in terms of the relation of grounding, which, as it is commonly perceived, is a transitive relation. It should be recalled that the problem we are dealing with here is whether the presence of strong conceptual premises in the previous syllogism is capable of vitiating the prospect of legal truthmakers. This fear of 'contamination', so to speak, is grounded in the truthmaker project's core idea that truth must somehow be responsive to extra-linguistic and extra-logical, worldly facts. If conceptual facts are implicated in the chain of arguments that explain the grounds of legal truth, it will be more figurative than literal to assert that legal truths really depend on facts about the world rather than facts about our conceptual understanding. This alarming conclusion becomes plausible as soon as we take on board the idea that the relationship between the truth of a proposition and its grounds (the existence of a legal norm) – as it figures in point (1) – and the relationship between the grounds (the existence of a legal norm) of a truth (legal proposition) and their own grounds (social facts) – as it figures in point (5) – are of exactly the same nature such that if the latter relation is transitive, so is the former.

As a rejoinder to this assimilative correlation between truthmaking and grounding, I will repeat what is being frequently invoked in the relevant literature[24] in support of their disassociation, namely, the fact that whereas the relata of truthmaking involve entities of a different kind (a linguistic representation of the world or proposition and a fact), the relata of grounding are both of the same kind, namely, facts. As a result, the transition from a proposition-to-fact relation to a fact-to-fact relation is not mediated by some restrictive principles, including the one that the relation of truthmaking is not transitive. To see why this is not the case, let us suppose that truthmaking is indeed a variety of the grounding relation. Then, from the previous syllogism we get:

(1) That [social fact] grounds [existence of legal norm Y] is conceptually true.
(2) [Existence of legal norms] grounds [<directive X constitutes legal norm Y> is true].
(3) [Social fact] grounds [<directive X constitutes legal norm Y> is true].

The syllogism fails because there is a crucial shift from <that [social fact] grounds [existence of legal norm Y]> to [social fact]. These two statements are not identical. The former points to a conceptually necessary proposition, while the latter points to a contingent social fact. Consequently, even in light of the grounding account of truthmaking, the relation of truthmaking remains intransitive precisely because it is a cross-categorical relation.

The combination of all the above results in a hybrid truthmaking explanation of legal propositions: conceptual facts may be implicated in the grounding of the truth of assertions of legal content, but they are not explanatorily direct in the sense that legal propositions cannot be true simply by virtue of the obtaining of these conceptual facts. This is not the place to fully evaluate the intricacies of Raz's reconceptualization of authoritative directives as pre-emptive directives, but it suffices to say that insofar as explanations of propositional truths are not entirely grounded in tautologies or analytical entailments, it is permissible to categorise them as instances of truthmaking explanations.[25]

[24] For a contrastive analysis, see Rodriguez-Pereyra (2005); and Schaffer (2009).

[25] Barry Smith illustrates this point, particularly with regard to the grounding of what he calls impure logical truths, by remarking that there is a class of logical truths 'which do bear specific existential presuppositions, such as "John is hungry or it is not the case that John is hungry" … These truths are made true (in the strict sense of [truthmaking]) by the existence of the entities named' (Smith and Simon 2007: 94).

Leaving behind this lengthy prelude, I shall offer a template[26] of how one may identify oneself as a legal propositionalist. As a first approximation, a legal propositionalist perceives her foundational work as a task that involves the derivation of the truthmakers of legal propositions from the logical regimentation of assertions of legal content. In other words, her foundational quest can be traced back to explaining the truth of simple statements such as 'In the State of California any person who, by means of deceit, intentionally deprives another person of property worth more than a thousand dollars shall be imprisoned for not more than six months' in terms of the postulation of a legal fact that depicts the logical structure of this sentence. There are at least three distinct routes for qualifying as a legal propositionalist. All three routes count as instances of legal propositionalism insofar as they ultimately purport to derive a truthmaker from some account of truth conditions. Their difference lies in the immediacy of their result.

The first route is available for those legal philosophers who would be eager to label themselves as non-reductive realists about legal facts. In other words, they believe that facts featuring legal properties (legality), legal relations (legal obligation) or legal objects (legal norm) are a legitimate addition to a theory's inventory of ontologically licensed entities. From a metaontological perspective, non-reductive realism about legal truthmakers is a theoretical option that is strongly compatible with a quantificational conception of ontological commitment. The selected truthmaker is a token of what our theory is ontologically committed to and its constituent (legal norm, legal relation or legal property) lies within the relevant domain of quantification. This way of responding to the question of what makes propositions about legal content true purports to protect the integrity of a domain of discourse – in our case, a theory of legal content – which makes reference to these entities.

To animate the emerging map, I would venture to classify both Mark Greenberg's moral impact theory of law and Joseph Raz's exclusive positivist theory as instances of non-reductive legal propositionalism.[27] For example, according to Greenberg, legal obligations are those moral obligations created by the actions of legal institutions. In this regard, relations of legal obligation are not reducible to relations of moral obligation precisely because the latter may

[26] I owe this idea to Dyke (2008).

[27] This metajurisprudential taxonomy is not meant to deflate the stark opposition between these two theories at the level of substantive jurisprudence. It can still remain the case that Greenberg and Raz occupy radically different substantive positions on the positivism-antipositivism spectrum in much the same way that a deontological ethical theory that postulates the existence of an irreducibly normative property of rightness can arrive at remarkably different conclusions about what is the right thing to do vis-a-vis a consequentialist theory that is equally affirmative of the existence of a non-natural property of rightness. Nevertheless, this metajurisprudential convergence will be an informative addition to our way of decoding the substantive dispute, mainly because it facilitates the advancement of a substantive objection to both theories on the basis of their common metajurisprudential premise rather than on their substantive merits.

obtain as a result of *any kind of action* (that is, even morally wicked actions) on the part of legal officials, whereas the moral facts that constitute the content of the law must come about in *the legally proper way*.[28] In a similar vein, on Raz's account, legal norms are not reducible to authoritative speech acts. The fact that a norm is authoritatively pronounced is not modally sufficient for its being a valid legal norm precisely because legally valid norms are abstract objects that also stand in hierarchical relations to superior norms with which they may conflict (eg, cases of unconstitutional legislation or formally deficient legal enactments). In this respect, it could also be argued that legal norms are existentially distinct vis-a-vis their constituents, namely, authoritative pronouncements.[29]

Fortunately, the range of options for the legal propositionalist is not exhausted by the path of staunch realism. If the legal propositionalist does not want to dismiss the veridicality of our discourse about legal content but is at the same time suspicious of the possibility of the existence of legal entities, she may proceed by proposing a *reduction* of truths about legal content to truths about another kind of entity. If this endeavour proves successful, she can come up with a theory whose sentences are not legal-content-committing. More precisely, she will be able to declare her commitment to the entities serving as the reduction base of her legal-norm talk such that sentences like 'according to the law of S it is obligatory to Φ' can be eliminatively reduced into a sentence of the form 'according to X it is obligatory to Φ'. As a result, given her propositionalist inclination of deriving truthmakers from truth conditions, she will claim that, strictly speaking, the truthmaker for the proposition 'according to the law of S it is obligatory to Φ' is the fact that X requires so precisely because the legal authority to issue such norms is reducible to X.

This moderate yet legal-truth-preserving strategy is not without its supporters. Scott Shapiro's planning theory of law is an excellent illustration of this view. This can be clearly evidenced by Shapiro's reductive plan to unpack the modal profile of legal norms by reducing them to a type of (sub)plan authorised by an institutionalised master plan. His strategy of reducing talk about legal norms to talk about plans serves as primary evidence of how we could elicit his own response to the question of what makes statements like 'according to the law of S it is obligatory to Φ' true.[30] The latter truth will be reducible to the

[28] Greenberg does not offer a systematic account of the legally proper way of triggering moral obligations, but he adamantly supports the idea that moral obligations that are triggered in legally improper or, as he calls them, paradoxical ways fail to constitute legal obligations. See Greenberg (2014: 1321–23).

[29] Raz alludes to the sortal and modal distinctness of valid legal norms vis-a-vis their constitutive material (authoritative directives) when he remarks that: 'Not all exclusionary reasons are norms. We have noted that *all authoritative utterances are exclusionary reasons, and yet they are not all norms*. It seems that norms and other exclusionary reasons do not differ in any way which is relevant to practical reasoning. *The difference is primarily ontological. We talk of norms as entities*' (Raz 1999b: 77–78, emphasis added).

[30] There are many places in *Legality* where it becomes evident that the connection between legal norms and plans is intimate. By way of providing some guidelines for his readers, Shapiro notes that

truth that 'according to the master plan of S it is obligatory to Φ' such that, strictly speaking, the truthmaker for the latter proposition will not be a legal fact, but a fact about the existence of a particular plan. Despite the elimination of talk about legal norms and legal facts, Shapiro's position can still be construed as a reductionist variant of legal propositionalism precisely because it remains faithful to the idea that propositional truth is ontologically committing to its constituent properties or objects, *whichever they turn out to be*.

Nonetheless, if our imaginary legal propositionalist is utterly pessimistic about the prospect of either safeguarding the existence of legal norms or offering a plausible reduction, she may move on to declare all sentences of the form 'according to the law of S it is obligatory to Φ' as literally false. This *error-theoretic* response is still in line with the rationale of legal propositionalism as it is motivated by the acknowledgement that sentences about the content of legal norms or legal obligations *imply*, albeit infelicitously, the existence of facts about the existence of legal norms or the obtaining of legal obligations. Such claims about legal content must be systematically false precisely because legal norms do not exist. In a further step, the propositionalist error-theorist is free to suggest an alternative truth-conditional content which, nonetheless, will serve as the template from which she will read off the appropriate truthmaker. Consequently, she may 'renew her vow', so to speak, to the truth of sentences that are not ontologically offending. In other words, she may argue that we do not ordinarily use sentences about the content of legal norms or legal obligations in order to assert the propositions they literally express; instead, there exist genuine semantic alternatives that can assist us in expressing our true thoughts about law.

In some respects, there is room for arguing that Ronald Dworkin could be classified as a legal propositionalist who would favour an error-theoretic response to the question of whether statements featuring legal entities are true. More precisely, we may read Dworkin's claim that legal practices cannot be identified independently of the legal content they produce as evidence of his error-theoretic orientation. In other words, on a charitable understanding of Dworkin's interpretivist theory of law, it is implausible to assign numerical distinctness to the pre-interpretive material that furnishes legal content. The inextricable tie between what Dworkin calls the dimension of fit and the dimension of justification can be formally unpacked into the claim that we cannot disassociate what the aspects of political practices contribute to the content of the law from legal content per se.[31] As a result, it will be an imprecise assumption to believe that

his 'purpose here is not to draw an analogy between laws and plans but to flesh out an implication. The existence conditions for law are the same as those for plans because the fundamental rules of legal systems *are* plans' (Shapiro 2011: 119).

[31] Legal interpretivism maintains that aspects of past political practices qualify as contributing to the content of the law by virtue of their being *instances* of the set of principles embodied in a particular political community. According to this picture, principles of political morality do not stand in a relation of *grounding* to the contributory aspects of legal practices, but in a relation of *instantiation*,

our assertions of legal content purport to communicate the constitutive interplay between pre-legal and legal entities precisely because legal content cannot be abstractly coincident with non-legal determinants.

A more familiar upshot of this metaontological position is Dworkin's substantive claim that assertions of legal content are properly understood as assertions about the instantiation of the principle of integrity. In other words, from the viewpoint of a legal interpretivist, the type of statements we should be evaluating for their truth are statements about the requirements of political morality rather than statements about what a *legal* authority requires. A first-hand indication of Dworkin's generic understanding of legal propositions is provided by his consistent appeal to the notion of 'figuring in' or 'following from' an integrity-realising scheme of principle. In *Law's Empire*, we read that '[according] to law as integrity, propositions of law are true if they figure in or follow from the principles of justice, fairness, and procedural due process that provide the best constructive interpretation of the community's legal practice'.[32] On this understanding, by uttering 'X does not constitute a legal norm (or legal obligation)', an interpretivist can meaningfully engage her opponents by inviting them to reconsider their inflationary understanding of the entities that are implicated in the generation of legal content. Her claim that 'X constitutes a legal norm' is not what we really assert when we say that 'it is legally obligatory to φ'. This is not a reductive position insofar as an understanding of legal discourse in terms of authoritative requirements would be treated by Dworkin as systematically delivering false statements. For him, the language of legal authority must be replaced by the language of instantiations of integrity precisely because the former is an erroneous guide to explaining what is actually at stake when legal officials act in particular ways.

IV. LEGAL PROPOSITIONALISM WITHOUT LEGAL TRUTHMAKERS

As was briefly noted in section II above, legal philosophers might – even though I doubt they would ever explicitly embark on this quest – disagree about the relation of legal truth to reality or, alternatively, the nature of legal truth. I have somehow expeditiously taken a stance in favour of a deflationary account of legal truth by way of arguing that it suffices to spark some intelligible controversy among legal philosophers who in one way or another believe that the grounds of legal truth are extra-propositional or non-linguistic in nature. That said, it would be an unfair move to forestall anyone's sincere proclivity

much like laws of nature are thought to have actual events as their instances. By denying that the pre-interpretive (to use Dworkin's jargon) material is identified independently of its contribution to the content of the law, the legal interpretivist argues that we cannot disagree about the sources of law independently of the principles of political morality which the content of the law instantiates.

[32] Dworkin (1986: 225).

to experimenting with a neo-Fregean account of legal facts such that the ensuing dispute over their grounds becomes a question of what best explains the concept of a legal norm. For the neo-Fregean legal philosopher,[33] legal facts would feature concepts rather than properties or objects as their constituent parts. Taking on board a standard version of the Fregean context principle, it could turn out that only *within the context of a legal utterance* does the concept of a legal norm acquire meaning. As a result, any further question with regard to the existence status of legal norms is stamped as a futile attempt to detach the lexical item 'legal norm' from its propositional environment, thus violating the context principle.

Consequently, the crucial question is whether legal propositionalism as a metaontological theory of jurisprudential commitment necessitates a robust account of legal facts as being eligible for two tasks, namely, for operating as the grounds of facts about the truth of legal propositions and for being grounded in more fundamental non-legal facts. Whereas I do believe that the truth-maker variant of legal propositionalism provides the most accurate depiction of familiar jurisprudential arguments about the grounds of legal truth, there is no principled reason for ascribing to this hypothesis universal scope. More precisely, there can be a line of argument to the effect that legal facts may exist not by virtue of their being part of the fabric of reality, but because they can be successfully accommodated by our privileged conceptual scheme. On this broadly Fregean picture, of course, there will be no room for grounding talk as there will be no distinction between truth-bearers and truth-makers. A Fregean legal fact is nothing more than a true legal thought (a legal proposition) and, as such, it falls short of standing in grounding relations to other Fregean facts. That said, the neo-Fregean legal philosopher could still be classified as a legal propositionalist precisely because, like her Quinean metaphysical counterpart, she purports to decipher the question of what exists by answering the question of what the truth conditions of legal sentences are. But beyond this minimal point of convergence, the neo-Fregean pursues a radical departure from non-trivial appeals to existence.

In the likeness of its traditional application in the ontology of arithmetic, a neo-Fregean account of the metaphysics of law could represent the grounding counterpart of the relationship between legal facts and their determinant non-legal facts by means of an abstraction principle. The latter principle will express a bridging, so to speak, conceptual fact about when certain obligations, rights, powers and so on necessarily obtain. The structure of this conceptual fact can ordinarily feature a universally quantified biconditional denoting a function from facts cast in sociological vocabulary to facts cast in jurisprudential

[33] Carsten Heidemann provides a pithy reconstruction of Hans Kelsen's theory of norms premised on a linguistic account of facts about the existence of legal norms as true legal judgments; see Heidemann (1997). For an overview of neo-Fregean approaches to ontology, see Eklund (2006).

vocabulary. This is a purely mental process that purports to attain a new idea of an abstract object by contemplating other objects and attempting to abstract therefrom the features that distinguish them.

To illustrate this option, we could perhaps reconstruct Shapiro's process of reducing legal norms to plans in a non-ontologically loaded way such that by observing institutional and non-institutional practices of planning agency, we push aside or abstract from the respects in which they differ, thereby acquiring an abstract conception of 'legal norm-hood'. This can work if we consider the case that the singular term *legal norm* has the logical form of a functional expression such that we can talk about a legal norm prescribing or allowing X-ing. This can be read as a function from an abstract object to a type of action. If, as expected, a legal norm designates an abstract object, there may exist an equation (abstraction principle) such that we get a functional regimentation of the form $(\forall x)(\forall M)(\Sigma(x)= \Sigma(M \supset x) \leftrightarrow E(x,M))$ where x is a variable denoting act types, M is a plan-denoting variable, Σ is a functional operator and E is an equivalence relation over items of the given type. To illustrate this description, let us assume for a moment that Shapiro would be eager to impersonate the neo-Fregean legal philosopher I have in mind.[34] Then he could proceed to defend the following conceptual claim (let us call it CC):

> A legal norm X = a rational requirement that {if one accepts M, one X's} iff X-ing is authorised by a shared master plan M.

The idea will then be that CC being an explanation of the concept of a legal norm, the existence of a legal norm requires nothing more than that a course of action required by the norms of instrumental rationality is authorised by the shared master plan of a planning organisation. The two sentences flanking the biconditional are somehow identical in terms of the content they express. Consequently, for the neo-Fregean legal philosopher, grounding *just is* a form of reconceptualisation. Being poor with words capable of summarily reviewing the background of this strand of thought, I will rely on a pithy description of the process of reconceptualisation offered by Bob Hale and Crispin Wright; according to their viewpoint, this process is premised on the idea that 'it is permissible to fix the truth-conditions of one kind of statement as coinciding with those of another – "kind" here referring to something like logical form – in such a way that the overt *existential* implications of the former exceed those of the latter, although the *epistemological* status of the latter, as conceived in

[34] Plunkett (2012) offers an extensive account of how Shapiro's Planning Theory can accommodate Greenberg's rational determination requirement by way of assigning to conceptual truths the role of making intelligible the determination of legal facts by social facts. Plunkett's analysis is geared towards engaging Greenberg's own terminology, but nothing in his line of reasoning prevents us from taking the intelligibility-enabling role of conceptual facts to be understood in terms of a more familiar abstraction principle, provided that Plunkett's reading of Shapiro can do without the literal use of the concept of grounding.

advance, is inherited by the former'.[35] In the present example, the statement that is fraught with existential implications is the left-hand-side sentence that a particular legal norm exists. Thus, the neo-Fregean legal philosopher will arrive at the conclusion that a particular legal norm X exists in S just by reconceptualising the sentence 'X is authorised by the shared master plan of S'. A good instance of reconceptualisation will be one where truth conditions are preserved right to left across the abstraction schema.

The metaontological implication of this strategy is indeed strikingly similar with the quantificational understanding of legal propositionalism, yet it falls short of counting as a focal instance of the latter mainly because not only does it countenance the dependence of reference on truth, but it also takes the further step of trivialising the prospect of ever exiting into the extra-conceptual space. Since we are dealing with linguistic entities, any resort to the vocabulary of grounding will retain its intelligibility on the explicit condition that we take it to be nothing more than a form of conceptual translation. From this perspective, the ontological commitment to the reality of legal norms is conceptually necessitated by the sameness of truth conditions across the biconditional. The argumentative challenge for the neo-Fregean legal philosopher lies in substantiating her claim that the content expressed by the sentence that X is authorised by the shared master plan of S is informatively reconceptualisable and this is not a trivial task.

[35] Hale and Wright (2009: 181). For an earlier formulation of this position, see Hale and Wright (2001).

3

Relating Legal Facts to Legal Propositions

JURISPRUDENTIAL DISAGREEMENT APPEARS stratified. At the most abstract level, legal philosophers disagree about the proper methodology of jurisprudence. For instance, opinions are divided as to whether the proper method of philosophical inquiry about law consists in refining our description of what a legal practice is or, conversely, justifying the practice of law from a normative vantage point. Further downstream, jurisprudential disagreement tends to focus on more substantive questions. On the one hand, controversy erupts with regard to the concept or the nature of law. Debates in this domain are usually cast in modal or essentialist terms such that the main question becomes whether legal validity can be attributed to norms promulgated by morally wicked governments or whether, by its essence, law serves a moral aim. On the other hand, there are philosophers of both a positivist[1] and antipositivist[2] persuasion who are sympathetic to the possibility of theoretical disagreement about which kind of non-legal facts ground legal facts. The scope of the latter dispute relates to the nature and role of more fundamental, social and/or normative facts by virtue of which facts about the content of the law of a given jurisdiction obtain. For instance, two judges may converge in their interpretation of a particular statute or precedent, but disagree about what the law is because they diverge in their beliefs about whether statutes and precedents are the sole determinants of legal content.

Currently, the most prominent antipositivist account of theoretical disagreement in law undeniably originates from Ronald Dworkin's elaboration of law as an interpretive concept. Dworkin does not begin by dissecting concept of law, but by attributing to legal practice the essential property of being argumentative. Thus, he claims that: 'Every actor in the practice understands that

[1] See Shapiro (2011: 282–306). Joseph Raz also seems to allow for some limited theoretical disagreement about law when he remarks that facts about the nature of legal authority are relevant for determining which interpretative theory is correct. He notes that his Authoritative Intention Thesis 'turns on our understanding of the notion of authority and its conceivable justifications' (Raz 1999a: 259).

[2] Dworkin sets out to defend the possibility of theoretical disagreement about the *grounds* of law by arguing that law is an interpretive concept; see Dworkin (1986: 13 ff) and (1997).

what it permits or requires depends on the truth of certain propositions that are given sense only by and within the practice; the practice consists in large part in deploying and arguing about these propositions.'[3] He then makes a first step towards regimenting the structure of this argumentative practice by drawing a distinction between what he calls 'propositions of law' and the 'grounds of law'. The former are statements about what the law requires, permits, prohibits or empowers one to do, whereas the latter, he argues, are the determinants of the truth or falsity of those propositions.

Equipped with this first distinction, he goes on to distinguish between two ways in which legal practitioners may disagree about the determinants of the truth of propositions of law. The first type of disagreement which he identifies as a kind of empirical disagreement is not about the grounds of law, but about whether those grounds obtain in a particular case. The second type of disagreement, which he calls theoretical, is the most interesting one as it directly relates to the grounds of legal truths. The rest of the story is too familiar to be rehearsed in detail here. Dworkin's conclusion is that theoretical disagreement is a real phenomenon and that the available theories of law fall short of accounting for the pervasiveness of this type of disagreement. His solution is to suggest that law itself is an interpretive concept that already encodes in its conditions of application the possibility of disagreement about when it is applicable.

In his recent insightful advocacy of legal positivism,[4] Scott Shapiro puts forward perhaps the most comprehensive-cum-reconciliatory positivist move towards accommodating Dworkin's argument from theoretical disagreement. He admits that, precisely because the ultimate grounds of law are not conventional, the process of ascertaining the grounds of law is inherently attributive in the sense that, more often than not, it may involve genuine disagreement over the purpose of a legal practice. Nonetheless, *pace* Dworkin, the dispute is kept alive thanks to Shapiro's qualification that the nature of the relevant disagreement over the grounds of legal facts is descriptive (rather than normative) in the qualified sense that it relates to the identification of 'the objectives set by the planners of the system in light of their judgments of competence and character'.[5] In the spirit of this positivist accommodation of the argument from theoretical disagreement, we may intelligibly disagree about the identification of the descriptive (social or intentional) facts by virtue of which facts about legal requirements

[3] Dworkin (1986: 13).

[4] Shapiro (2011: 282–306).

[5] ibid 382. Shapiro further unpacks the aspects of this type of descriptive disagreement, noting that: 'Participants in a practice can disagree over proper interpretive methodology because they disagree about whether their practice is best described as an authority or an opportunistic system, and hence to whose judgments they ought to defer. Even if they agree about the general nature of the practice, they can differ about any of the three steps of meta-interpretation. They might disagree about the demands imposed by particular methodologies, the ideological purposes of the system, its distribution of trust and distrust, or which methodology best harmonizes with such purposes and judgments of competence and character' (ibid 382).

obtain, *but not* about the normative considerations on which the lawmakers based their decisions.

Tellingly, what both sides appear to deny is that we can intelligibly disagree about whether legal facts are conjunctively or disjunctively grounded in descriptive and/or normative, non-legal facts. The latter is an instance of what I will refer to as *inter-jurisprudential* theoretical disagreement. On the standard picture described above, theoretical disagreement about the grounds of law is inherently *intra*-jurisprudential, thereby bifurcating into two mutually exclusive variants. The reason for this is obvious: for positivists, legal facts are descriptive facts about the existence of legal norms or whatever these norms are reducible to, whereas antipositivists take legal facts to be less fundamental but nonetheless normative facts about the obtaining of legal obligations, rights and powers. The descriptive variant affirms the possibility of disagreeing about the social and other descriptive facts by virtue of which (descriptive) legal facts obtain, whereas the normative variant treats theoretical disagreement as an instance of normative disagreement about the responsibilities of government vis-a-vis its citizens. On this picture, an episode of inter-jurisprudential theoretical disagreement featuring a positivist and an antipositivist interlocutor will inevitably be classified as an instance of *verbal* or trivially semantic disagreement insofar as each side has a radically different conception of what is to be grounded.

In what follows, I plan to argue that at least part of what makes the relevant discourse so unfit for serving as a platform of inter-jurisprudential disagreement about the grounds of legal facts is a set of irreconcilable *positivist* accounts of the relevance of a distinctly legal point of normative assessment for determining the propositional content expressed by legal utterances.[6] Consequently, on this positivist approach, what legal facts or legal truthmakers make true are not legal propositions *simpliciter*, but legal propositions with a semantically or pragmatically inbuilt legal point of normative assessment. Henceforth, I shall adopt the term *jurisprudential perspectivalism* with a view to designating a class of competing positivist explanations of whether and how the evaluation of the truth or the assertability conditions of legal statements is sensitive to the obtaining of a contextually supplied, distinctly jurisprudential perspective on which governance by law is morally binding or reason-giving.

The crux of my argument will be that by modelling legal propositions as conveying (by semantic or pragmatic means) a perspective on the normative force of law, legal positivists prematurely inject into the semantics of a

[6] Provided that legal propositions are made true by legal facts – that is, provided that the constituents of the truthmakers of legal propositions reflect the structure of legal propositions – it becomes evident why the content and scope of the metaphysical dispute about the non-legal facts (descriptive and/or normative) that ground legal facts are crucially sensitive to semantic verdicts about the role of the legal point of view. Jurisprudential perspectivalism as a semantic view about the truth or assertability conditions of legal propositions can be ontologically committing insofar as one is willing to subscribe to a familiar metaontological position according to which a proper metalinguistic regimentation of natural language can carve reality at its joints. See, among others, Cameron (2010).

metaphysical disagreement about the grounds of the truthmakers of legal propositions – namely, *legal facts* – presuppositions about the grounds of the *normativity* of the truthmakers of legal propositions (legal facts) or, in other words, about the grounds of facts about the reason-giving force of legal facts.[7] The latter normative presuppositions about the normative force of legal facts trivialise episodes of inter-jurisprudential disagreement about the grounds of legal facts *proper* precisely because they communicate metaphysically committing information about the normative nature of legal facts. More precisely, they represent legal facts as *extrinsically* or circumstantially reason-giving, thereby prematurely excluding from consideration the antipositivist conception of legal facts as inherently normative facts.

Upholding the distinction between legal facts and facts about the reasons provided by legal facts can be used as a basis for revising the terms on which legal philosophers of competing jurisprudential allegiances may *intelligibly* disagree about what grounds legal facts. The main idea is that if there is a *non-perspectival* alternative to regimenting the *verificandum* – namely, legal propositions – there is room for arguing that there may also be an *inter-jurisprudential* alternative to modelling disagreement about the grounds of the *verificans* – namely, legal facts or, more broadly, the truthmakers of legal propositions – which supervenes on the available intra-jurisprudential (descriptive and normative) variants. The possibility of entailment between a non-perspectival account of legal truth and an inter-jurisprudential account of theoretical disagreement about the grounds of the truthmakers of legal propositions (legal facts) will become more visible as soon as we get a clearer picture of which variants of jurisprudential perspectivalism are endorsed by legal positivists who are well disposed towards the possibility of accommodating a sizeable amount of descriptive theoretical disagreement in law.

Before outlining the structure of this chapter, I ought to be more precise about the scope of my argument vis-a-vis the established methodology of accommodating jurisprudential disagreement. On the emerging picture, any taxonomy based on slicing up the continuum from exclusive positivism to traditional natural law theories will be a poor guide to understanding what is really transpiring in the exchange of arguments and counter-arguments between legal philosophers. The solution I propose does not purport to favour either variant (descriptive and normative) of theoretical disagreement about the grounds of law. More precisely, I do not intend to explore which of the two variants (the descriptive or the normative) is better at escaping an analogical application of the 'sting' of Dworkin's famous argument against jurisprudential criterialism.

[7] Whereas theoretical disagreement, at least as initially conceived by Dworkin, regards the grounds of legal facts themselves rather than the grounds of facts about the reason-giving force of legal facts, I see no principled objection to the possibility of enlarging the scope of grounding disagreements in law. In section IV below, I shall briefly explore a challenge resulting from keeping this distinction on the surface of jurisprudential theorising.

On the latter view, semantic competence with legal concepts like *validity*, *legal system* or *norm* consists in sharing a rule setting out criteria for applying these concepts such that, as Dworkin describes this view, 'unless lawyers and judges share factual criteria about the grounds of law there can be no significant thought or debate about what the law is'.[8] Before briefly explaining how this argument could work out, it is crucially important to emphasise that Dworkin's 'semantic sting' argument cannot be *directly* applied to the type of dispute under discussion precisely because his argument appears to presuppose that in light of their criterialist inclination, positivist theories of law cannot accommodate genuine disagreement about the grounds of legal facts.[9] By sharp contrast, the dispute at hand between positivist and antipositivist proponents of theoretical disagreement about the grounds of law rests on the common assumption (shared by some legal positivists and antipositivists) that theoretical disagreement *is* possible in the case of law. What is at stake on this occasion is whether theoretical disagreement about law is descriptive or normative, not whether positivist theories of law can accommodate a considerable amount of theoretical disagreement about the grounds of law.

The argument I aim to pursue instead is a modest instance of a common form of philosophical argument that draws on intuitions of disagreement to reach semantic conclusions.[10] It is modest in the sense that it is not oriented towards defending a wholesale semantic theory for the use of nominal constructions like 'legal duty' and 'legal validity', deontic constructions like 'legally ought' or predicative constructions like 'legally obligatory',[11] but rather it aspires to considerably downsize the scope of eligible interpretations of ascriptions of

[8] Dworkin (1986: 44).

[9] Dale Smith provides a comprehensive defence of the view that Dworkin's 'semantic sting argument' purports to explain why 'semantic theories of law' invoke criterialism in support of the view that legal officials cannot in principle disagree about the grounds of legal facts. See Smith (2010).

[10] In this regard, my argument reverses the order of methodological explanation favoured by proponents of jurisprudential perspectivalism. In the latter case, semantic verdicts about the perspectival nature of legal statements serve to ground further verdicts about the nature of metaphysical disagreement over the grounds of legal facts.

[11] Such a wholesale treatment would require a comprehensive account of how a non-expert speaker can come to satisfy a set of criteria of folk linguistic and semantic competence with the use of jurisprudential vocabulary. The semantic proposal at hand is meant to operate in the service of jurisprudentially informed speakers precisely because it aspires to capture a particular class of cases of linguistic exchange which could be aptly classified as jurisprudential disputes, that is, disputes about the determinants of legal content. In this specific context, the speakers involved genuinely disagree with each other about the truth of a given legal utterance, even though they may not converge in their jurisprudential understanding of a given case. For instance, it remains an open question whether an average speaker's ability to convey determinate information about legal content depends either on an implicit deference to the actual practice of a community of jurisprudential experts or, alternatively, on an individual's 'armchair' a priori reasoning about which properties, relations, kinds or objects would count as being legal, provided that one engaged in full jurisprudential and perhaps socio-cultural reflection or, finally, on an individual's psychological capacity to identify a posteriori a given item as relevantly similar to paradigmatic instances of legality. For a critical rejection of semantic deferentialism in law, see Coleman and Simchen (2003).

legality with a view to making the jurisprudential discourse of the sort described above intelligible. In the course of this elimination, my main target will be two formally distinct variants of a distinctly perspectival understanding of ascriptions of legality precisely because, as it will turn out, perspectival analyses unnecessarily limit the scope of theoretical disagreement in law.

Before getting started, a few more paragraphs are required on the remaining structure of this chapter. The chapter is divided into four sections. First, I shall locate a semantic and a pragmatic variant of jurisprudential perspectivalism with which I shall associate positivist philosophers who are more or less eager to accommodate – in positivist terms – Dworkin's seminal argument from theoretical disagreement. More precisely, I plan to correlate Scott Shapiro's theory of perspectival legal statements and Joseph Raz's elaboration of the notion of the legal point of view with a semantic and a pragmatic conception of jurisprudential perspectivalism respectively. Consequently, I shall explore the ways in which each variant prematurely rules out the possibility of inter-jurisprudential disagreement.

In the spirit of challenging the idea that perspectival theories trivialise episodes of inter-jurisprudential disagreement, I will then move on to address the question of how a refutation of perspectivalism, as is eloquently defended by these two prominent legal positivists, can pave the way for detailing in Chapter 4 the possibility of a global, inter-jurisprudential variant of theoretical disagreement which can serve as a hospitable common platform for positivist and antipositivist theories of law alike. To this end, I shall take the liberty of suggesting an alternative semantic regimentation of ordinary legal statements that can accommodate meaningful exchange between speakers with competing jurisprudential mindsets. On this alternative approach, ordinary legal statements of the sort that could serve as a template of inter-jurisprudential theoretical disagreement can be remodelled in the likeness of non-perspectival, *constitutive* statements we encounter in the context of metaphysical disputes about whether an object of kind A constitutes a material or abstract object of kind B. On this alternative regimentation, the linguistic accommodation of a distinctly legal perspective of normative assessment becomes redundant precisely because a metaphysical (constitutive) modelling of legal statements is non-committal on the question of whether and how law is normatively assessable.

In sections III and IV respectively, I shall address two particularly poignant objections. The first regards the intelligibility of theory-sensitive, constitutive disagreements in law and the second highlights the implications of a constitutive semantics for legal discourse for its eminently practical character. With respect to the first objection, I shall argue that constitutive disagreements in law are theory-sensitive in a way that prevents them from lapsing into a verbal type of disagreement. With respect to the second objection, I shall argue that construing statements of legal content as conveying metaphysical rather than practical information does not result in the elimination of the agent's point of view. The reason for this is that this alternative regimentation leaves room for a second class of jurisprudential statements about the normative force of law and its grounds, the content of which can also figure in episodes of theoretical disagreement.

I. TWO HYPOTHESES ABOUT JURISPRUDENTIAL PERSPECTIVALISM

Ordinary legal discourse appears to be rather rich in syntactic variations of ascribing legality to objects, actions, persons or relations there among. Locutions like 'A has a legal obligation to φ', 'A legally ought to φ', 'not φ-ing is illegal', 'the law requires that one φ's in circumstances C', 'there exists a legal norm to the effect that one φ's in circumstances C', 'the rule that one is obligated to φ is legally valid' are used interchangeably in the invariable context of our reports of what the content of the law is or entails in a given circumstance. As one may reasonably expect, it is legal positivists who bear the brunt of accommodating the use of normative or prescriptive language in law in a way that does not vitiate their core commitment to how descriptive facts make law. In the service of disassociating what the law is from what the law ought to be, analytic legal positivism offers an impressive gamut of linguistic frameworks for accommodating the normative flavour of legal discourse. The first and more traditional view is Joseph Raz's analysis of deontic statements made from a legal point of view. Being motivated by the concern of how to preserve the normative flavour of legal statements without allowing value-based intuitions to vitiate his positivist enterprise, Raz favours a pragmatic account of legal statements featuring normative predicates. The second positivist approach has found its most sophisticated defence in Scott Shapiro's perspectival account of legal statements. Shapiro's approach is truth-conditional rather than pragmatic, arguing that, despite appearances, legal statements featuring normative predicates are descriptive by virtue of their being *de dicto* rather than *de re* deontic truths.

A. Pragmatic Perspectivalism

Beginning with Raz's account of the legal point of view, it is worth quoting his explanation of why the semantics of legal statements are notoriously recalcitrant to assimilation by general accounts of normative statements. He remarks that:

> [The] beginning of wisdom is to allow that such statements are not reducible to one or the other of the basic types. Such statements simply state what one has reason to do from the legal point of view, namely, what ought to be done if legal norms are valid norms. *But they do not state this conditional* … [t]hey are like statements made on the *assumption* that something is the case. They do not state that if the law is valid

> that is what ought to be done. Nor do they state what ought to be done. *They do not presuppose that the law is valid.* (Emphasis added)[12]

On the one hand, legal statements featuring deontic modals (ought, must, may) or predicates (obligatory, permissible) are not conditional descriptive statements merely reporting what is logically entailed if the normative viewpoint of the law holds. On the other hand, their standard jurisprudential use seems to be echoic,[13] in the sense that the ordinary speaker does not use this sentence truth-conditionally – that is, she does not purport to represent it as true – but attributes it to a particular legal practice, thereby expressing an attitude of detachment with regard to whether the fact that the law requires that φ is always a normative reason to φ.

This type of metalinguistically (non-truth-conditionally) conveyed detachment is precisely the type of attitude referred to by Raz in his argument about the 'detached point of view'. Raz comments that '[legal] scholars – and this includes ordinary practicing lawyers – can use normative language when describing the law and make legal statements without thereby endorsing the law's moral authority. There is a special kind of legal statement which, though it is made by the use of ordinary normative terms, does not carry the same normative force of an ordinary legal statement'.[14] This is a pragmatic, not semantic, analysis of legal statements as it permits the echoic mention of moral content by way of taking a detached stance towards the fact that the law *qua* source of requirements is either contingently or essentially normative.

At the same time, Raz is willing to make room for committed legal statements. He asks us to consider the case of a vegetarian who sincerely believes

[12] Raz (1999b: 175).

[13] As Robyn Carston explains, '[a] representation is used echoically when it reports what someone else has said or thought and expresses an attitude to it' (see Carston (1996: 320)). In the present context, Joseph *echoes* Thomas' utterance with a similar content to the one expressed in his utterance, in order to express a critical attitude to it in the accompanying rectifying clause. The term 'echoic mention' was has been coined by Sperber and Wilson (1981).

[14] Raz (2012: 156). Jules Coleman makes exactly the same point when he argues about the 're-description' of legal content *qua* moral content. He notes that a statement of the form 'mail fraud is illegal' should be analysed in terms of the sentence '[from] the law's point of view by acting in such a way as to make mail fraud illegal the law warrants re-describing mail fraud as morally wrong' (Coleman 2007: 597). Whereas Coleman describes his view as the 'moral semantics thesis', this should not misguide us into believing that his argument is literally semantic. A charitable way to read his argument is that he purports to accommodate the truth-conditional challenge of real moral claims within the peculiar context of legal discourse. He describes his thesis as 'a claim about how the content of the law can be (accurately or truthfully) described. The moral semantics thesis is the view that the content of the law can be truthfully re-described as expressing a moral directive or authorization … The moral semantics claim is that 'mail fraud is not to be done' can be re-described truthfully as 'mail fraud is morally wrong' (ibid 592). I take it that what he means by 'warranted re-description' is that the utterance 'mail fraud is illegal' *implies* (in the pragmatic sense) that a given legal practice purports to represent its content as morally true. The attitude conveyed by the echoic, non-truth-conditional use of 'mail fraud is illegal' is that of a *distanced report* of what moral re-descriptions are implied by syntactic occurrences of legality.

that it is wrong to consume meat. Whereas his carnivore interlocutor will use the sentence 'you should not eat this dish because it contains meat' in a detached or echoic manner, the vegetarian will use the very same sentence truth-conditionally. I believe that Raz's description of the latter type of statement as committed is not expressivist, but cognitivist. This is to say that the vegetarian does not express an attitude of disapproval towards the act of consuming meat, but purports to make a truth-apt statement about what is wrong with eating meat. If this interpretation is correct, then it cannot remain an option for Raz to claim that committed statements of legal content are *literally legal* statements that happen to entail a moral statement; rather, they are full-fledged *moral* statements that re-appropriate legal content in normative truth-conditional terms.[15] To assume otherwise is to expose the long-cherished social facts thesis to great peril. The reason is that if committed legal statements *entail* a moral claim and the moral claim is false, then the asserted legal proposition must also be false. It then follows that the truth of legal propositions is partly determined by appeal to moral standards, which is obviously unacceptable to the legal positivist.[16]

It appears then that the most charitable reading of Raz's account of the legal point of view forces him to accept the following distinction. On the one hand, legal content can indeed be conveyed by normative statements in an echoic or non-truth-conditional fashion. Detached speakers merely echo the normative aspiration of a legal system by expressing their disassociation from the question of whether the fact that the law requires that φ is necessarily or essentially a reason to φ. On the other hand, committed or literal or truth-conditional uses of legal content necessarily have moral truth-conditions and as such they cannot be genuine legal statements unless interpreted in antipositivist terms.

On this reconstructive interpretation, Raz's claim that legal propositions are inherently perspectival has to be qualified accordingly. What is ultimately truth-evaluable for the positivist is not the echoically used normative content of the

[15] Richard Holton espouses a similar understanding of Raz's distinction between committed and detached legal statements. He rejects the idea that 'there is a class of committed legal statements, where this is understood as a class of legal statements that, by their very meaning, commit the speaker to the moral authority of the law. Rather, by making a legal statement an actor might pragmatically implicate that they are committed to the moral authority of the law' (Holton 1998: 618). Raz seems to validate this interpretation when he remarks that 'I find it impossible to resist the conclusion that most internal or committed legal statements, at any rate those about the rights or duties of others, are moral claims' (Raz 1981: 455).

[16] Richard Holton prefers to read Raz as landing himself voluntarily in contradiction. He attributes to Raz the fallacious assumption that committed legal claims are *legal* claims with moral content and then proceeds to highlight this error (Holton 1998: 613–14). Raz seems to license the alternative interpretation that I favour when he expresses his doubt as to whether '[it] is possible that while officials believe that legal obligations are morally binding this is not what they say when they assert the validity of obligations according to law. It may be that all they state is that certain relations exist between certain people and certain legal sources or laws. Their belief that those relations give rise to a (moral) obligation may be quite separate and may not be part of what they actually say when asserting obligations according to the law. But such an interpretation seems contrived and artificial' (Raz 1984: 131).

form 'according to the law it is obligatory to φ', but the conversationally implied descriptive content that 'the law of S requires that φ'.[17] This is precisely the content that Raz's commitments license him to evaluate for truth or falsity. This content will be taken by the positivist to be a descriptive statement about what the law requires precisely because on the positivist view, the sortal entity law *qua* source of requirements is not intrinsically normative. The latter content will be true *iff* 'there is, in the legal system referred to, a norm which requires the action which is stated to be one which ought to be done'.[18] These truth conditions make no reference to (a representation of) the reason-giving capacity of legal norms and are perfectly compatible with the positivist's descriptive account of the grounds of law.

B. Semantic Perspectivalism

The second option is to explain the use of normative language in law in semantic terms. This is the avenue chosen by Shapiro when he draws the distinction between adjectival and perspectival uses of the term 'legal'. Whereas Shapiro concurs with Raz in treating adjectival uses of 'legal' as full-fledged moral claims,[19] he takes a different approach with regard to what he refers to as perspectival statements of legal content. He introduces the notion of perspectival claims by remarking that:

> [O]n the perspectival interpretation of the word 'legal', statements of legal authority, legal rights, and legal obligations are *descriptive*, not normative. *They describe the normative point of view of the law.* Statements such as 'X has legal authority

[17] Luís Duarte D'Almeida offers an alternative reconstruction of Raz's account of the use of normative language in law. Whereas he confirms the view that the piece of truth-evaluable semantic information conveyed by legal statements is a descriptive content of the form 'the law requires that φ', he proceeds to remark that 'it would be pointless to adopt any particular "point of view" in order to utter it' (D'Almeida 2011: 189). More precisely, he rejects the claim that legal statements are inherently perspectival on the grounds that 'to make a statement that the law requires you to φ … is nonetheless and merely to report a social fact. In order to utter a statement like (4L) one does not need to accept that the requirement concerned is justified and ought to be complied with, nor does one need to feign such acceptance' (ibid 192). Whereas my proposal concurs in that legal statements do not necessitate a perspectival regimentation (semantic or pragmatic), I remain charitably doubtful about the defensibility of D'Almeida's semantic inflationism. In D'Almeida's words, there is a use of the language of 'rights' and 'duties' in legal statements, which is moreover the characteristic and disseminate use in the legal context, in which those terms have quite a different sense from the one they have in the "moral context"' (ibid 198). For a comprehensive defence of the implausibility of an inflationary semantic account of normative concepts, see Chrisman (2012). For a reductive account of semantic monism about 'ought', see Finlay (2014: 48–84).

[18] Raz (1999b: 177).

[19] '[What] are we imputing to someone when we say that she has "legal authority"? One possibility is that we are imputing a type of moral authority. On this reading, the word "authority" means the same as it does in moral contexts, roughly speaking, the power to impose moral obligations and confer moral rights, and the word "legal" functions as an adjective, identifying this kind of moral power. We are saying, then, that the person in question has moral authority in virtue of being an official in a legal institution. Call this the "adjectival" interpretation' (Shapiro 2011: 185).

> over Y in S' are true just in case it is true that *according to S's point of view* X has moral authority over Y. (Emphasis added)[20]

How is this possible? The critical step for Shapiro is to assume that the perspective on which legal norms are represented as morally binding figures in the truth-conditions rather than the implicated (non-truth-evaluable) content of legal utterances. He maintains that, despite the use of overtly normative language, 'statements of legal authority, legal rights, and legal obligations are *descriptive*, not normative'.[21] He then proceeds to dispel the oddity of this claim, noting that the descriptive character of perspectival legal statements consists in that '[t]hey *describe* the normative point of view of the law' (emphasis added).[22] For him, the normative point of view of the law with respect to a particular legal system 'is the perspective of a certain normative theory … that holds that the norms of that system are morally legitimate and obligating'.[23] In other words, we may say that the legal point of view of S designates a set of normative propositions (normative theory) according to which the norms of S provide reasons for action. Although Shapiro refrains from any further elaboration of this idea, his explanation is far from trivial. A charitable reading of this claim can elicit an original contribution to the debate on the linguistic role of the legal point of view.

My critical argument begins from the assumption that Shapiro would concur that there is an informative distinction between instances of *referring* to (or rendering truth-evaluable) and instances of *describing* in a detached fashion the normative point of view of the law. This is strongly evidenced by Shapiro's elaboration of perspectival appeals to the normative aspirations of a legal system's officials. In his words: 'The normative theory that represents a system's point of view is not a complete account of morality … [it] may be false from a moral perspective … the legal point of view always *purports* to represent the moral point of view, even when it fails to do so.'[24] The idea seems to be that perspectival invocations of the normative force of the law operate in a way that renders the evaluation of the actual capacity of legal norms to be morally binding semantically (that is, truth-conditionally) irrelevant.[25] Taking this assumption on board, there is room for advancing the further argument that the distinction

[20] ibid 188.
[21] ibid.
[22] ibid.
[23] ibid 186.
[24] ibid 187.
[25] At this point, I would dare to suggest that a further unpacking of this idea could bring Shapiro's argument much closer to David Kaplan's account of vivid representation. Kaplan's argument is about the possibility of quantification in opaque contexts – as presumably the legal context is. More precisely, he construes names and descriptions – as is 'a legal obligation to Φ' – in opaque contexts as performing two types of referential function: they can refer to their normal referents (*de re*) – in our case, a moral obligation obtaining in virtue of the actions of legal institutions – and they can also refer to themselves (*de dicto*). To this effect, Kaplan draws a distinction between representational and non-representational names and descriptions on the basis of whether they satisfy the following

between adjectival and perspectival uses of the word 'legal' needs to be qualified in a more committed way that refines the conditions for evaluating the truth of claims featuring the normative point of view of the law both in the adjectival (moral) and perspectival (juridical) contexts.

More precisely, I would like to suggest that a direct implication of the former, explicit distinction between adjectival and perspectival legal statements is that deontic modifiers like 'legally' or predicate modifiers like 'legal' are opacity-inducing, in the sense that they create a linguistic environment that does not always permit the truth-preserving – *salva veritate* – substitution of descriptive (definite or indefinite) constructions like 'a legal obligation', 'the legal authority', 'a legal right' for their moral counterpart expressions 'a moral obligation', 'the moral authority' and 'a moral right' respectively. The opacity associated with this distinction licenses a redescription, in more formal language, of the two modes in which an agent can stand in a legally qualified relation to an action. In the adjectival case, it could be argued that an agent A stands in a *de re* 'legal obligation', 'legal entitlement' or 'legal authorisation' relation to an action Φ just in case the agent stands in the relation of being 'morally obligated', 'morally entitled' or 'morally authorised' to Φ. We may then say that attributing this deontic relation to agent A is semantically *de re* in the sense that the description 'legal obligation' is intersubstitutable *salva veritate* with the description 'moral obligation'.[26]

In the perspectival case, the idea seems to be that an agent stands in a *de dicto* 'legal obligation', 'legal entitlement' or 'legal authorisation' relation to an action Φ just in case the *proposition* 'A has the moral obligation/moral right/moral authority to Φ' has the property of being represented as morally necessary by officials of legal system L.[27] Consequently, the *de dicto* use of 'legal' or 'legally' is perspectival precisely in the sense that the truth of a proposition

two conditions: (a) they are *of* an object; and (b) they are sufficiently vivid. In order for a description or name to be of an object for a user, that object must play an appropriate *causal* role in the user's acquaintance with the name or description. Moreover, a name or description is a vivid representation of an object x when, in Kaplan's words, it is 'the conglomeration of images, names, and partial descriptions which Ralph [his fictional subject] employs to bring x before his mind' (Kaplan 1969: 201). In Kaplan's spirit, we could say that the description 'a legal obligation to Φ' plays a distancing function whenever it plays no causal role in a speaker's endorsement of a legal system's moral legitimacy and, moreover, it is not employed as a way of reviving the speaker's evaluation of a legal system.

[26] On such occasions, the term 'legal' is attributive (or adjectival in Shapiro's terminology) in the sense that it operates as a predicate modifier such that predications like 'A has legal authority' or 'A has a legal obligation' are shorthand for the expressions 'A has moral authority *qua* being an official in a legal institution' and 'A has a moral obligation in virtue of its being part of the content of the law of system S'.

[27] Shapiro alludes to the truth-conditional irrelevance of the normative theory designated by the legal point of view when he describes the relationship between the legal point of view and a legal system's master plan. In his words: 'The relation between the legal point of view and the master plan can be rendered like so … From the point of view of S, X has moral authority over Y with respect to subject matter Z ↔The master plan of S authorizes X to plan for Y with respect to Z' (Shapiro 2011: 187). On the most charitable interpretation of this passage, the relationship described refers

of the form 'A has a legal obligation to Φ' is a function of how A's obligation to Φ is *described*, namely, a function of whether the contextually supplied viewpoint of legal officials of a given system *represents* A's Φ-ing as being made morally right by the norms of that system. We may then say that attributing a 'legal obligation' relation to agent A is semantically *de dicto* in the sense that the expression 'legal obligation' is not truth-preservingly interchangeable with the expression 'moral obligation'. In other words, the by now familiar distinction between adjectival and perspectival uses of legal language appears to rest on the idea that two expressions – in our case, 'a legal obligation to Φ' and 'a moral obligation to Φ' – *need not* have the same denotation in a given context if they usually (namely, in most contexts) have the same denotation.

C. Perspectival Theoretical Disagreement

In the remainder of this section, I will try to demonstrate that, despite appearances, perspectival regimentations of legal statements entail that any episode of *inter-jurisprudential* theoretical disagreement about the grounds of law featuring a positivist and an antipositivist disputant will be classified as merely verbal. For the purpose of my argument, I shall adopt a more committed view with regard to the verbalness associated with instances of inter-jurisprudential disagreement premised on perspectival semantics. Perspectival disagreements about the grounds of law are verbal in the qualified sense that perspectival interpretations of legal statements end up violating *semantic neutrality* in a way that depicts legal philosophers as talking past each other. By introducing the notion of semantic neutrality, I intend to flag up the importance of distinguishing between the semantics and metaphysics of legal talk.[28] It is at least plausible to assume that a basic desideratum for legal semantics is that it remains neutral with regard to the substantive criteria that determine the extension of

to the truth-conditions of perspectival legal statements such that the sentence 'from the point of view of S, X has moral authority over Y with respect to subject matter Z' *is true if and only if* the master plan of S authorises X to plan for Y with respect to Z. On this construal, it becomes evident how the normative theory designated by the legal point of view is truth-conditionally irrelevant; it is irrelevant insofar as it *does not* figure in the truth-conditions of a perspectival legal statement.

[28] In other words, this distinction points to the view that propositions are not semantically transparent to their truthmakers. The latter does not presuppose anything with regard to the question of whether, for instance, every legal proposition has a distinct truthmaker or whether its truthmaker is a fact about the very same propositional content asserted by a legal utterance; it only commits us to the idea that every legal proposition has some truthmaker or other. For instance, there can be predications such as 'the electron is spin up' whose truthmakers depict their fundamentality. In such a case, a plausible truthmaker would be the very fact that the electron is spin up. This overlapping of propositional content and truthmakers is not necessary, but can be a function of the fundamentality of the truth asserted. To paraphrase Alex Silk's similar remark on the semantics of moral terms, 'the sorts of truth conditions that reflect what it takes to know what a [legal] sentence means are conditions on how things might be [legally]. By contrast, what conditions must obtain *in the world* for a [legal] sentence to be true is a substantive issue' (Silk 2013: 201).

jurisprudential terms. Consequently, the bar of semantic competence raised by any theory in this domain should not be elevated beyond the point of what is true in an ideally accessible world. Packing the metaphysically proper ordering into the truth conditions of jurisprudential terms would amount to assigning semantics with the task of solving or presupposing solutions for philosophical problems about how facts make law.

In the present context, the type of metaphysical information that is prematurely packed into the semantics of legal discourse regards the normativity of the truthmakers of legal propositions (legal facts), namely, the question of whether and how facts about legal content provide reasons for action. By virtue of the fact that they endow legal statements, by pragmatic or truth-conditional means, with a perspective on which the law is reason-giving, perspectival theories inject jurisprudentially committing verdicts about the *normativity* of law into the structure of metaphysical disputes about the *grounds* of law.

In what follows, I shall try to illustrate how both the pragmatic and semantic variants of jurisprudential perspectivalism are directly implicated in what trivialises episodes of inter-jurisprudential disagreement. To see how this connection emerges, we can imagine two episodes of theoretical disagreement. In the first episode, Ronald, a devout legal antipositivist, is confronted by Joseph, a legal positivist, who espouses the pragmatic variant of jurisprudential perspectivalism. In the second episode, Ronald is confronted by Scott, a legal positivist who espouses the semantic variant of jurisprudential perspectivalism. Now suppose Ronald utters (1):

(1) Ronald: A is legally obligated to Φ.

For the sake of argument, we may suppose that Ronald is a legal interpretivist; in other words, he believes that a legal obligation obtains because its actual or prospective enforcement is morally consistent with past instances of enforcement by the legal institutions of a given system. We may also suppose that, being informed about Ronald's jurisprudential allegiances, Joseph utters (2):

(2) Joseph: A is not legally obligated to Φ; that Φ-ing signals satisfaction of some descriptive criteria of legal validity does not entail that it is a reason to Φ.

A plausible way to understand Joseph's objection is to decipher this episode of disagreement in metalinguistic (ie, pragmatic) terms. This interpretation is compatible with his pragmatic conception of statements of obligation made from a legal point of view. Recall that for a pragmatist perspectivalist, legal statements uttered in the context of jurisprudential discourse pragmatically convey the speaker's detachment vis-a-vis the question of whether the fact that the law requires that A Φ's is also a reason for A to Φ. In the preset context, we may argue that Joseph's negation of (1) is metalinguistic. Borrowing Väyrynen's definition, metalinguistic negation (as opposed to truth-conditional negation) is 'a device for objecting to a previous utterance on the basis of its presuppositions, implicates, or linguistic form or manner, rather than its content'.[29] It looks very plausible that the second half of (2), which conveys Joseph's perspectival detachment towards the normative force of legal requirements, channels the negation expressed in the first half specifically to the normative content pragmatically associated with 'legally obligated' by Ronald. A metalinguistic denial of (1) would involve an utterance identical to (2), but this time it would be interpreted as denying a previous utterance on the basis of its presuppositions rather than its content. To paraphrase Väyrynen's application of the same notion,[30] the material under the scope of the negation in the first half seems to be naturally heard as echoing an actual or potential positive utterance by another speaker, followed in the second half by a rectifying clause that expresses a comment on some aspect of that utterance. In the relevant case, the aspect that serves as the ground for metalinguistic denial is the *presupposed* theoretical claim that a legal requirement provides a reason for official enforcement on demand.

As a result, the use of 'legally obligated' in (2) will echo its use in (1) such that (2) and (1) do not express logically inconsistent propositions. The material falling within the scope of 'not' in the utterance 'is not legally obligated to Φ' is echoically mentioned or metarepresented rather than used. It thereby appears that Joseph's denial of the presupposition expressed by (1) is nevertheless felicitous precisely because according to the metalinguistic model, the denied presupposition is defeasible. The rectifying clause *that it signals satisfaction of some descriptive criteria of validity does not mean that it is a reason to Φ* preserves the felicity of his response insofar as we subscribe to the view that the evaluation he objects to is not part of the semantic content of 'legally obligated', but merely a conversationally defeasible presupposition.

However, is this really how the resolution of episodes of meaningful interjurisprudential disagreement between positivists and antipositivists is supposed to work? My contention is that the pragmatic variant of jurisprudential perspectivalism fails to accommodate intelligible disagreement across the entire spectrum of philosophical accounts of the grounds of law.[31] By relegating the dimension of evaluation from the domain of asserted content to the domain of presupposed content, participants in this dialogue are misrepresented as agreeing that despite lexical appearances, the predicate 'being legally obligated' denotes a *descriptive* property, but disagreeing with regard to its normative implications. Thus, Joseph appears to convey the idea that nothing of normative importance *essentially* follows from the fact that something is legally required, whereas Ronald is, incorrectly, portrayed as a *normative positivist* who claims that there is something essentially valuable in the fact that something is legally

[29] Väyrynen (2012: 254).

[30] ibid 253.

[31] This is not to say that jurisprudential discourse can never feature metalinguistic instances of theoretical disagreement between positivists and antipositivists, but that such instances can feature a small portion of views on both sides of the positivist–antipositivist divide.

required.[32] But this is not what a genuine legal antipositivist like Ronald would want to say! For him, the evaluation determines the extension of 'legally obligated' and, as such, it cannot but figure into its semantic rather presuppositional content. Construing legal statements as descriptive assertions accompanied by normative presuppositions is only a partial invitation to theoretical disagreement about the grounds of law. It is partial precisely because it forces opponents of hardcore positivism to affirm its core premise, which is the thesis that legal content is determined by social facts alone.

As I am about to argue, an even more restrictive result occurs in Ronald's confrontation with Scott, who, as hypothesised above, is a legal positivist espousing the semantic variant of jurisprudential perspectivalism. It is more restrictive because the semantic modelling of perspectival disagreement cannot even accommodate the inclusion of the normative variants of legal positivism, thus necessitating a bifurcation of theoretical disagreement into positivist and antipositivist variants. To see why semantic perspectivalism excludes *tout court* the possibility of inter-jurisprudential disagreement, it is worth recalling that for a semantic perspectivalist like Scott, there is a lexical ambiguity in syntactic occurrences of the word 'legal'. Whereas in some contexts legal statements can be directly paraphrased into full-fledged moral statements about the normative impact of the actions of legal institutions, 'genuine' instances of jurisprudential discourse feature descriptive propositions about the content of the law whose truth consists in the fact that legal officials represent an action as being morally mandated or authorised by the norms of a given system. Now suppose that Scott utters (3):

(3) A is not legally obligated to Φ.

In sharp contrast with his pragmatist counterpart, Scott's utterance cannot count as a felicitous negation of (1) precisely because his use of the adverbial 'legally' in (3) has an entirely different meaning. Consequently, he cannot intelligibly disagree with Ronald about the grounds of the fact that A is legally obligated to Φ. The reason is that Scott's use of the adverbial 'legally' is adjectival rather than perspectival;[33] in other words, it has no jurisprudential

[32] That said, there is more than one kind of normative legal positivism that this semantic modelling can accommodate; for instance, (1) could be metalinguistically negated by someone who believes that legal positivism is an intrinsically good thing that ought to be promoted, or, alternatively, by someone who advances the methodological claim that acknowledging that the determination of legal content is a matter of social fact is quite compatible with certain morally impactful features of law. For the former view, see Waldron (2011); for the latter view see Perry (2009).

[33] An alternative route for rescuing this episode from triviality is to remodel their disagreement as an instance of metalinguistic negotiation revolving around the normative issue of which of a range of competing *concepts of law* should be used in a given conversational circumstance. This is a view recently expounded by Plunkett and Sundell (2013). Metalinguistic negotiations are conceptual disagreements transpiring at a higher level of abstraction and, as such, they are in principle convenient devices for enlarging the scope of jurisprudential disagreement. That said, it would make little

meaning, but expresses a moral evaluation of governance by law such that Scott and Ronald are destined to appear as talking past each other. For a semantic perspectivalist, the information conveyed by Ronald's assertion is not about the content of the law, but about the fact that the actions of legal institutions at system L make A's Φ-ing morally right. As a result, Scott's negation of (1) fails to deliver a direct objection to Ronald's account of the grounds of law insofar as the perspectival regimentation of their confrontation ascribes two radically different meanings to the use of 'legally' in (1) and (3) respectively.

II. NON-PERSPECTIVAL JURISPRUDENTIAL STATEMENTS

To adumbrate a few ideas on the way forward, I plan to argue that a way out that can push both positivists and antipositivists onto a platform of meaningful disagreement is to forgo the prospect of trying to regiment legal statements in the likeness of *perspectivally qualified practical* claims and instead explore the option of understanding jurisprudential statements as carrying *metaphysical*, so to speak, rather than practical information about 'recipes' for making law. In this regard, the jurisprudential variant of constitutive or 'recipe-making' discourse will feature utterances whose logical structure is represented by propositions of the form <X constitutes a *law* (of system L)>, where X will stand for whichever abstract object or kind encapsulates the propositional content identified by the speaker's jurisprudential background as the determinate general content of the law at a particular time in a particular jurisdiction.[34]

Irrespective of its linguistic regimentation, the legal point of view is a perspective on whether and how the law is practically normative or, in other words, whether legal facts are intrinsically or extrinsically (contingently) normative. In this regard, part of what could explain the looming verbalness of instances of theoretical disagreement about the grounds of legal facts is

sense to insist that the present episode of disagreement represents a *metajurisprudential* negotiation about whether the adverbial modifier 'legally' should be used adjectivally or perspectivally in the given context. The reason is the adjectival variant has no jurisprudential use and can only be used in a purely moral context. In this regard, even at this higher level of abstraction, this disagreement is not jurisprudential in any informative sense.

[34] In what follows, I shall defer for later (Chapter 4, section I.B) the question of how Dworkin's interpretivist model of theoretical disagreement could be reconstructed on the basis of a constitutive rather than perspectival regimentation of legal statements. The reason for this is twofold. First, the proposal I seek to unpack is not co-extensive with Dworkin's conception of interpretive disagreement precisely because it rejects the premise that jurisprudential disagreement is intelligible only insofar as it involves the employment of normative, political argument. Second, legal interpretivism treats any ontological distinction between law as an institutional practice and law as a set of principles of political justification as metaphysically spurious. That said, a legal interpretivist can intelligibly participate in constitutive disputes about law at a second-order level by virtue of adopting an error-theoretic stance towards the possibility of legal constitution. In other words, she can claim that despite the fact that constitutive regimentations of legal statements are truth-apt, they are systematically false.

the fact that perspectival treatments of legal statements prematurely inject into the semantics of jurisprudential discourse metaphysically committing verdicts about the normative relevance of law. By regimenting legal statements in perspectival terms, positivists like Joseph Raz and Scott Shapiro appear to settle the question of whether legal facts are intrinsically normative at the level of semantics, thereby excluding the possibility of engaging with their antipositivist critics in meaningful metaphysical disputes about whether legal facts are intrinsically normative and, consequently, whether legal facts are grounded in descriptive or descriptive *and* normative facts. In this regard, it would make little sense to insist on conditioning instances of disagreement about the grounds of law on semantically channelled presuppositions about the normativity of law.

I believe that I am not making a daring step when I assume that all parties to this dispute converge in their disposition to settle this matter at a theoretically more committing level. The purpose of establishing a common semantic platform remains visibly valuable. It ensures the meaningfulness of the disagreement between positivist and antipositivist accounts of the grounds of the *truthmakers* of legal propositions. Without a commonly acceptable logical regimentation of assertions of legal content, talk of legal facts would irresolutely vacillate between semantically irreconcilable theoretical claims. Fortunately, there is no conclusive reason to feel aggrieved by the semantic recalcitrance of 'law'. The elusive semantic behaviour of this syntactically versatile concept is first-class evidence that perhaps we have been unnecessarily hasty in associating representations of legal content with familiar patterns in moral semantics. In this regard, I would invite the reader to provisionally join me in entertaining the hypothesis that legality's syntactic interactions with action-denoting predicates or with deontic predicates or modals should not incline us to be driven by the force of surface analogies. In other words, we should resist for a moment the thought that we should look for semantic models that have already been tested for concepts like morality or rationality, which seem to display similar syntactic behaviour.

There is still, I believe, an alternative way to determine in a principled manner the semantic value of typical syntactic manifestations of legal content without tilting the debate between legal positivists and antipositivists. This is precisely the context within which I would like to flag the importance of evaluating an alternative semantic route in the light of this caveat about settling metaphysical questions at the level of semantics. Whereas the question of where to determine the bar of value-neutrality is equally applicable in discussions about moral semantics, I would dare to remark that in the legal case, their relevance is more intricate in a way that justifies refraining from analogical applications of available semantic models. The reason is that there is an unpronounced difference in the way in which the normative flavour of moral language and the normative flavour of legal language pose a challenge for the meta-ethicist and the legal philosopher respectively.

On the one hand, it is not just that there is little doubt that morality is normative in a more or less robust sense, but it would also sound absurd to claim that merely adopting this view can vitiate the task of providing a value-neutral semantics for this type of discourse. Deontologists, consequentialists and virtue-ethicists do not seem to be worried by the fact that taking the normativity of moral discourse as a given for the purpose of constructing a semantic theory will eventually result in smuggling a Trojan horse into someone's neighbourhood. Their threshold of alertness is high enough to accommodate this premise as a non-alarming factor. By contrast, substantive disagreement in moral semantics kicks in as soon as the nature and possibility of moral truth are subject to evaluation. The prospect of tilting the debate between different substantive moral theories starts to become visible following the emergence of questions about the semantic role of 'ought' and its context-sensitivity. For instance, a deontologist may be favourably disposed towards a predicative reading of 'ought',[35] which can better account for the agent-centred aspect of moral deliberation. Conversely, a consequentialist may be more inclined to favour a more traditional treatment of 'ought' as a propositional operator[36] or as a dyadic relationship between agents and propositions rather than actions.[37]

On the legal side of the spectrum, the challenge is considerably different. Whereas there is a growing consensus among legal philosophers that legal language has a normative flavour, this hypothesis does not encompass the further assumption that law is normative in any robust sense. In other words, there is a consciously preserved gap between the normative flavour thesis and the normativity thesis that any account of legal semantics seeks to accommodate. The reason is obvious: if someone's anticipation of the normativity of law is already affirmed by the way in which legal discourse is semantically regimented, it would immediately signal an alarm for positivist participants in this debate. By the same token, it would be an unwelcome result for defenders of legal antipositivism if someone's deflationary or flatly dismissive account of legal normativity is already portrayed by the semantic value we assign to syntactic manifestations of legality. On this picture, the pool of semantic alternatives becomes considerably shallower, unfortunately at the expense of achieving a more fine-grained regimentation of legal talk.

By excluding the possibility of analysing legal talk so finely that it can emulate the granularity of moral talk, we come closer to becoming aware of the limits of informative appeals to extra-legal analogies in thinking about the semantics of legal discourse. At the same time, we come closer to realising that legal talk has its own subtleties that remain suppressed for as long as we insist on regimenting legal discourse in the likeness of other types of normative discourse.

[35] For a concise presentation of the literature in support of the predicative reading of 'ought', see Schroeder (2011).

[36] See, for instance, Kratzer (1981); and Williams (1981: 114–23).

[37] See Wedgwood (2006); and Broome (1999).

More precisely, I plan to argue that a solution that can keep both positivists and antipositivists on a platform of meaningful disagreement is to abandon the semantic typology of jurisprudential perspectivalism and instead explore the option of understanding statements of legal content as carrying purely metaphysical rather than practical information about recipes for making law.

In what follows, I will be focusing on the application of my alternative proposal in the semantics of universal legal statements. By universal legal statements, I mean any statement to the effect that something is generally the case in a particular legal order. Universal legal statements are repeatedly exemplifiable such that all universally quantified claims about what rights, obligations, prohibitions and institutional powers obtain within a specific juridical domain qualify as universal legal statements. More specifically, I shall argue that legal claims carry information about recipes for constituting legal content. This kind of recipe-making represents a moment of creation, so to speak – it is as though we are told: take some substance S and add some structure to it and you will get a piece of legal content.

After this meandering chain of arguments, I am in a better position to invite the reader to consider the possibility that this is what statements of legal content are all about and, consequently, that this is the information we as legal philosophers try to test for truth. I do not intend to use this 'recipe' jargon as a metaphor, but as literally as it gets. What we are actually communicating by means of advancing universal legal claims is that somehow the propositional contents contributed by the sayings, doings and thoughts of some particular individuals or collectivities are capable of producing a sortally distinct content-bearing entity.

To see the analogy with the lump of clay and a statue of Goliath, it is helpful to consider how the two entities can be thought of as sharing the same intrinsic non-sortal properties and yet radically depart in their possession of sortal and persistence or modal properties. In the same sense that a particular lump of clay has intrinsically the *same shape* as the statue of Goliath it constitutes but is sortally distinct (one is a lump of clay, the other is a statue) and persistence-wise distinct (the lump of clay does not have its shape *essentially* whereas the Statue of Goliath is essentially Goliath-shaped) a propositional-content-bearing entity P can have the same constituents with those furnishing a legal norm with its content, but at the same time it can differ with respect to its sortal and persistence or modal properties. Accordingly, assertions of legal content are assertions of which pre-legal content constitutes legal content and, as such, they perfectly qualify for being labelled as recipe-making or, in more formal language, constitutive claims.[38]

[38] The idea of casting the semantic information conveyed by constitutive claims in recipe-like terms is not mine; I owe this term to Stephen Barker and Mark Jago. In their own illustrative prose, '[claims] of material constitution carry information about recipes for making things. If we tell you that the cardigan is made of one piece of thread, then we convey the information that one way of

More precisely, my proposal delivers a logical regimentation of legal propositions that vaguely resembles our ordinary language assertions of legal content. A promising way to obviate the lexical ambiguity encountered in syntactic constructions purporting to convey semantic information about the content of the law is to consider the possibility of using the logical form of constitutive claims like 'A constitutes B' as a metalinguistic template for representing the structure of legal propositions. In this regard, an ordinary syntactic occurrence like 'it is legally obligatory to φ in legal system S' is logically regimentable as 'the proposition that φ-ing is obligatory constitutes a law of S'. The latter analysis will deliver a logical regimentation representing a copular sentence which features a definite proposition description ('the proposition that …') as the subject term and the referring expression 'a law of S' as the predicate complement. The resulting logical form can be represented as PD*L, where PD stands for a propositional description, * is the symbol for the copula and L is a referring expression.

A critical aspect of this alternative scheme regards the implications of using the nominal construction 'the proposition that …' as a dummy sortal term[39] that needs to be further fleshed out in terms particular to the jurisprudential vocabulary used by different theorists. The sortal description 'the proposition that' falls within the same class of descriptions like 'thing', 'physical object', 'non-human entity' and 'felicific substance'. Dummy sortals lack the criteria of identity that individuate their instances. Even though they behave grammatically as count nouns, they do not also behave logically as such, as evidenced by the unintelligibility of questions pertaining to their enumeration ('exactly how many things made up the universe?') or their persistence conditions ('is the substance that makes you feel happy still in your bloodstream?').

At first approximation, all occurrences of both the noun phrases 'the proposition that it is obligatory to φ' and the corresponding that-clause 'that it is

getting a cardigan is to take some thread and process it in a certain way. A single wool thread is part of at least one recipe for a cardigan. This kind of making-recipe says: take some substance and add some structure to it. In the cases that interest us, the original substance survives the change in its structure: the thread remains, now structured to make up a cardigan. Crucially, such constructive making-recipes are asymmetric. They involve the addition of structure: the cardigan is the wool with suitable structure added. One cannot add structure to a cardigan to obtain a single thread' (Barker and Jago 2014: 190).

[39] A 'dummy sortal' is a term that functions grammatically (ie, it is modified by articles and quantifiers) as a sortal, but whose truth value is not a real kind. For instance, terms like 'substance', 'thing', 'body' or 'object' are standardly described as dummy sortals in the sense that they cannot make any semantic contribution independently of more specific terms subordinate to them. David Wiggins explains this distinction in terms of an identity principle. He notes that '[i]f a is the same as b, then it must also hold that a is the same something as b' (Wiggins 1980: 47); see also Wiggins (1967: 29–35)). In other words, to say that a term does not express a real sortal is to say that it is not a proper answer to the question 'same what?'. By the same token, being a proposition does not settle the identity conditions of an entity endowed with propositional structure. For a critical analysis of this distinction, see Marcus (2006).

obligatory to φ' seem to designate the same proposition, namely, <it is obligatory to φ>. As a result, one could remark, the truth or falsity of the utterance 'the proposition that it is obligatory to φ is a law of S' in a particular circumstance will ultimately depend on the properties possessed by the proposition < it is obligatory to φ> at the same circumstance of evaluation. This would be a non-starter at least for the legal positivist, as it would make the truth of legal assertions transparent to the truth of one of their constituents, namely, the noun phrase 'the proposition that it is obligatory to φ', whose referent would be a contingently true or false normative proposition. Hopefully, this is not a semantic factum, as it remains a valid possibility to assume that in its current use, 'the proposition that it is obligatory to φ' is not inter-substitutable *salva veritate* with the corresponding that-clause, nor does there exist a semantic imperative that this noun phrase should directly refer to the proposition <it is obligatory to φ>.

As it stands, the description 'the proposition that it is obligatory to φ' is a dummy sortal term in the sense that it does not have much content of its own, but instead it is *sortally dependent* on whatever turns out to be the proper sortal instance that is capable of constituting legal content. The proper logical function of the dummy sortal 'the proposition that' is that of a variable or placeholder that awaits to be occupied by a genuine sortal instance. To illustrate its logical behaviour, let us assume that the nominal construction 'the proposition that' operates as a placeholder. Then a more formal regimentation of the sentence 'the proposition that it is obligatory to φ constitutes a law of S' will be something like '_____ to φ constitutes a law of S'. Until we inject a determinate sortal term, the latter sentence is not truth-evaluable.

The only semantic constraint with regard to which kind of content-bearing term could replace 'the proposition that is obligatory' in actual assertions of legal content is that it be sortally and not singularly referential. What prompts me to emphasise that the proper terms must be sortal and not singular is that otherwise, we would be led to the counter-intuitive conclusion that when we disagree about what constitutes a legal norm, we disagree about whether it is this or that particular *text* (constitutional, statutory, executive, judicial or administrative) or a *speech act instance* performed by a particular person to which a legal norm owes its content. A reliable way of distinguishing individually referring terms from sortally referring terms is to ask whether a chosen term has further instances. As EJ Lowe remarks:

> According to the definitions of *individual* and *sort* suggested above, what distinguishes the individual *Dobbin* from the species or sort *horse* is that Dobbin has no instances (except, quite possibly, himself) whereas the horse does. That is, 'horse' *divides its reference*, but 'Dobbin' does not. It is indivisibility of *reference* rather than *material* indivisibility that, it seems clear, the notion of 'individuality' implies, when we employ it in speaking of 'individual' as opposed to 'sortal' terms. Dobbin is, of course, not 'indivisible' in the sense that he cannot be cut into pieces, merely in the sense that nothing (apart perhaps from Dobbin himself) – such as any one of these

pieces – qualifies as an *instance* of Dobbin. There is no plurality of different *Dobbins*, in the way that there are many different *horses*.[40]

This is not an unwelcome consequence of stretching the logical regimentation of legal claims beyond plausibility. It is exactly the result that this analysis invites us to anticipate. What makes it the right moment to evaluate this result is what has just preceded its emergence. Thus, for instance, in a hypothetical linguistic exchange between a moral impact theorist, an exclusive legal positivist and a plan positivist, this dummy nominalisation will deliver on the truth-conditional side of our analysis three distinct *shell* nominal constructions, namely, 'the fact that it is obligatory to φ' (moral impact theory), 'a directive to φ' (Razian positivism) and 'a rational requirement to act on the plan to φ' (plan positivism) respectively.[41] All replacements are sortally (and not individually) referential in the sense that they can be further instantiated. A general and abstract authoritative directive is instantiated by individual orders, a universal fact about the content of general obligations is instantiated by atomic facts pertaining to the particular obligations of concrete individuals, and a general rational requirement can likewise be instantiated by individually addressed requirements.

On the one hand, the moral impact theorist purports to represent the normative content syntactically expressed by the use of the term 'obligatory' as truth-evaluable. On the other hand, the Razian positivist will use the same syntactic construction echoically. Despite surface syntax, she expresses her metalinguistic (conversationally triggered) detachment from the question of whether a directive to φ *also* constitutes an obligation to φ![42] Lastly, the plan positivist can account for this syntactic manifestation in semantic terms insofar as she is willing to endorse a wide-scope analysis of rational requirements such that to say that a rational requirement to act on the plan to φ obtains is to say that one is rationally required [if one represents the plan to φ as morally binding, to intend to φ].[43]

[40] Lowe (2009: 39–40).

[41] All alternative substitutions of the dummy sortal 'the proposition that …' are semantically cognate in the sense that they operate as shell nouns. In linguistic theory, shell nouns such as 'fact', 'decision', 'requirement', 'idea' and 'problem' are devices for encapsulating propositional content by way of reducing complex pieces of information expressed by clauses. In the present case, the relevant piece of information regards the propositional content – normative as in 'it is obligatory to φ' or descriptive as in 'one φ's' – contributed by law-determining practices. The choice of the shell noun that will be used to encapsulate this propositional content will vary depending on the jurisprudential background of the speaker. The shell metaphor comes from Schmid (2000).

[42] Consider the analogy with the case of promissory utterances. Many philosophers share the view that metaphysically speaking, a promissory utterance of the form 'I promise to φ' constitutes a promise, namely, an abstract object that encapsulates the promisor's commitment to particular performance. It is a further question whether the same promissory utterance also stands in a relation of abstract constitution to a promissory obligation such that the promise is vested with the normative authority to demand the promisor's performance.

[43] More precisely, the wide-scope construal of rational requirements amounts to the claim that one can equally satisfy the requirement by revising any one of the relevant conflicting attitude states. There is no preference either as to what *outcome* among the permissible ones should be brought

Taking stock of what has been said so far, it is worth noting that the type of legal claim that figures in actual jurisprudential disputes is theory-sensitive in a way that would exclude a non-legally-trained person from qualifying as a semantically competent participant without at least implicitly deferring to one of the sides figuring in the relevant dispute. Instances of full-fledged jurisprudential disagreement are such that not all kinds of speaker can be meaningfully engaged. This result should not go by unnoticed. Upon proper reflection, it may turn out that there can be a layperson-privileged description of law's constitutive material that allows ordinary speakers to have a priori access to reference-fixing criteria for their use of legal vocabulary, but only a posteriori access to the words' associated modal profile.

That said, I believe that this is not a bullet a proponent of a unified semantics for jurisprudential disagreement must bite; it is precisely what our theory should anticipate and explain. There is nothing wrong or counter-intuitive in claiming that genuine legal disputes are just not open for anyone. This is a linguistic division of labour that a subject matter as intricate as the determination of legal content necessitates. What appear to be instances of disagreement featuring legal assertions made by non-trained speakers are instead testimonial disagreements about what *the law around here is* rather than about what *makes it the case what the law around here is*.

III. ARE CONSTITUTIVE DISPUTES MERELY VERBAL?

I see no reason why the fact that the semantics of legal statements are sensitive to the findings of jurisprudential inquiry is an alarming indication that there is something deeply mistaken about our methodology. Even if our best rational reflection cannot deliver a reference-fixing description of legality to which every ordinary speaker is capable of accessing a priori, I cannot see how the rejection of law as a deferential concept on metasemantic grounds[44] can decisively

about or as to what the ideal *means* for reaching an outcome is. For a more extensive defence of the wide-scope formulation see, among many others, Brunero (2010); Dancy (2000); and Way (2010). Scott Shapiro cautions about the thinness of the normativity of legal plans when he remarks that 'the normativity of the master plan of a legal system is of a very limited sort. While legal officials are rationally required to conform to their shared plan, it is also true that those who do not accept the law are not similarly bound. Furthermore, the master plan of a legal system may be morally illegitimate and hence not capable of imposing a moral obligation on anyone to obey' (Shapiro 2011: 182).

[44] Jules Coleman and Ori Simchen associate their rejection of the reliance of semantic competence with 'law' on jurisprudential expertise with a traditional understanding of semantic deference. They note that 'a term will exhibit linguistic deference when there is widespread trust within the linguistic community that there is a received expert doctrine on the nature of the things to which the term refers that is thought to contribute to speakers' capacity to negotiate the world' (Coleman and Simchen 2003: 23). More precisely, they express their concern about the prospect of treating law as a deferential concept when they focus on what they call the 'pedestal view' about the metasemantics of law. According to this view, 'in the same way that scientists uncover the nature of water, philosophers of law uncover the nature of law – just as the best theory of the nature of water determines

constrain our best understanding of the site of theoretical disagreement about the grounds of law and, consequently, our best understanding of the semantic modelling of this disagreement. The argument, as it stands, is based on the following syllogism:

(a) The extension of 'law' is determined by recourse to legal theory.
(b) If (a), wide semantic competence with the doctrinal extension of law must be deferential.
(c) There is a pervasive dispute between alternative theories of law.
(d) If (c), law is not a deferential concept.
(e) Because of (d) and (b), the extension of law cannot be determined by recourse to legal theory.

I believe that the fallacy that plagues this syllogism lies in an unpronounced assumption that those who believe that the semantics of legal claims are theory-sensitive also believe that the content of their best theoretical verdict must figure into the semantic content of 'law'. For instance, if in light of a particular theory, law is essentially made of authoritative pronouncements, this latent assumption would predict that the notion of an authoritative pronouncement is at least part of what we mean when we use the word 'law'. This, however, is a seriously mistaken conclusion. Whereas jurisprudential disagreement is clearly focused on scrutinising verdicts like this one, the content of this verdict need not be encoded in our use of the word 'law'. By modelling legal claims as claims about *what* constitutes the abstract object *legal norm* or *part* or *legal content*, it is easier to predict how an instance of disagreement can indistinctly and thus genuinely engage all jurisprudential viewpoints without legitimising the assumption that the semantic content that corresponds to what constitutes law is also part of the semantic content of law itself.

The crucial distinction lies in what distinguishes the semantics of legal claims construed as constitutive claims from the semantics of the word 'law'. Properly speaking, it is the former but not the latter semantics that is theory-sensitive in the sense that matters here. To see how this distinction can work, I suggest we subject a claim of the form 'an authoritative directive to φ constitutes a legal norm' to a 'mere verbalness' test. For the sake of simplicity, we may name the particular authoritative directive 'Directive'. Stating the obvious, my choice of casting the example in Razian terms is completely random. Exactly the same experiment can be conducted by replacing the dummy sortal 'the proposition that it is obligatory to' with other referents like 'the fact that it is obligatory to φ'

the content of "water", the best theory of the nature of law determines the content of "law". This approach expresses the idea that jurisprudence somehow figures in the semantics and metasemantics of "law"' (ibid 38). Their argument is basically that law cannot be a deferential concept because the lack of a received jurisprudential doctrine about the nature of law severely undermines their confidence that they will ever qualify as being semantically competent with 'law' by relying on one rather than another competing doctrine.

or 'a rational requirement to φ'. That said, suppose that we witness the following dialogue between Gonzo, a Razian positivist, and Froddo, a Greenbergian antipositivist:

(a) Gonzo: Directive constitutes Legal Norm.
(b) Froddo: Directive does not constitute Legal Norm.

Instead of taking sides with either Gonzo or Froddo, one may proceed to claim:

(c) The deflationist: Something is going really wrong with the debate.

This latter claim purports to describe the dispute between Gonzo and Froddo as merely verbal. To test this line of reasoning, I shall employ Eli Hirsch's necessity condition for verbalness according to which 'a dispute over the truth of a sentence *D* is merely verbal if there are two undisputed sentences *U1* and *U2*, one true and one false, such that one side holds that *D* is (*a priori* necessarily) equivalent to *U1* and the other side holds that *D* is equivalent to *U2*'.[45]

To show how the verbalness test fails in the case of legal constitution, I shall properly modify Karen Bennett's incisive criticism of Hirsch's deflationist strategy.[46] For the purposes of our modified example, let *D* be 'Directive constitutes Legal Norm'. *U1* could be something like 'Legal Norm *strongly supervenes* on Directive', whereas *U2* could be something like 'Legal Norm existentially depends on Directive'. Gonzo argues that *D* is true *iff* Legal Norm *strongly supervenes* on Directive and that because *U1* is obviously true, *D* is true as well. By contrast, Froddo argues that *D* is true *iff* Legal Norm *existentially depends* on Directive and that because *U2* is patently false, *D* is false as well.[47]

Whereas U1 is a claim that Gonzo would eagerly take on board, *U2* is presented as what Gonzo believes that Froddo, falsely, believes that *D* entails. A preliminary objection is that it is not entirely clear that we can safely attribute to Froddo the belief that the sentence 'Directive constitutes Legal Norm' entails that 'Legal Norm existentially depends on Directive'. The problem, as Bennett notes, is that 'because [in disputes over composition and constitution] it is not clear that there is in either case an undisputed falsehood U2 to which the low-ontologist [Froddo] takes D to be equivalent, it is not clear that these disputes meet [Hirsch's] sufficient condition (H). If they do not we have been given no reason to think that they are verbal disputes'.[48]

The relevant worry is that it will always be controversial how the conversational background of a dispute over constitution can furnish the indisputable

[45] Hirsch (2005: 83).
[46] Bennett (2009).
[47] The latter claim is indisputably false, as the existence of Directive does not necessitate or ground the existence of Legal Norm. For instance, it is possible that a particular authoritative directive has been issued that is considered to be invalid according to the criteria set by the rule of recognition of a given legal system. In this case, the directive will exist even though it is invalid, but there will be no legal norm coming into existence.
[48] ibid 52.

falsehood that a low-ontologist like Froddo purports to attribute to a high-ontologist like Gonzo. Before proceeding to explain why the indisputable truth (*U1*) about Legal Norm's supervenience on Directive fails to threaten the substantive character of the dispute between Gonzo and Froddo, it should be noted that as it stands, it may reasonably cause confusion as the relation of supervenience is standardly taken to hold between families of properties and not objects. This is not a fatal restriction as one can specify the constitutional type of supervenience as a three-place relation. For instance, Kathrin Koslicki provides a partial analysis of constitution in terms of strong supervenience as follows: '(C) *Partial Analysis of Constitution*: For any objects, x and y, and any kinds, K1 and K2, such that x is of kind K1 and y is of kind K2, y *constitutes* x only if x is *constitutionally supervenient* on y with respect to the family, A, of x's and y's S-properties.'[49]

Now, let us take a look at how the case of legal constitution might be fitted into this mould. We may assume that the family A of the properties of Legal Norm and Directive features intrinsic properties like 'having a particular propositional content C', extrinsic properties like 'being part of legal system S', modal properties like 'being repealable' and temporal properties like 'being effective as of 1 June 2014'.

According to Hirsch's verbalness principle, the disputed sentence 'Directive constitutes Legal Norm' must be a priori and necessarily equivalent to the sentence (*U1*) 'Legal Norm is constitutionally supervenient on Directive with respect to the family A of Legal Norm's and Directive's intrinsic and extrinsic properties'. In the light of this equivalence principle, Bennett poignantly objects that the application of Hirsch's principle can be a sufficient condition on a dispute's being merely verbal if and only if the same principle entails a further principle, namely, that:

> If Legal Norm is constitutionally supervenient on Directive with respect to the family A of Legal Norm's and Directive's intrinsic and extrinsic properties, then it is a priori, necessarily, *and analytically* true that Directive constitutes Legal Norm.

Bennett's related concern is that there is no evidence whatsoever that the above conditional is analytic in Gonzo's language. In the present example, the equivalence principle is clearly synthetic in the sense that whereas the relation of constitutional supervenience is obviously symmetric, the relation of legal constitution is asymmetric. Consequently, the sentence 'Legal Norm is constitutionally supervenient on Directive with respect to the family A of Legal Norm's and Directive's intrinsic and extrinsic properties' is at best a *partial*[50] analysis

[49] Koslicki (2004: 345).

[50] This precisely how Kathrin Koslicki understands the claim about constitutional supervenience. She notes that: 'The relation of constitutional supervenience as defined in (CS) has a feature which it shares with other supervenience-principles and which was already brought up in discussion earlier: it is by itself, i.e., without the addition of further conditions, not an asymmetric principle' (ibid 347).

of 'Directive constitutes Legal Norm'. As it stands, Gonzo's assumption that Legal Norm is constitutionally supervenient on Directive is ontologically non-committal, as nothing in the formulation of this claim suggests that the related objects in question must be numerically distinct. On the other hand, Gonzo's main claim that 'Directive constitutes Legal Norm' is ontologically committing precisely by virtue of its asymmetric character. What Gonzo's main claim clearly entails is that Directive is numerically distinct from Legal Norm. An analytic interpretation of the equivalence principle would amount, as Bennett remarks, 'to saying that *we can define things into existence*. But surely an analytic claim cannot be existence-entailing in this way; surely the existence of a new object cannot follow *by meaning alone*. Who knew ontological arguments were so easy?'[51]

IV. CONSTITUTIVE DISAGREEMENT AND THE PRACTICAL POINT OF VIEW

The implications of this alternative proposal are not meant to serve as an alternative theory of the semantics of legal discourse, but as a heuristic semantics of jurisprudential disagreement. This can be evidenced by the criteria upon which I have based my rejection of the semantic and pragmatic variants of jurisprudential perspectivalism. Both variants have been scrutinised by reference to whether they respect semantic neutrality to the maximal degree possible. Whereas I do believe that an eventual theory of legal semantics must also include the criterion of neutrality among its premises, I chose not to press this point any further mainly because our present concern is about how to convince all major contributors of a broadly cognitivist persuasion to sit around the same table. The object of this negotiation is not what will eventually qualify as a correct semantic theory for law, but whether we can refine our understanding of the mechanics of our disagreement by discovering points of convergence that do not correspond to the traditional coarse-grained intersections between positivist and antipositivist theories.

In place of a summary of this semantic digression, it is worth belabouring a point that is crucially relevant for capturing the general payoff of this alternative approach. As I have tried to demonstrate, it is at least possible to regiment legal statements as metaphysical rather than practical statements of legal constitution. The semantic information encoded by such statements is similar to what is being conveyed by ordinary utterances involving the constitution of material or abstract artefacts. A powerful objection to my preferred route for regimenting legal statements is that the model of metaphysical constitution fails to capture the distinctly practical dimension of jurisprudential discourse. In the

[51] Bennett (2009: 56).

end, a critic would remark, legal statements are about what ought to be done by citizens, legislators, judges and so on. By expunging this normative perspective from the metalinguistic analysis of legal statements, we lose sight of the practical standpoint of those subject to legal requirements. Consequently, the urge to rescue inter-jurisprudential disagreement from triviality at any cost results in a counter-intuitive trivialisation of the normative relevance of agency for our grasp of how facts about legal content bear upon practical reasoning.

Albeit powerful, this objection is not devastating insofar as we are willing to consider the possibility that the logical form of grounding disagreements in law is more fine-grained than initially assumed. In other words, the notion of ground – be it descriptive or normative – is general enough to encompass at least two metaphysically distinct questions about law. The first question, which the entirety of this chapter has dealt with, relates to the grounding of the truth-makers of legal propositions (legal facts) in descriptive and/or normative facts. This question occupies the bulk of the controversy diving legal positivists from legal antipositivists and, as such, it has been traditionally treated as exhausting the subject matter of theoretical disagreement in law. But this is a rather hasty verdict which, as evidenced by the trivialising effect of perspectival accounts of jurisprudential discourse, neglects the granularity of legal talk and thought.

A further equally metaphysical question which has not been traditionally associated with the controversy over theoretical disagreement regards the grounding of facts about the normative force of legal facts. Whereas the former question pertains to the grounding of legal facts *themselves*, the latter question invites us to ponder about what explains the further fact that a given legal fact is *practically relevant*. It is precisely the latter question that captures the practical dimension of the law. Consequently, I would like to suggest that although the class of practical judgments we commonly associate with assertions of legal content are paradigmatically jurisprudential, they do not literally convey information about the content of the law in a given jurisdiction but rather about the legal, so to speak, reasons for action provided by the content of the law.

What I purport to argue is that perspectival accounts of legal statements unnecessarily end up conflating *two* equally important kinds of asserted legal content conveyed by jurisprudentially informed speakers. The first kind regards the *building*, so to speak, of law from pre-legal 'materials' (normative facts, authoritative directives, planning requirements etc), whereas the second kind regards the *sources* of legal normativity, namely, whether the same materials qualify as sources capable of generating legal reasons for action.[52] My contention is that we can accommodate both questions in the context of intelligible jurisprudential disagreement without packing into the *semantics* of assertions

[52] Consequently, theoretical disagreement about the first kind of assertion relates to the grounds or foundations of what is being built (legal content), whereas theoretical disagreement about the second kind relates to the explanation of why a given law-making source (derivative or non-derivative) provides a legal reason for action.

of the first kind metaphysical verdicts entailed by assertions of the second kind. In Chapter 7, I will engage with these worries head-on, but, for now, a short adumbration of how we can obviate these concerns will suffice.

In the spirit of preserving a semantic continuum between statements of legal content and statements of legal normativity, a practical (as opposed to metaphysical) occurrence[53] of a statement like 'A is legally obligated to Φ' can be regimented as 'the proposition that A is obligated to Φ is a legal reason to Φ'. As explained above, this is a semantically empty construction which, depending on the jurisprudential context of a given utterance, delivers truth-evaluable statements of the form 'a directive to Φ provides a legal reason to Φ in context C', 'the fact that Φ-ing is morally obligatory provides a legal reason to Φ in context C' or 'a rational requirement to Φ provides a legal reason to Φ in context C'. Formalisations like the above are non-committal with respect to whether the reason-providing source (institutional morality, authority or rationality) of legal reasons for action is derivatively or non-derivatively normative. In other words, nothing about the *essence* of the sources of legal normativity[54] is retracted from the baseline of genuine disagreement about what explains why a given source (derivative or non-derivative) qualifies for providing a legal reason for action. Consequently, episodes of disagreement featuring such statements are anything but trivial, as they do not semantically encode into the concept of a 'legal reason for action' metaphysically committing information about the status of legal reasons for action as being generated by intrinsically or extrinsically normative entities.

Last but not least, it is crucially important to notice that the grounding explanations invoked within the context of the former dispute about the grounding of legal facts cannot migrate to the metanormative debate about the nature and grounds of legal normativity. More precisely, there are two important differences that block a collapse of the latter dispute into the realm of the former dispute. The first difference regards the facts whose grounding is being contested. Whereas the facts that call for grounding in the former dispute (legal facts) can be descriptive or normative, depending on which side one is willing to take in the relevant controversy, the grounded facts in the latter dispute (facts about the normative import of legal facts) are by their very nature normative precisely because they are about the binding effect of facts about legal content! The second difference uniquely affects the local dispute among competing

[53] In other words, two lexically identical statements of the form 'A is legally obligated to Φ' can admit one of two formalisations: one corresponding to a proposition about the content of the law and one corresponding to a proposition about the normative force of legal content.

[54] A similar implication has been encountered in the context of the alternative regimentation of statements of legal content. As I argued above, the principal virtue of the constitutive model is that it does not semantically encode into the concept '(a) law' or 'content of the law' metaphysical verdicts about the normative or descriptive nature of facts about legal content. Consequently, it enables meaningful inter-jurisprudential disagreement *about* their status as normative or descriptive facts!

antipositivist accounts of law as it relates to the relationship between the non-legal normative facts that ground legal facts and the non-legal normative facts that ground facts about the normative force of legal facts.

Ronald Dworkin aptly illustrates this problem in his effort to distinguish between the grounding relevance of integrity in the context of the generation of legal rights and obligations, and its grounding relevance in the context of how these facts about legal content acquire the force of reasons for enforcement on demand. In this regard, he notes that integrity in the latter context is not always sufficient to ground the normative force of legal facts, as exceptional circumstances may require the inclusion of considerations of justice and fairness as trumping determinants of the outcome. In this regard, he invokes the Fugitive Slave Act case to describe an exceptional occasion where what determined *what the law was* before the American Civil War failed to also give *normative force* to this law. The best illustration of this exceptional divergence is given by Dworkin in his latest work, where he observes that:

> The United States Congress (let us assume) was sufficiently legitimate so that its enactments generally created political obligations. The structuring fairness principles that make law a distinct part of political morality – principles about political authority, precedent, and reliance – gave the slaveholders' claims more moral force than they would otherwise have had. But their moral claims were nevertheless and undoubtedly undermined by a stronger moral argument of human rights. So the law should not have been enforced.[55]

[55] Dworkin (2011: 411).

4

Two Levels of Disagreement about the Metaphysics of Law

In place of a summary of the previous chapter, it is worth highlighting three points that are crucially relevant for what follows. First, it is at least possible to regiment legal statements as statements of legal constitution. The semantic information encoded by such statements is similar to what is being conveyed by ordinary utterances involving the constitution of material or abstract artefacts. Second, my semantic proposal purports to offer a maximally inclusive semantic model for regimenting competing arguments about legal content. In other words, my proposal is meant to be utilised as a semantics for legal arguments without extending an invitation to apply this model to the case of ordinary, context-bound legal sentences. Third, although my proposed semantics respects jurisprudential neutrality, it is theory-sensitive in a qualified sense. It respects neutrality because it avoids thick interpretations of legality as a property or sortal entity that pack jurisprudentially committing information into its extension. At the same time, it acknowledges the theory-dependence of competing legal claims by integrating into what is called a modestly committed[1] doctrinal reference to the sources of legal content.

With this semantic apparatus in place, I will try to show how my initial proposal about reconfiguring the site of jurisprudential disagreement can affect the orientation of our dispute about the nature of law. More specifically, I intend to show how the emerging variety of new types of disagreement, both first-order and second-order, supervenes on a taxonomical variety of theories of law that goes beyond the modalised conception of whether and how law is related to morality. The guiding idea is that elevating the site of jurisprudential disagreement at the more abstract level of what grounds the truthmakers

[1] I highlight the modestly committing character of the terms that replace the dummy sortal 'the proposition that it is obligatory to' because nothing definitively rests on which genuine sortal instance will figure in a constitutive relation to legal content. For instance, one may adopt the view that legal norms are made out of authoritative directives and maintain at the same time that what enables an authoritative directive to constitute a legal norm is its being constitutionally capable of serving as a standard of rational conduct. Alternatively, on a positivist reading of the same semantic content, it is a brute fact that an authoritative directive constitutes a legal norm in the sense that there are no explanatory intermediates between the obtaining of a legal norm and the issuance of an authoritative directive.

of legal propositions carries substantive implications for both the scope and content of our dispute. The structure of this chapter will be divided into three sections focusing on the co-variation pattern between the discursive and taxonomical aspects of each of the three constituents of the reconfigured site of jurisprudential disagreement: the possibility and nature of legal constitution, the truthmakers of legal propositions and the grounding of the truthmakers of legal propositions. In each section I will contrastively develop the arguments that each one of our four exemplary jurisprudential theories can offer in response to the discursive challenges posed by the three thematic domains I have just identified. The alternative grouping of these four theories is the result of a functional association between different levels of disagreement and distinct taxonomical identities.

By order of emergence, the problem of legal constitution gives rise to a first-order, 'recipe-type' disagreement about what legal norms are made of and a second-order disagreement about whether legal constitution is possible. The taxonomical output of answers to the first-order question will not overlap with the familiar division between positivist and antipositivist theories; instead, it will deliver four possible versions of the impact of law-determining practices resulting from each theory's distinct way of articulating the metaphysical or legal-content-determining impact of facts about the sayings, doings and thoughts of legal officials. With regard to the second-order question about whether there is such a thing as a legal constitution, the competing answers can be categorised into three theoretical pathways. A first informative surprise will be the common attribution of non-reductivism about the existence of legal norms/parts of legal content to Raz's authority-based conception of legal norms and Greenberg's moral impact theory of legal obligation. Shapiro's planning theory of law will be identified as an instance of reductivism about the possibility of legal constitution, and Dworkin's theory of law as integrity will be associated with an error-theoretic rejection of the possibility of preserving as numerically distinct law's constituting material and legal content proper.

The next problem that will serve as a platform of informative divisions is the relation of legal propositions to the world. Again, the methodological pattern remains constant. A first-order type of disagreement revolves around the question of what makes legal propositions true. Besides Shapiro's reductive understanding of legal facts as facts about the obtaining of plans, the other three exemplary theories will deliver a univocal commitment to legal facts as the proper truthmakers of legal propositions. That being said, it is imperative to clarify that despite their common individuation as *legal* facts – as opposed to, say, facts about the existence of plans – Greenberg's and Dworkin's account of facts about the obtaining of legal obligations, rights or powers are radically different from Raz's conception of legal facts as facts about the existence of legal norms. The former are essentially normative, whereas the latter are only contingently so.[2] The second-order question pertaining to the relation of legal propositions to the world is about whether legal truth is laden with ontological commitments. In this regard, all four theories will fall under the category of legal propositionalism, which, as explained above, maintains that logically regimented legal claims or whatever these claims are reducible to commit us to the existence of the entities that figure in their content.

The last problem will re-introduce a more refined version of the traditional distinction between legal positivism and legal antipositivism. The generic formulation of this problem is already familiar; it asks what grounds legal facts or, in my preferred terminology, the truthmakers of legal propositions. By the same token, this question can be of a first-order and second-order specification. On the one hand, we may ask what grounds the fact that a legal norm exists, that a plan exists or that a legal obligation exists. The types of answer we should expect to receive are roughly co-extensive with the arguments that distinguish each theory as positivist or antipositivist. For instance, on Raz's theoretical account, the fact that a legal norm exists is grounded in the fact that an authoritative directive has been issued that is validated by a particular system's rule of recognition, whereas on Greenberg's view, the fact that a legal obligation obtains is grounded in the fact that a moral obligation has been triggered in the legally proper way. On the other hand, we are also entitled to ask what grounds or, as Greenberg would say, what makes intelligible the fact that the obtaining of a legal obligation or the existence of a legal norm is grounded in the legally proper triggering of a moral obligation or the validation of an authoritative directive by a rule of recognition respectively.

Greenberg is well known for his concerted effort to vindicate the requirement of making grounding explanations in law rationally intelligible, whereas a similar effort in the positivist field can be attributed to Shapiro's conceptual argument about the relationship between legal institutions and legal norms and its utility in making the grounding of facts about planning rationally intelligible. On the other hand, more traditional defenders of legal positivism and antipositivism like Joseph Raz and Ronald Dworkin respectively resist the postulation of explanatory facts that are not already part of the set of facts that ground legal facts.

[2] For Raz, like any other legal positivist, legal facts are properly speaking descriptive facts that are contingently reason-giving by virtue of normative facts. For instance, according to Raz's theory of legal authority, the fact that a legal norm exists is a reason to act accordingly *iff* the Normal Justification Thesis applies in this particular case. In other words, the fact of the existence of a legal norm provides a reason for action only by virtue of the normative fact that by taking this fact as reason-giving, one is more likely to comply with what one has most reason to do independently of the creation of a legal norm.

I. LEGAL CONSTITUTION AND ITS DISCONTENTS

Before proceeding with the presentation of the first type of jurisprudential disagreement, I would like to reiterate that the semantic proposal I am defending here will not be used as an alternative theory of the semantics of ordinary legal discourse, but as a heuristic semantics of jurispurdential claims as they figure in an argumentative context. By this, I do not purport to exclude the possibility of generalising the use of my proposed semantics, but this is not a commitment anyone has to shoulder in order to engage in some meaningful disagreement about what grounds the truthmakers of legal propositions. To see why the latter does not necessitate the former, I shall begin with explaining an episode of disagreement over whether 'the proposition that it is obligatory to φ constitutes a law of system S'. I shall deliberately keep the nominal construction 'the proposition that' as a placeholder in order to highlight that the ensuing disagreement can be meaningful irrespective of how one would prefer to specify it.

Starting from the vocabulary used to frame the familiar dispute between proponents and opponents of the possibility of spatiotemporally or abstractly coincident objects, it is worth noting that the outstanding problem for those who wish to explain material coincidence or constitution is not literally identical to the problem faced by those who wish to explain the possibility of there being abstractly coincident objects. Whereas the former problem is about the possibility of materially coinciding objects sharing their matter, occupying the same spatiotemporal region whilst remaining numerically distinct, the latter problem is about the very possibility of creating abstract objects such that a particular sound pattern can be said to constitute a musical work via the creative intervention of the artist. On the one hand, the creativity claim occupies centre stage for anyone daring enough to talk about the ontology of artworks. On the other hand, it is an ontological platitude that abstracta cannot be created; there is no creative moment such that if it is true at any time that an abstract object *a* exists, then it is not true at all times that *a* exists.

There is no doubt, I believe, that if a problem of constitution arises in the case of law, it must be a problem of abstract rather than material constitution. More precisely, the problem would take the form of a prima facie inconsistent propositional triad: (a) laws are created; (b) laws are abstract objects; and (c) abstract objects cannot be created. With regard to the first proposition, it is worth mentioning that any legal philosopher of a broadly cognitivist conviction would accept that there is a creative moment in the existence of a law that more or less exactly overlaps with its enactment. The familiar division of opinion is not about the necessity of enactment, but about the way in which it becomes relevant for determining the content of the law.[3] With regard to the

[3] This intuition also applies with regard to the obtaining of legal custom as, despite the absence of an enacting moment, there still exists a diachronic activity or practice of endorsing and

second proposition, it should be clear by now that this categorisation as well as the entirety of this exposition is meant to have some bearing on the questions that divide legal philosophers who already countenance the possibility of legal truth. It would be no surprise then that this entire talk about the constitution of abstract legal norms would be nonsensical for non-truth-conditional theories, like legal expressivism or legal realism.

That being said, there will be no need to delve into terminological distinctions that carve the division of opinion about the problem of constitution precisely because the dividing line in both versions of the problem is defined with respect to the numerical criterion of ontological distinctness rather than the nature of the contribution of the creator or manufacturer. Dismissive and defensive responses to this puzzle tend to be classified under the terms 'monist' and 'pluralist' respectively, such that those who take constitution to be nothing more than identity restrict their ontological commitments to the existence of one object – be it the constituting bronze or the constituted statue – whereas those who take constitution to be a distinct metaphysical relation are eager to take on the ontological board both a bronze (constituting) object and a statue (object).

A. First-Order Disagreement over Legal Constitution

The first type of disagreement over locutions of the form 'the proposition that it is obligatory to φ constitutes a legal norm' is about what constitutes what. I would dare to say that it is akin to the mode of disagreement we can witness between two chefs arguing about the proper ingredients in a recipe. By the same token, claims about the constitution of abstract artefacts like musical or literary works can be equally represented as carrying recipe-like information. Whereas it remains controversial whether some abstract artefacts (like musical works) can literally be created rather than mentally discovered or tracked, constitutive talk is no less frequent in aesthetic discourse. For instance, on Jerrold Levinson's modest account of musical Platonism, a musical work is constituted by a sound-structure-as-indicated-by-x-at-y.[4] This may be characterised by frugal metaphysicians as an ontologically inflationary approach, but given the present framework of discussion, it remains an open question whether constitutive claims have truthmakers that feature ontologically 'offending' entities like indicated sound structures or musical works. That being said, Levinson's approach is not an ad hoc amalgamation of his intuitions; this sortal description can be easily moulded into a more general pattern like Kit

implementing a standard as a custom which from an ontological perspective can be still be regarded as a process of creation.

[4] Levinson (1980).

Fine's theory of *qua* objects[5] such that, as Simon Evnine remarks: 'Levinson's indicated structures can be taken as qua objects that have sound structures for their bases and properties of the form *indicated by x at t* as their glosses. The works will inherit many properties of their bases including, of course, the property of sounding a certain way when realised.'[6]

To see how the controversy over the relationship between spatiotemporally or abstractly coincident objects such as a lump of bronze and a statue, or a sound pattern and a musical piece can animate our local controversy over the nature and possibility of legal constitution, it is imperative to begin with a brief comment on the intricacies of constitution. As already noted, one of the major puzzles that seem to have been keeping the controversy over statues and musical works alive is the distinctness of the modal and sortal profiles of two otherwise perfectly identical objects. So, for instance, a statue and the piece of bronze out of which it is made share the same space at the same time, have the same fundamental components (molecular structure), the same weight, shape, colour and texture as well as the same extrinsic properties, like the property of being placed in a museum room or the property of being five metres from the entrance to the room. At the same time, the lump of bronze and the statue seem to be strikingly divergent with regard to their persistence conditions – the lump of bronze but not the statue can survive being squashed because the latter but not the former is *essentially* shaped in such a way, whereas the former has the same shape *accidentally* and so – and their sortal or sortal-related properties – for instance, a particular statue *qua* statue may be worth a fortune and be aesthetically sublime, even though the piece of bronze is of negligible monetary or aesthetic value.

Keeping analogies in sight, is it plausible to think that the challenge for 'legal constitution' can be articulated by means of the same problematic pairing of intrinsic/extrinsic similarity and modal/sortal disparity? A brief examination of the available readings of this relation can confirm our suspicions. To facilitate this illustration, I will briefly scrutinise one positivist and one antipositivist modelling of legal constitution with a view to showcasing that irrespective of their truth-conditional analysis, statements of legal constitution pose a challenge that is similar to the one faced by monist and pluralist accounts of material constitution.

On one available positivist interpretation, statements of the form 'the proposition that it is obligatory to φ is a law of S' express the proposition that an authoritative directive to φ constitutes a legal norm of S. Thus, provided that this statement is true, the abstract object *authoritative directive to φ* stands in a relation of abstract constitution to the abstract object *legal norm of S*. Their intrinsic similarity becomes immediately apparent by noticing that they share the same content, namely, the agential property of φ-ing.

[5] See Fine (1982a) for the theory of *qua* objects in general. See also Fine (1982b) for its application to literary works and, as he notes in passing, to musical works as well.

[6] Evnine (2009: 205).

Moreover, they do not seem to differ from the point of view of their extrinsic properties; for instance, both are amenable to the same institutional practice (S). At the same time, their modal profiles are strikingly divergent: the issuer of an authoritative directive employs the imperative mood to express the obligation to φ, whereas the constituted legal norm refers to the same obligation in the declarative mood. Consequently, they also differ with regard to their satisfaction conditions: the imperative speech act of issuing an authoritative directive is satisfied just in case it is obeyed, whereas the assertable content of a legal norm is true if it meets its target of capturing how things are. From a sortal perspective, the differences are even more perspicuous: legal norms are essentially valid, whereas authoritative directives are only contingently so, as it is always possible for the latter to become devoid of normative consequences if they conflict with directives instantiating superior norms.

An antipositivist way of exemplifying the same relation is not radically different with respect to the puzzle it produces. For the sake of argument, we can sample the model of legal constitution that could plausibly accommodate Greenberg's moral impact theory of law. As noted earlier, a charitable semantic regimentation of the latter theory would entail that <the proposition that it is obligatory to φ is part of the content of the law of S> is true *iff* the moral fact that it is obligatory to φ constitutes a part of the content of the law of S or, in simpler terms, a moral obligation to φ constitutes a legal obligation to φ. Whereas in the previous example we had an abstract object (authoritative directive) as the constituting object, in the present example the dummy sortal <the proposition that it is obligatory to φ> is taken to refer to the moral fact that it is obligatory to φ. Moreover, instead of the atomic reference to legal norms, we have assumed that a holistic reference to the content of the law is more in line with Greenberg's antipositivist account. Despite different appearances, this alternative parsing is fraught with the same problem.

On the one hand, both the constituting normative fact and the constituted legal content have the same compositional structure. At the extrinsic level, they are also enabled by the actions (sayings, doings, thoughts) of particular legal officials: the activity of the latter changes the morally relevant circumstances, thus affecting both what we are morally and thus legally obligated to do. However, from a modal perspective, the distance between normative facts and (parts of) legal content seems to grow exponentially. In Greenberg's own jargon, legal obligations are not just any moral obligations that are created by the actions of legal institutions, but only those moral obligations that are produced in the 'legally proper way'. As a result, in paradoxical cases where the actions of legal officials result in a deterioration of the moral situation in a way that creates a moral obligation to compensate for the bad government action, the latter moral fact fails to constitute part of the content of the law.[7] Consequently, the fact that the

[7] Greenberg (2014: 1321–23).

government is obligated to provide compensation will necessarily result whereas no legal obligation to compensate will manage to 'survive' the paradoxical impact of a legally improper gerrymandering of the moral profile.

I am not entirely convinced which kind of abstractly constituted entity law resembles the most, but for the sake of evading lofty innovations, I could easily resort to Dworkin's famous analogy between law and literary works. My invocation of this analogy has no ontological underpinning whatsoever, nor does it imply my espousal of Dworkin's account of constructive interpretation. The only reason I am dragging this analogy to the surface is to act as an illustration; the idea I intend to convey is that we are already familiar with analogies that implicate in more or less direct ways the relation of material or abstract constitution. Dworkin's correlation between law and literature is only one of numerous other analogical arguments employed by legal philosophers in the service of their diverse argumentative ambitions. In the positivist literature, related examples feature associations between the constitutive power of promissory utterances and the relationship between official enactments and the obtaining of legal norms, or the affinity between legal rules and the constitutive rules of games. Natural law theorists have also contributed informative analogies mainly by way of likening the function of laws to the function of what Judith Jarvis Thomson calls 'goodness-fixing' kinds.[8] For instance, it is customary in natural law theory to encounter comments on the constitutional capacity or incapacity of laws to count as reason-giving norms.

Keeping these analogies in mind, we may ask how we can identify an episode of constitutive disagreement about law. To facilitate the adjudication of this dispute, let us assume that two imaginary jurisprudes, Gonzo and Froddo, are engaged in a first-order disagreement over legal constitution. A typical instance of this disagreement would take the form of the following exchange:

> Gonzo: X constitutes a legal norm (or a part of the content of the law).
>
> Froddo: X does not constitute a legal norm (or a part of the content of the law).

At first sight, there is no conclusive reason to dismiss this disagreement as an instance of a merely verbal dispute. As previously explained (see Chapter 3, section III), constitutive disagreements are substantive disagreements to the extent that the participants therein do not take their claims to be analytically entailed by unpronounced premises. Moreover, I have kept the constituting object argument place empty with a view to exploring the taxonomical implications of engaging in this type of disagreement.

According to one interpretation, Gonzo's disagreement with Froddo is about what legal norms (or parts of legal content) are made of. They do not disagree about the existence of legal norms or the possibility of their being abstractly

[8] See Thomson (2008: 21).

coincident with other entities. In its current formulation, their disagreement is about the 'materials' that make or constitute law. Admittedly, it is easy to confuse the constituting entities that figure in claims of legal constitution with what is commonly known as the sources of law like constitutional and statutory texts, judicial rulings, administrative regulations and the like. But the object of this disagreement is considerably more refined than a heap of texts, utterances and the products of other institutional activities.

To see how the taxonomical impact of this type of disagreement can be spelt out, let us assume that Gonzo is a Razian exclusive positivist and Froddo a moral impact theorist. At various points in the course of this exposition, I have seized the opportunity to disclose my intention of treating both Raz's authority-based account of legal norms and Mark Greenberg's moral impact theory of legal obligation as instances of non-reductive realism about legal propositions. The main idea is that both theories can be charitably read as associating the effect of institutional activity with the constitution of legal content. By effect, I mean the metaphysical role of authoritative pronouncements or facts about the actions of legal institutions in determining the content of the law.[9] Non-reductivist theorists share the belief that our ontological inventory should be capable of accommodating the existence of 'legal things' and that the ontological profile of these legal things is distinct from the ontological profile of their constituting materials. Given the reconstructive nature of this taxonomical endeavour, I carry the burden of providing some textual grounds for my proposal to interpret these two starkly opposed theories of law as sharing a common metajurisprudential background.

Beginning with Joseph Raz's theory of legal norms, it is worth emphasising that he makes no explicit reference to a relation of abstract constitution holding between authoritative directives and legal norms. His standard way of relating these two entities is by using the verbal predicates 'issue' or 'prescribe'.[10] Consequently, the connection that seems to result is not between authoritative

[9] My use of the notion of constitutive effect is not synonymous with Greenberg's understanding of *moral impact*. As Greenberg notes, 'the Moral Impact Theory holds that the law is the moral *impact* or *effect* of certain actions of legal institutions – i.e., the moral obligations that obtain in light of those actions' (Greenberg 2014: 1301, emphasis added). Greenberg's notion of moral impact or effect is explanatorily upstream of the constitutive effect of law-constituting 'material'. According to my favoured interpretation, the 'is' that connects legal content with moral impact is that of constitution rather than that of identity or instantiaton. Facts about the actions of legal institutions change the morally relevant circumstances, thus effecting a change in what we are morally obligated to do (moral impact). The resulting obligations are not legal obligations merely by virtue of the fact that they are the result of moral impact. Whereas all actions of legal institutions are morally impactful, it is only instances of moral impact that have been brought about in the legally proper way that also qualify as instances of 'legal impact', so to speak. In this sense, my association of the notion of impact or effect with the relation of legal constitution regards this latter notion of *legal impact* rather than the explanatorily prior notion of moral impact.

[10] 'A norm is prescribed if it is set by an individual or a group as a norm to guide the behaviour of some other person or persons. A prescribed norm is one set by a speech-act intended to be taken by the norm subjects as an exclusionary reason for action' (Raz 1999b: 82).

directives and legal norms, but between an authority *qua* creating entity and legal norms as the product of its creative activity. The word 'issue' is commonly understood as a success term, such that if a pair of relata – eg, an authority and a legal norm – falls within its extension, it follows by way of entailment that a legal norm exists. What I am about to argue is that this depiction is very close to licensing a constitutive interpretation given some additional premises. The latter are to be found in Raz's distinction between authoritative utterances and norms. To illuminate his point, I shall quote in full a pivotal passage from *Practical Reason and Norms* where it clearly appears that whereas authoritative utterances are intimately related to the creation of legal norms, they remain modally and sortally distinct. According to Raz:

> Not all exclusionary reasons are norms. We have noted that *all authoritative utterances are exclusionary reasons, and yet they are not all norms*. Let us suppose that being completely ignorant in the matter I always invest my money according to the advice of a friend who is an expert on the Stock Exchange. His advice is an exclusionary reason for me and I regard him as my authority. And yet he is not issuing norms when he gives me advice … all orders are, in a sense, exclusionary reasons. But they are not always norms. It seems that norms and other exclusionary reasons do not differ in any way which is relevant to practical reasoning. *The difference is primarily ontological. We talk of norms as entities*. (Emphasis added)[11]

The above passage is a clear indication that Raz does not take the copular sentences of the form 'an authoritative utterance is a legal norm' as identity statements. Not only would the meaning of his description not be affected, but perhaps it would become more accurate if we replaced 'is' in the previous sentence with 'constitutes'. Much in the same sense that a piece of statue-shaped rock does not always constitute a statue – as it may have acquired this shape by virtue of a physical phenomenon – an authoritative directive or utterance need not always constitute a legal norm. In the case of law-making, the question of whether an authoritative directive succeeds in constituting a legal norm is ultimately settled by recourse to the particular legal system's rule of recognition or set of rules of recognition.[12] Moreover, on Raz's account, the content of an authoritative directive and the content of a legal norm are identical, thus validating the intuition that constitutively related objects are intrinsically similar. This is a direct implication of combining the Sources Thesis with his

[11] ibid 77–78.

[12] Raz explicitly acknowledges the theoretical fecundity of Hart's concept of a rule of recognition when he remarks '[that] the rule of recognition sets up some criteria of validity is clear. There must be in every system some criteria of validity that, although legally binding, are not legally valid; hence they must be set in the rule of recognition' (Raz 2012: 95). Furthermore, he adds two important qualifications: first, rules of recognition may be incomplete such that more determinate criteria of legal validity must be established by legal norms validated by a rule of recognition; and, second, a legal system may have more than one rule of recognition each pertaining to a different source of law (legislation, precedent and custom). See ibid 95–96.

view of what determines the content of legal sources. According to the Sources Thesis, '[all] law is source-based … A law is source-based if its existence and content can be identified by reference to social facts alone, without resort to any evaluative argument'.[13] It thereby follows that to establish the content of the law *just is* to establish the content of a source of law. In Raz's own words, '[to] establish the content of the statute, all one need do is to establish that the enactment took place, and what it says. To do this one needs little more than knowledge of English (including technical legal English), and of the events which took place in Parliament on a few occasions'.[14]

On the other hand, Greenberg's allusion to the possibility of legal constitution is evidenced by his remarks on the relationship between moral obligation and legal obligation.[15] Greenberg mainly illustrates this relationship in normative rather than strictly metaphysical terms, but the point he tries to make has a clear constitutive flavour. There are very few occasions where he speaks directly of legal obligations being constituted by moral obligations. One of these occasions is strongly evocative of a metaphysical use of the predicate 'constitutes'. In his words:

> The Moral Impact Theory's approach to this issue begins from an intuitive notion that the moral obligations in question are not brought about in the right sort of way to *constitute* legal obligations. Intuitively, for example, bringing about changes in the moral profile paradoxically is not the way in which legal systems, by their nature, are supposed to change the moral profile. Thus, the Moral Impact Theory holds that there is a distinctive way or ways in which legal institutions are, by their nature, supposed to create obligations. Call this the legally proper way. The obligations that come about in this way *constitute* legal obligations. Obligations that come about in other ways do not. (Emphasis added)[16]

In most cases, Greenberg spells out the same relationship in normative terms by postulating a hypothesis which he terms the 'Bindingness Hypothesis'. According to this hypothesis:

> a legal system is supposed to operate by arranging matters in such a way as to reliably ensure that, *for every legal obligation, there is an all things considered moral obligation with the same content – but not necessarily so that for every moral obligation, there is a corresponding legal obligation* … An intuitive way of putting the point is that the law is supposed to be binding, where that means genuinely binding all things considered – not just legally binding (which the law trivially is). Let's call the relation between law and morality that the law is supposed to ensure – *that there be for every*

[13] Raz (1994: 210–11). For an alternative formulation see Raz (2012: 39 and 47). For a critical analysis of their difference, see Atria (2002: 65–67).

[14] Raz (1994: 221).

[15] In what follows, I will adopt Greenberg's metaphysical talk of legal obligations instead of the metaphysically neutral term 'part of the content of the law' that (alternatively with the atomistic term 'legal norm') figures in the logical regimentation of legal utterances.

[16] Greenberg (2017: 282).

> *legal obligation a moral obligation with the same content – bindingness*, and the hypothesis *the bindingness hypothesis*. (Emphasis added)[17]

Greenberg's gloss on the way in which determinate moral obligations are related to determinate legal obligations allows us to infer that it is metaphysically possible that there simultaneously exist a moral obligation triggered by the actions of legal institutions and a legal obligation with which it shares the same content. What would ensure that the intimate relationship between triggered moral obligations and legal obligations proper is constitutive is a positive answer to the question of whether the former can exist without the latter also existing. That would confirm the constitutive role of the copula that Greenberg uses when he emphatically says that '[legal] institutions take actions to change our moral obligations by changing the relevant facts and circumstances ... With important qualifications, the resulting moral obligations *are* legal obligations' (emphasis added).[18] According to this picture, the relationship between legally triggered moral obligations and legal obligations is asymmetric in the sense that the existence of the former cannot depend on the existence of the latter.

The constitutive asymmetry between these two entities can be safely affirmed by the way in which Greenberg proceeds to qualify their relationship. He carefully distinguishes between legally proper and legally improper ways of triggering moral obligations such that only those that come about in the legally proper way *are* legal obligations. My argument is that the italicised copula can only have the meaning of 'constitutes'. Greenberg rejects the pure identity between legally triggered moral obligations and legal obligations when he clarifies that 'legal obligations are not just any moral obligations that are created by the actions of legal institutions. We need to limit the relevant moral obligations to ones that come about in the appropriate way – what I call the *legally proper* way'.[19]

Greenberg is careful to qualify his understanding of institutionally generated moral obligations when he acknowledges that there seem to be occasions where legal obligations such as the prohibition of assault, murder or rape correspond to pre-existing moral obligations which do not obtain by virtue of the proper actions of legal institutions. In such cases, a cursory reading of the moral impact thesis would entail that these pre-existing moral obligations cannot constitute legal obligations precisely because they have not been generated by the actions of legal institutions. Greenberg's way of obviating this paradox is to include in the cohort of legally fashioned moral obligations a list of moral obligations that are not modified but normatively *reinforced*, so to speak, by the actions of legal institutions. In his words:

> In addition to altering pre-existing moral obligations, a legislative enactment of a criminal prohibition (on conduct that is already morally prohibited) typically results

[17] Greenberg (2011: 85).
[18] Greenberg (2014: 1294).
[19] ibid 1321.

> in new reasons for not engaging in the relevant conduct … For example, the legislative action will often add reasons of fairness and democracy to the pre-existing moral reasons. When reasons are added for engaging in conduct that is already obligatory, let us say that the pre-existing obligations are *reinforced*. The Moral Impact Theory holds that moral obligations that are reinforced by the actions of legal institutions are among the moral obligations that are legal obligations.[20]

It is worth emphasising that Greenberg does not offer a systematic account of the legally proper way of altering or reinforcing moral obligations, which in their turn constitute legal obligations, but he adamantly supports the idea that moral obligations that are triggered in legally improper or, as he calls them, paradoxical and/or irrelevant ways fail to constitute legal obligations.[21] In a very general way, he remarks that:

> If legal institutional action, by making the moral situation worse, generates obligations to remedy, oppose, or otherwise mitigate the consequences of the action, such obligations to mitigate have not come about in the legally proper way. Call this general way of changing the moral profile *paradoxical* (because the resulting obligations run in the opposite direction from the standard case). Moral obligations that are produced in the paradoxical way are not legal obligations.[22]

It thereby follows that Greenberg's line of reasoning offers a clear indication that he would not at least object to a piecemeal reconstruction that replaces his copular references to the relationship between properly triggered moral obligations and legal obligation with a constitutive predicate.[23] Moral obligations that are properly (non-paradoxically or relevantly)[24] triggered by the actions of legal institutions are capable of constituting legal obligations with the same content.

After this necessary exegetical digression, we may return to our initial example of an episode of legal disagreement featuring the use of the expression 'X constitutes a legal norm'. We may now be able to convert this empty

[20] ibid 1321.

[21] One may recall the analogy with the statue and the piece of rock. A rock being hit by a lightning is not a 'statue-proper' way of constituting a statue, even if it comes to acquire a statue-like shape.

[22] Greenberg (2014: 1322).

[23] Greenberg's reconstructed position could be modelled in the likeness of Lynne Rudder Baker's relational account of the possibility of constituted objects. Baker remarks that 'here is the reason that Piece and David differ in their essential properties even though they are intrinsically just alike: There are relational properties that David has essentially but that Piece does not have essentially' (Baker 2000: 107). Using a modest analogy, we could attribute to Greenberg the view that the relational property of making the moral situation better *essentially* applies to 'legal obligation', but not to 'moral obligation' because the latter can be the result of a deterioration of the moral situation.

[24] Besides the paradoxical deterioration of the moral situation by the actions of legal institutions, Greenberg also mentions another kind of case where 'legal institutions' actions lead through an extended chain of events to moral obligations that are intuitively too far downstream to qualify as legal obligations. For example, the actions of legal institutions in setting up a tax system might lead me to promise to help you fill out your tax returns. As a result of my promise, I may have a moral obligation to help you. Although this moral obligation traces back (rather indirectly) to the actions of legal institutions, intuitively it is not brought about in the right way to constitute a legal obligation' (Greenberg 2017: 281–82).

statement into a substantive claim. The example will feature Gonzo uttering the sentence 'an authoritative directive to φ constitutes a legal norm' and Froddo will deny Gonzo's substantive claim. Depending on the context of this episode of disagreement, the target of Froddo's denial may strike a course in two distinct directions. On the one hand, if he does not wish to challenge the Razian model of legal metaphysics head-on, Froddo may courteously object that this particular directive is invalid either because it conflicts with another superior directive or because its source – for instance, the minutes of a ministerial meeting – is not a source of law in the contextually specified legal system. On the other hand, as a devout moral impact theorist, Froddo may direct his objection to the fact that although the particular source of the authoritative directive is among the recognised sources of law of their legal system, the metaphysical role of authoritative directives does not consist in their *constituting* legal norms.

In other words, Froddo does not question the existence or validity of the particular authoritative directive, but its aptness to assume the role of a law-constituting object. In this particular example, Froddo may endorse Greenberg's approach according to which the constitutive role is properly assumed by normative facts about the impact of authoritative directives on the moral profile. According to this latter view, the fact that an authoritative directive exists is not directly implicated in the constitution of legal content, but it may change the moral context in such a way that a new moral obligation results; it is the latter *moral obligation* that according to Greenberg's account constitutes a legal obligation with same content.

As a result, the first-order version of a constitutive disagreement about law encompasses two possible questions: (i) whether a legal-content-constituting object O originates from a valid source of law (source question); and (ii) whether O is capable of having the effect of constituting a legal norm that shares the same content (effect question). A crucial implication of this making-recipe type of disagreement is that meaningful participation is reserved only for non-reductive pluralist about legal constitution. In other words, as it stands, any exchange of the form '"X constitutes a legal norm" "No, X does not constitute a legal norm"' conversationally implies that both parties agree that in the context of the dispute, there exist two coincident abstract objects, one of which is a law or a piece of legal content. The regimentation of this discourse creates a slot for those theories of law to which we can attribute a non-reductive pluralist view about legal constitution.

Consequently, only two out of the four exemplary theories of law can figure in the first-order version of this dispute. On the one hand, on Joseph Raz's authority-based account, legal norms are directly constituted by authoritative directives in the sense that a directive which is validly issued by a legal authority constitutes a legal norm with which it shares the same linguistic content. On the other hand, according to Mark Greenberg's moral impact theory of law, legal obligations are constituted by moral obligations whose obtaining is triggered in what Greenberg calls 'the legally proper way'. Despite their radical divergence with regard to the nature of law's constituting material, both theories converge in their espousal of the possibility of legal constitution. In other words, both theories agree that from an ontological point of view, there exist both a constituting object (an authoritative directive or moral obligation respectively) and a constituted object (a legal norm or legal obligation respectively), which under constitution-favourable circumstances are related in this particular way.

B. Second-Order Disagreement over Legal Constitution

The most robust implication of this model is probably its exclusionary effect. Given how the discussion is presently decoded, a plan positivist or an interpretivist cannot intelligibly participate in the current version of the dispute without rendering it merely verbal. On the one hand, if someone like Shapiro believes that legal norms are reducible to a class of institutionalised plans, he cannot come across as meaningfully disagreeing with Gonzo if he utters 'X does not constitute a legal norm'. The reason is that for him, a sentence like 'X constitutes a legal norm' acquires meaning only if we accept that it is paraphrasable into a sentence of the form 'X constitutes a plan'. On the other hand, a theorist like Dworkin believes that there is no constitutive moment at which what justifies a legal practice as a whole *creates* a legal obligation. For a Dworkinian, what justifies the practice and what one is legally obligated to do are two sides of the same coin, each one describing a particular aspect of law-making. In this regard, for a Dworkinian theorist, a sentence of the form 'X constitutes a legal obligation' is literally false (or metaphysical bogus, as she may remark) as there is no matter of fact about the existence of two abstractly coincident entities.

This line of reasoning places a significant burden of justification. If this is the finishing line of my argument, one may reasonably get the impression that a plan positivist or an interpretivist can never meaningfully disagree with a Razian positivist or a moral impact theorist about the sources of law or the effect that facts about these sources have on the determination of legal content. This is certainly not the case. Against this misunderstanding, I would like to affirm the possibility of their disagreement by remarking that the suggested model of disagreement about legal constitution correctly predicts that a source or effect objection on the part of a plan positivist or an interpretivist cannot be voiced as a first-order denial. In both cases, their objections about what is made of what are being addressed to their opponents from a higher level of abstraction.

I shall begin with the case of an interpretivist objector, as it displays the highest degree of recalcitrance to a unified semantics of legal disagreement. Its recalcitrance is evidenced by the interpretivist's error-theoretic reaction to constitutive claims about law. The objection of literal falsehood is a legitimate choice that poses a serious challenge for those who are willing to make the platform of legal disagreement as inclusive as possible. Hopefully, this challenge can be met as soon as we allow that disagreement over legal constitution is versatile enough to switch levels of abstraction depending on who enters the debate. By the end of this section, I will also try to explain how a reductivist about legal norms like Shapiro can also participate in constitutive disputes about law. My argument will be similar to the one employed vis-a-vis the interpretivist objector, but it will be subject to considerably less strain for the simple reason that in essence, Shapiro's hypothetical objection is not targeted against the understanding of legal claims as constitutive claims, but rather against their featuring legal norms instead of plans as their proper constituted object.

Let us begin with the question of what happens when an interpretivist retorts that 'X does not constitute a legal norm'. The idea I have in mind is that her denial is centred on the very possibility of drawing a numerical distinction between the materials of law and law proper. This second-order objection about the possibility of legal constitution has a dual content. On the one hand, it expresses an error-theoretic view about the truth of claims of legal constitution. It rejects these claims as literally false. For an interpretivist, it is not just the case that talk of legal constitution can be paraphrased into a non-constitutive kind of talk; rather, it fails to report any truth whatsoever. Instead of providing a sentence that is synonymous with the ontologically offending 'X constitutes a legal norm', the interpretivist believes that Gonzo and Froddo do not ordinarily use constitutive claims to assert the propositions they literally express. In this regard, she carries the burden of telling us what interlocutors like Gonzo and Froddo really assert in their ordinary use of claims about legal constitution. This error-theoretic stance does not amount to the attribution of systematic error to speakers like Gonzo and Froddo with regard to their capacity to grasp what is at stake in the relevant domain of discourse. What it conveys instead is the idea that many of the sentences that are being used in this domain are systematically false.

On the other hand, this qualification brings us to another, more crucial aspect of the interpretivist's objection to assertions of the form 'X constitutes a legal norm'. In the immediately preceding paragraphs, I endorsed the concern that by regimenting legal claims as claims about legal constitution, we exclude too early positions like those of Dworkin or Shapiro from figuring in disputes about the sources of law or their effect. Now, I believe that I can appease this reasonable criticism by adding the qualification that the interpretivist's denial of 'X constitutes a legal norm' also serves as an affirmation of the possibility of an alternative position about the individuation of the sources of law and their effect on the determination of legal content. This idea becomes plausible the moment we think that the vehicle for expressing this alternative position is what the interpretivist believes we really assert when we say that it is legally obligatory to φ. Given that it is imprecise to exhaustively associate legal interpretivism with Dworkin's particular theory of law as integrity, I will confine my analysis to Dworkin's theory for the sake of theoretical economy.

According to Dworkin, aspects of past political practices qualify as contributing to the content of the law by virtue of their being *instances* of the set of principles embodied in a particular political community. According to this picture, principles of political morality do not stand in a relation of *grounding* to the contributory aspects of legal practices, but in a relation of *instantiation*, much like the laws of nature are thought to have actual events as their instances. By denying that the pre-interpretive (to use Dworkin's jargon) material is identified independently of its contribution to the content of the law, the legal interpretivist argues that we cannot disagree about the sources of law independently of the principles of political morality which the content of the law instantiates. How can this position be adumbrated by what the interpretivist believes we really assert when we make a legal statement? The crucial evidence, I believe, lies in Dworkin's generic understanding of statements of legal obligation as expressing propositions about which obligations instantiate the principles of political morality that are applicable in a legal system.

A primary indication of Dworkin's generic understanding of legal propositions is provided by his consistent appeal to the notion of 'figuring in' or 'following from' an integrity-realising scheme of principle. In *Law's Empire*, we read that '[according] to law as integrity, propositions of law are true if they figure in or follow from the principles of justice, fairness, and procedural due process that provide the best constructive interpretation of the community's legal practice'.[25] On this understanding, by uttering 'X does not constitute a legal norm', an interpretivist can meaningfully engage her opponents by inviting them to reconsider their inflationary understanding of the entities that are implicated in the generation of legal content. Her claim that 'X constitutes a legal norm' is not what we really assert when we say that 'it is legally obligatory to φ'.

There are two major implications following from this way of translating Dworkin's positive claim. The first is that legal content-contributing aspects and principles of morality have to be of the *same kind* if the latter are to be instantiated by the former. By its very essence, the relation of instantiation holds between kinds and their instances or properties and their instances. As such, their instances cannot be of a different kind vis-a-vis their generic sources, but only a world-bound actual exemplification of a universal kind or property. The second implication is itself implied by the first one as the homogeneity between legal-content-contributing aspects and their generating principles seems to make the existence of legal facts themselves spurious. In other words, if for some reason some aspects of law practices come to qualify as instances of principles of political morality, there is no intermediate space left for facts about what legal obligations, rights or powers exist to figure into this picture.

It seems that somehow the contributory aspects of law practices and legal obligations proper are ontologically indiscernible. I will refer to this implication

[25] Dworkin (1986: 225).

as the *Indiscernibility Thesis*, which I aim to unpack in a way that it can be understood as a formal, ontological regimentation of Dworkin's familiar claim that interpreting the law practices consists in assigning to them the content that best fits and justifies them. On the most charitable reading of Dworkin's gloss on the structure of legal interpretation, there does not exist a strict division between a pre-interpretive and an interpretive stage of legal reasoning. As Nicos Stavropoulos remarks:

> The interpretivist does not accept, nor does the fit-justification distinction properly understood entail, a distinction between the data and their reading that is prior to and independent of interpretation ... No aspect of the practice can be taken as a non-interpretive given. Rather, they are both parts of the interpretive, *thoroughly normative account*. (Emphasis added)[26]

It is crucial to note that for Dworkin, these two aspects are theoretically indistinguishable despite their epistemological disassociation in ordinary descriptions of legal practice. He emphatically explains this misconception when he remarks that he intends this 'distinction not as a phenomenological report but an analytic device to help understand the logic of interpretation ... the two dimensions of fit and value represent different aspects of a single overall judgment of political morality'.[27] With these caveats in place, it would not be exegetically far-fetched to reconstruct Dworkin's hypothetical response to the dispute between Gonzo and Froddo as involving the claim that what they really assert or deny is the proposition that a legal obligation succeeds or fails to instantiate a determinate conception of the principle of integrity. Instantiation is crucially generic in much the same way that a person's life achievements or diachronic behaviour instantiate a particular ethical virtue.

The idea that may emerge by following this route will be that the focal points of content-contributing practices, legal facts and principles of political morality form a potentially virtuous circle. To see how this might work, we may ask what Dworkin's reply would be to the question of what makes legal propositions *construed as constitutive claims* true. In other words, we can ask what kind of fact is the truthmaker for a constitutive claim of the form *the contribution of S constitutes a part of the content of the law of S*. Featuring Dworkin in a reconstructed confrontation with a hypothetical question is definitely a serious detour from a more exegetical understanding of his argument. As a result, I would be insincere if I neglected the immediate objection that I am attempting to decipher Dworkin's thought by allowing it to be infiltrated by ideas that he never entertained. There is no doubt that he did not take any interest in providing a semantically meticulous analysis of legal statements mainly because he thought that this would be an unnecessary distraction from the evaluative orientation of legal discourse.

[26] Stavropoulos (2008).
[27] Dworkin (2006: 15).

My response to this legitimate concern is twofold. First, I do not intend to commit Dworkin to a constitutive account of the semantics of legal statements, but to animate his hypothetical rejection of this view in a way that reveals his actual understanding of how law is made. In that sense, my invocation of this semantic alternative is contrastive and not indicative of how Dworkin would presumably argue about the semantics of legal statements. Second, and most importantly, my purpose is to offer a reconstructive account of the interplay between law, practices and normative facts that does justice to Dworkin's first-order argument about the relevance of law practices by way of ascending to a higher level of abstraction.

To see how the previous semantic digression can unpack the first interpretive hypothesis about the metaphysical role of law practices, let us see whether and how the familiar operative concepts of Dworkin's theory can be used to respond to this hypothetical challenge. My calculated guess is that Dworkin would have a cogent response to whether we should *reject* a constitutive understanding of legal discourse and that this same response would be an epitome of his own unpronounced metaphysical commitments. It is the latter aspect of Dworkin's response that I intend to marshal in support of the 'strategy' I have attributed to him.

Given that for Dworkin, there is no strict divide between the descriptive and normative aspects of legal philosophy,[28] it is reasonable to expect that he would reserve an error-theoretic response to the question of what makes the proposition that *the fact that the contribution of S is the obligation to φ constitutes a part of the content of the law of S* true. He would say that as it stands, this proposition is literally false, not because he does not believe in the reality of legal facts, but because this constitutive way of representing the reality of law is false. His objection would simply be that the aspects of practices that contribute legal content are indiscernible from the normative content they contribute, such that it is a plain fallacy to assume that our discourse is about two numerically distinct entities standing in a relation of abstract constitution. By rejecting the constitutive account of legal discourse, Dworkin would be ipso facto classified as a monist with regard to the possibility of legal, so to speak, constitution. In other words, he would most probably remark that as it stands, the proposition that the contribution of S constitutes a part of the content of the law of S is literally an *identity* statement and nothing more.

At first sight, postulating the identity of these two purported objects can raise the Moorean concern that it implies a collapse between the descriptive and the normative aspect of law-making. It would seem, so the objection goes, that the interpreted content of the sayings, doings and thoughts of legal officials is already endowed with the normative status of legal obligation. Whereas this

[28] Given his unified account of value, Dworkin would offer the same comment with regard to the other two branches of practical philosophy, namely moral and political philosophy.

would not be a problematic conclusion in the case of a lump of clay and a statue (both are just material objects), it is undoubtedly an undesirable result for our understanding of Dworkin's normative conception of legal discourse.

Hopefully, there is a way to retain Dworkin's classification as an error-theoretic monist about legal constitution without shouldering the undesirable complications of identifying the normative with the descriptive or vice versa. A helpful analogy comes from the discourse about the possibility of material constitution. In Michael Burke's *dominant kind* view,[29] it is both true that a lump of clay and a statue cannot be spatiotemporally coincident *and* that there is a sense in which they remain numerically distinct. Burke claims that an object can be a statue and a lump of clay if and only if it has the persistence conditions associated with the dominant sortal profile of the object. In Burke's own words, 'an object's dominant sortal is the sortal … whose satisfaction entails possession of the widest range of properties'.[30] For instance, the sortal *statue* but not the *lump of clay* entails possession of aesthetic properties in addition to microphysical properties.

Prior to the creation of the statue, there only existed a lump of clay, since this was the available dominant sortal. Let us now call the lump of clay that exists before the creation of the statue 'Lump' and the lump of clay that exists after the creation of the statue 'Lump*'. Lump* is identical to the statue ('Goliath'), but not Lump! In Burke's view, by way of sculpting a lump of clay into a statue, the ordinary lump of clay ceases to exist and is replaced by another object, namely Goliath. Goliath is also Lump*, but Lump* is numerically distinct from Lump because they have different persistence conditions.

How could this analogy from the ontology of material objects illuminate Dworkin's Indiscernibility Thesis? We could say that before the onset of our interpretive work, the only thing that exists are ordinary descriptive facts about the sayings, doings and thoughts of some actual persons in a given community. At this stage, even the institutional designation of these persons *qua* legal officials is not available. Let us call the set of these descriptive facts *Activities*. By the time we set out to subject a set of descriptive facts to legal interpretation, *Activities* ceases to exist as such and is replaced by *Activities**. Now *Activities** is just a part of the content of the law (for the sake of brevity *Law*) because *Law* is a dominant sortal in the sense that it entails possession of a wider range of properties. To name a few, *Law* but not *Activities** is – in Dworkin's view – enforceable, reason-giving and, most importantly, instantiates a select set of principles of political morality – that is, it realises the value of integrity.

In other words, there is no point in trying to locate a constitutive continuum during which some descriptive facts stand in a relation of abstract constitution to some normative facts, namely facts about what legal obligations, rights or

[29] Burke (1994).
[30] ibid 610.

powers exist. The content-contributing aspects of the law practices and the obtaining legal obligations are *one and the same thing* insofar as the former acquire the persistence conditions of the latter. This 'modal absorption' by legal obligations is explained by the fact that the sortal *legal obligation* or *Law* is dominant vis-a-vis the sortal *content-contributing practices* or *Actvities**.

In the light of this analogy, how could Dworkin's hypothetical monism about the possibility of legal constitution lend support to the idea that interpretation occurs by way of a virtuous circle from judgements of fit to judgements of justification and vice versa? The answer is that it does so by eliminating the distinction between facts about what content law practices contribute and legal facts proper in favour of the latter. By way of this elimination, it deprives the objector of a course of attack that would accuse Dworkin of failing to provide a legal-content-independent account of what identifies law practices as such. Since facts about content-contributing practices (*Activities**) *are just* facts about legal content and since the sortal *legal obligation* is the dominant one, what actually instantiates principles of political morality are legal obligations.

This metanormative explanation helps to make it more intelligible how Dworkin purported to present his strategy about how law is made normative *all the way down*. According to the instantiation reading of his strategy, there is no point in trying to distinguish what Dworkin calls the dimension of fit from the dimension of justification precisely because the process by which law comes into existence is normative from beginning to end. Everything begins with the postulation of a single vision of political justice as it is amalgamated within the context of a particular political community. What follows is an interpretive circle that starts from a normatively privileged description of the practice *qua* content-contributing and ends with the determination of legal content *qua* normative fact.

Only normatively privileged facts about the sayings and doings of actual people within a particular community at a particular time can trigger the set of principles that actually embody the value of integrity within a given political community. As a result of this triggering effect, the same set of principles is instantiated by contingent normative facts about what legal obligations, rights or powers exist in a particular community at a particular time. In their turn, those legal facts obtain by virtue of the fact that they normatively explain *ex post* the occurrence of those practices that have qualified as being capable of triggering the political community's generative principles.

This could be a charitable depiction of the virtuous interpretive circle that Dworkin pointed towards by advancing the Indiscernibility Thesis. For Dworkin, to identify a practice as legal *just is* to assert that *this* practice and not another triggers the instantiation of principles of political morality by legal facts. Moreover, the latter facts justify the practices that qualified as triggers of integrity. This *triggering-instantiation-justification* circle is best explained I believe, by the reconstructive attribution to Dworkin of a *dominant kind* view of legal constitution.

On a charitable reading of this alternative view, a sentence of the form 'it is legally obligatory to φ in S' is true *iff* the obligation to φ instantiates a principle of S. Before proceeding with the unpacking of this claim, I must confess that Dworkin's writings do not provide conclusive evidence as to how exactly he would prefer to regiment the relationship between legal obligations, the principle of integrity and the totality of legal practices. That said, his prolific authorship is marked by a consistent reference to how legal obligations and rights are such that they simultaneously justify past political decisions and follow from the principles of morality that justify an actual legal practice.[31] On the one hand, legal obligations and rights *qua* best justifications of past political practice are those normative facts that 'deploy some argument why law on that conception [of integrity] provides an adequate justification for coercion'.[32] On the other hand, legal obligations and rights are themselves determinate instances of how an abstract principle of integrity is amalgamated in a particular political community.

The major implication of attributing to Dworkin a generic – as opposed to constitutive – account of legal propositions is that in his own theoretical universe, legal obligations and rights are not episodic instances of morally filtered or brute facts about the sayings and doings of legal officials, but generic instances of a specified principle of integrity that both individuates these practices as legal (dimension of fit) and justifies their coercive effect (dimension of justification). This conception can explain why a Dworkinian objector can meaningfully intervene in the exchange between Gonzo and Froddo. All that we need to grant her access to in this dispute is to agree that instead of reading her objection as a first-order comment about whether a particular pattern of activity is a proper material for constituting legal content, we shall interpret her objection as being targeted against the *separation of questions* of source (fit) from questions of their effect or impact (justification) on the content of the law.

Consequently, the interpretivist's reply that X does not constitute a legal norm is not given at the same level of abstraction as Froddo's homophonic response. It acquires a concrete communicable meaning as a *metajurisprudential* and not a jurisprudential or first-order negation of Gonzo's statement. Its informational contribution roughly consists in the claim that the appeal to the relation of constitution misleadingly disassociates the constituting from the constituted object. For the interpretivist, the inappropriateness of talk about legal constitution can be further explained by the fact that legal obligations do not piggyback on whatever the best theoretical account of a legal practice qualifies as being endowed with normative impact. Legal obligations and rights are ontologically inseparable from whatever qualifies as having a normative impact

[31] In one of his various glosses on the principle of integrity, Dworkin notes that 'rights and responsibilities flow from past decisions and so count as legal, not just when they are explicit in these decisions but also when they follow from the principles of personal and political morality the explicit decision presuppose by way of justification' (1986: 96).

[32] ibid 139.

on the content of the law because both aspects are abstractly enshrined in a set of principles of political morality. The inseparability of these two components and their common instantiation of a principle of integrity is what make both Gonzo's positive and Froddo's negative claim literally false.

Next comes the case of the plan positivist who wishes to intervene in Gonzo's and Froddo's brief exchange without giving the false impression that she sides with Froddo when she also utters the sentence 'X does not constitute a legal norm'. Again, as I am about to argue, the nature of her denial is meta-jurisprudential rather than first-order, but the route to her qualifying as a peer participant to this dispute is rather different from the interpretivist's path of error-theoretical denial. As I briefly noted at the beginning of this section, the challenge posed by the plan positivist's negation of Gonzo's claim is easier to address. The reason is that a plan positivist has no compelling reason to reject the possibility of abstractly coincident objects. On the contrary, this scheme of explanation can lend additional support to the kind of solution plan positivists like Shapiro favour with regard to the circularity problem arising for those who welcome into their ontology both facts about the exercise of legal authority and facts about the existence of power-conferring norms.

By reducing talk of legal norms to talk of subplans and master plans, a plan positivist need not eliminate her reference to relations of constitution. Both forms of talk remain constitutive, but only the latter is explanatorily basic. Given that my reparsing of legal claims as constitutive claims is reconstructive, I will confine my exegetical quest to adducing sufficient evidence for attributing to Shapiro a reductive view of legal norms. There are many places in *Legality* where it becomes evident that the connection between legal norms and plans is intimate. By way of providing some guidelines for his readers, Shapiro notes that his 'purpose here is not to draw an analogy between laws and plans but to flesh out an implication. The existence conditions for law are the same as those for plans because the fundamental rules of legal systems *are* plans'.[33]

Whereas throughout his argumentation Shapiro maintains the use of legality as a distinct property of norms, he does not seem to intend to imbue its use with a strong ontological undertone. There is a considerable volume of textual evidence suggesting that Shapiro treats legality as the formal, higher-order property of having some lower-order properties whose possession by a planning organisation or a plan is represented by the system's officials as serving the aim of solving 'those moral problems that cannot be solved, or solved as well, through alternative forms of social ordering'.[34] Among those lower-order properties are attributes such as compulsoriness,[35] self-certification,[36]

[33] Shapiro (2011: 119).

[34] ibid 225.

[35] For Shapiro, legal authority is compulsory in the sense that (like parental authority) 'consent is not a necessary condition for the applicability of its requirements' (ibid 212).

[36] A planning organisation is self-certifying to the extent that it is capable of '[enforcing] its rules without first demonstrating to a superior (if one exists) that its rules are valid. A planning

official character[37] and institutionality.[38] On the standard view of higher-order properties, their instantiation is generated by means of quantifying over some set B of lower-order properties plus a condition on what counts as membership of B.[39] We can further specify this general account to fit Shapiro's implicit endorsement of it as follows:

> Being legal just is the property of having some other properties P in B such that R(P), where R specifies a condition on members of B which is satisfied just by those properties in B that allow their bearers to be represented as serving a moral aim.[40]

This formal analysis can be charitably read as a reduction plan on Shapiro's part.[41] Shapiro's account of legality is reductive in the sense that it does not appeal to the property of legality in explaining what law is. By contrast, law can be understood in terms of a set of more basic properties borne by a class of planning organisations or plans that allow the representation of these organisations and plans as serving a moral aim.[42] According to this picture, the property of legality does not by itself enable the representation of a planning activity as serving a moral purpose, but merely points to the existence of other properties that do so. In the light of this understanding. Shapiro's remark that 'legal activity is the shared activity of social planning and that laws *are just* plans, or planlike norms' (emphasis added)[43] can be plausibly invoked as a summary of a reductive project.

organization, therefore, will be self-certifying whenever it is supreme or enjoys a general presumption of validity from all superior planning organizations' (ibid 221).

[37] 'It is an essential feature of an office, therefore, that holders of power are "fungible", namely, that the rights and responsibilities that attend the office do not depend on the identity of those who inhabit the office. If X and Y are both eligible to occupy office O, then X and Y will have the same rights and responsibilities when they occupy O' (ibid 209).

[38] '[The] normativity of law is "institutional" in nature, which is to say that the legal relations may obtain between people independent of the particular intentions of those people' (ibid 210).

[39] Kim (1998: 19–20).

[40] I have benefited immensely from David Plunkett's elaboration of the representational dimension of Shapiro's Moral Aim Thesis; see Plunkett (2013). This definitional scheme is extensively used in 'buck-passing accounts' of evaluative and deontic properties. The term 'buck-passing' has been initially adopted by Thomas Scanlon within the context of his reductionist account of value in terms of reasons (see Scanlon 1998: 95–98). The overall strategy of demystifying value continues a long tradition codified under the name 'fitting-attitude analysis of value'. For a comprehensive presentation of the fitting-attitude theorising about value, see Rabinowicz and Rønnow-Rasmussen (2004). In the present context, I have adapted Pekka Väyrynen's qualified restatements of Scanlon's traditional definition of buck-passing (see Väyrynen 2006: 300).

[41] Buck-passing analyses of properties are standardly treated as reductive. See Heuer (2006).

[42] Shapiro notes that: 'The law possesses the aim that it does because high-ranking officials *represent* the practice as having a moral aim or aims' (Shapiro 2011: 216–17, emphasis added). In a different context, Plunkett (2013) remarks that on pain of letting the planning theory of law collapse into a theory of moral planning, Shapiro must be committed to the view that the relationship between legal officials and the activities of legal planning is representational in the sense that the former represent the latter as serving a moral purpose.

[43] Shapiro (2011: 194).

How can this reading of Shapiro's theory of law fit into the discursive mould defended here? A crucial prerequisite for ensuring that this adaptation is informative and charitably reconstructive of Shapiro's argument is to verify whether his account leaves space for abstract coincidence. In this regard, I believe that the most telling piece of evidence lies in Shapiro's treatment of what he describes as the 'Chicken-Egg Problem'. His main concern is that there is a lurking circularity in the relationship between the concepts of power or authority and the concept of a norm that can threaten the very possibility of legal authority. To illustrate his argument, he presents this puzzle as a pair of inconsistent principles:

> *Egg*: some body has power to create legal norms only if an existing norm confers that power.
>
> *Chicken*: a norm conferring power to create legal norms exists only if somebody with power to do so created it.

On the one hand, based on the Egg Principle, if A1 has the power to create a set of legal norms, a norm must exist which confers that power on A1. On the other hand, the Chicken Principle dictates that somebody endowed with power to create this power-conferring norm actually created them. The puzzle arises as soon as we ask who created the power-conferring norm that confers power on A1. As Shapiro remarks, '[the] answer cannot be "A1" because he did not have the power to create any norms until n1 existed. In other words, it would be viciously circular to argue that A1 granted himself legal power, because n1 [the power-conferring norm] had to exist *before* A1 could have created it'.[44] If we postulate the existence of another authority A2 to explain the antecedent validity of the power-conferring norm, circularity is inevitable because by virtue of this pair of principles, that authority must also derive its authority from another source or body and so on ad infinitum.

Shapiro's solution to this puzzle is strongly indicative of a constitutive understanding of legal norms *qua* plans. Any possible solution must involve the rejection of either one of the two aforementioned principles. We must either reject the Egg Principle by postulating the existence of a body whose power does not derive from some norm or reject the Chicken Principle by locating a norm that confers powers to create legal norms, but which is not itself created by someone with a relevant power. Shapiro's solution features the rejection of the Chicken Principle in a way that strongly suggests that legal norms *qua* plans are constituted by norms that are not themselves created by anyone else. Below I quote the whole passage that encapsulates this idea:

> [The] Planning Theory is able to secure the existence of fundamental legal rules without generating vicious circles or infinite regresses. Legal officials have the power to adopt the shared plan that sets out these fundamental rules by virtue of the norms of

[44] ibid 40.

> instrumental rationality. *Since these norms that confer the rational power to plan are not themselves plans, they have not been created by any other authority. They exist simply in virtue of being rationally valid principles.* (Emphasis added)[45]

This remark clearly points to the existence of two kinds of norms – those of instrumental rationality and legal norms reductively construed as plans – which are crucially different with regard to their modal profiles in much the same way that abstract objects like an indicated sound structure and a musical work have different persistence conditions. Norms of rationality exist necessarily by virtue of their status as rational principles, whereas legal norms *qua* plans exist contingently by virtue of their being created by planning officials vested with the authority to plan for others. The final step is to see whether these sortally distinct norms can be constitutively related. Whereas Shapiro does not make any explicit move in this direction, there is nothing in principle that should dissuade us from supplementing his argument in this way. The relation of constitution is such that it crucially respects the modal dissimilarity of coincident objects and purports to put an end to the circularity of creation by virtue of the fact that constituted objects are asymmetrically dependent on their constituting counterparts.

The pivotal question is what the constituting material of legal norms *qua* plans can be. It certainly cannot be the set of abstract norms of instrumental rationality as their content is not exclusively specifiable in terms of the far more determinate content of legal norms. But this is not where our quest is doomed to end. Norms of instrumental rationality like the means-ends principle are regularly instantiated by local, world-bound rational requirements that specify what type of behavioural response is rational in a given context. These requirements typically take wide scope over the conditions of their application such that to say that one ought to intend to pursue the means Y that are conducive to the realisation of one's intention to X is to say that one is rationally required to [intend to Y, if X]. Crucially, this wide-scope formulation allows more than one valid response such that one can be said to satisfy this rational requirement either if one pursues the necessary means Y or if one revises one's intention to X.

In the case of law, local rational requirements of the relevant sort can be generated whenever the officials of a legal system adopt a subplan that is authorised by the jointly adopted master plan of their system. According to this picture, what comes first is the acquisition of an adoptive attitude on the part of legal officials towards the fundamental rules of a legal system, figuring in what Shapiro describes as the master plan of that system. The master plan of a legal system is an institutionalised shared plan that includes, among other things, 'new provisions that specify the formal conditions for the exercise of planning power'.[46] In other words, the master plan endows legal officials with

[45] ibid 181.
[46] ibid 168.

the proto-authority to plan for others and, moreover, it instructs them how to exercise this authority. According to Shapiro, its purpose is 'to guide, organize, and monitor the shared activity of legal officials. It seeks to overcome the enormously complex, contentious, and arbitrary problems associated with arranging a system of social planning'.[47]

This is the first episode in a chain of infinitely ensuing episodes of what Shapiro calls the 'inner rationality of law'. The initial adoption of this master plan triggers the obtaining of a series of more specific rational requirements committing legal officials 'to filling out the plan, to ensuring consistency with one's beliefs, subplans,[48] and other plans, and to not reconsidering it absent a compelling reason for doing so'.[49] These more specific rational requirements are crucially involved in the ordinary law-making process as they explicitly instruct legal officials to adopt the subplans that best realise the master plan or other more general adopted subplans of the system. Everything that follows from the proto-planning activity of legal officials is also a plan.[50] What emerges from taking this avenue of legal planning is a standard pattern of constitution of legal norms *qua* plans by local rational requirements. This pattern can be represented as follows:

A local rational requirement to φ constitutes a plan to φ.

A local rational requirement to φ obtains *iff* a legal official or a group of legal officials (i) accept(s) a shared master plan, (ii) adopt(s) a subplan that others[51] φ and (iii) believe(s) that the subplan that others φ serves to realise the master plan. In Shapiro's terms, an adoptive attitude towards a plan is not reducible to a corresponding intention to realise a plan. To illustrate the contrast between the two attitudes, he remarks that:

> [In] the case of individual planning, the process [of norm creation] is the psychological activity of intending. In institutional contexts, however ... a plan may be created even though the one who adopted it did not intend to create a norm. As long as the institutionally prescribed procedure is followed, he will be acting in accordance with a process that is supposed to create norms and will therefore be capable of adopting a plan.[52]

[47] ibid 177–78.

[48] Subplans carry the bulk of regulative work associated with legal norms. Their relation to the more fundamental plans of a legal system is instrumental. As Shapiro explains, '[these] plans are clearly related to one another. Buying food at the supermarket is a means to cooking dinner at home to night. When one plan specifies a means for accomplishing, or a way of realising, the end fixed by another plan, we will say that it is a "subplan" of the second' (ibid 121).

[49] ibid 183.

[50] 'If legal activity is the activity of planning, then it follows that all norms generated by this activity are plans' (ibid 225).

[51] By 'others', I do not intend to exclude legal officials themselves from the applicability of a legal plan. The latter are also part of the others, yet this time not by virtue of their capacity as legal officials, but as members of a legal community.

[52] Shapiro (2011: 128).

What triggers the normative impact of an obtaining local rational requirement that others φ is that legal officials exercise their planning authority in accordance with the procedures set out in the master plan of their legal system. Given the institutionalised structure of a legal system, they need not accept the end or purpose to which this particular legal plan is conducive. It is sufficient for a local rational requirement to constitute a legal plan that they exercise their planning authority according to the formal provisions of the shared master plan.

Returning to the case of the plan positivist who overhears the dispute between Gonzo and Froddo, we are in a better position to understand the nature of her metajurisprudential negation of Gonzo's claim that 'X constitutes a legal norm'. In sharp contrast to the interpretivist objector, she is not opposed to the very possibility of constitution, but aims her target at the ontological profile of the constituted object. Her denial of 'X constitutes a legal norm' is about the ontological superfluity of legal norms. What she invites Gonzo and Froddo to consider is the possibility of paraphrasing their talk of legal norms into talk of plans. Only by virtue of this necessary reduction can the constitutive claim of the form 'X constitutes a legal norm' acquire truth conditions.

From this new vantage point, the plan positivist can meaningfully disagree with Gonzo and Froddo about whether authoritative directives or facts about moral impact can have a constitutive effect on the content of the law. For the plan positivist, neither authoritative pronouncements nor the impact of actions of legal institutions on the moral profile can have the effect of constituting legal norms *qua* plans. In her view, this task is to be carried out by facts about the obtaining of rational requirements. By contrast with Greenberg's account of properly triggered moral obligations, rational requirements are triggered by facts about the adoption, revision or rejection of various (sub)plans rather than by facts about how the actions of legal institutions change the moral profile. Moreover, a plan positivist can voice her disagreement about whether a particular form of activity originates in one of the recognised sources of law of a given legal system. For instance, she may argue that a particular action of a legal official or legal institution fails to trigger a new rational requirement because the master plan of the legal system does not recognise it as a proper way of changing the content of other subplans.

What I have attempted so far is the application of one metaontological position, namely that ontological commitments must reflect the truth-conditional structure of ordinary language (legal propositionalism) to an ontological dispute about the nature (first-order) and possibility (second-order) of coincident objects (legal constitution). This is far from qualifying as a licence to make a step towards the further claim that participants – the opponents or defenders or, perhaps, both – in the ontological dispute over the possibility of material or abstract constitution are explicitly committed or logically inclined to subscribe to the view that the Quinean metaontologist is arguing for.[53] But, fortunately, such a strong assumption is unnecessary for the purposes of my more localised argument about law.

It would instead suffice to demonstrate that the majority of pluralist and monist responses to the problem of constitution *can* be read through the lens of a linguistically flavoured Quinean metaontology without endorsing the further assumption that, necessarily, the latter metaontological position settles the question of which account of material constitution one should endorse. This modest correlation is intended to be minimally offensive to those critics or supporters of constitution who do not portray themselves as Quineans in their metaontology or, even though they do so, their defence or rejection of the possibility of constitution is primarily based on other grounds.

II. OBJECTIONABLE JURISPRUDENTIAL COMMITMENTS

The next domain that may host a second round of first-order and second-order types of legal disagreement pertains to the relationship between veridical representations of legal content and the world. In section I in Chapter 2, I tried to draw our attention to the cursory treatment by the current literature of the truthmakers of legal propositions with a view to raising our alertness of their pivotal role in defining our metaontological commitments about law. In this section, I will try to substantiate this concern by showing how declining to skip the step that connects legal propositions to the grounds of law can broaden the spectrum of legal disagreement at two different levels of abstraction. Unfortunately, there is little if any textual evidence that contemporary contributors to the jurisprudential discourse are inclined to offer more fine-grained descriptions of legal facts beyond the obvious claim that legal facts are facts about legal content. My aim is to show that this is a necessary step towards developing a theory about the grounds of law.

At the first level, the relation of legal truth to the world may spawn an informative division of opinion with regard to what kind of entities legal philosophers should be ontologically committed to. These will be the entities that figure in the facts that a theory takes to be the truthmakers of legal propositions. Behind the effacing label of legal facts, there can be remarkably different objects of ontological commitment. With regard to the linguistic representation of legal content, legal philosophers of competing convictions utilise semantic conventions or models that can help them in accommodating the use of concepts that in principle seem to be in conflict with their metaphysical attachments. For instance,

[53] Namely, the view that a proposition carries a commitment to the existence of those entities which must feature in the proposition as the values of the variables bound by quantifiers in order for the proposition to be true.

as we previously observed, positivists like Shapiro and Raz do use normative concepts like 'obligation' or deontic modals in their respective theories of legal content. What licenses their use is not their ultimate commitment to normative determinants of legal content, but the evasive pathways that semantics or pragmatics may offer in order to make sense of episodes of linguistic usage that on some particular theories cannot withstand further metaphysical scrutiny.

As soon as our disagreement migrates from the level of representations of legal content to the level of what in the world makes these representations true, it becomes imperative to realise that our common vocabulary will be drastically downsized. This is not a worrisome result, but a natural consequence of letting our talk of legal content be succeeded by the talk of legal truthmakers. The latter talk takes place at the stage of jurisprudential discourse where our views of ontological commitment about law become visible. As a result, it is inevitable that our use of the same concepts cannot remain as ontologically innocent as before. For instance, both Shapiro's semantic account and Raz's pragmatic account of the use of normative language in law cannot extend their applicability to the question of what makes legal propositions true. At this level, the scope of their vocabulary is restricted to notions that are consonant with their descriptive accounts of legal truth.

Whereas on the traditional conception of legal disagreement it is the grounds of legal facts rather than legal facts themselves that gain our attention, this alternative model of legal disagreement allows controversy to erupt even with regard to the ontologically committing constituents of legal facts. According to this alternative method, any appeal to a generic notion of legal facts is metaphysically improper precisely because the symptoms of theoretical disagreement about law are already evidenced by the different avenues of ontological commitment that different theories of law suggest by their appeal to what makes legal propositions true. From the point of view of ontological commitment, Raz's conception of legal truthmakers as facts about the existence of legal norms and Shapiro's competing account of facts about the existence of plans are in direct disagreement. Despite their convergence in the advocation of exclusive legal positivism, the ontological underpinnings of their theories are remarkably disparate. Shapiro is a reductivist about legal norms, believing that ontological parsimony dictates the elimination of talk of legal norms from our ontological vocabulary and its replacement by the explanatorily wider notion of a plan or subplan.

The same contrast can be witnessed in comparing Dworkin's account of legal facts to Greenberg's account. Whereas both cherish the antipositivist legacy of earlier natural law theories, their ontological commitments are not on the same level. On the one hand, Greenberg's non-reductivism about legal constitution leads him to a wholehearted espousal of normative facts about the obtaining of legal obligations, rights and powers as the truthmakers of legal propositions. For Greenberg, the sum total of the legal content of a particular system consists in the totality of legal obligations, rights and powers currently in force within a given system. On the other hand, Dworkin's error-theoretic rejection of legal constitution is perhaps the most challenging position with regard to legal truthmaking. In the previous section, I suggested that Dworkin's rejection of the possibility of legal constitution must be accompanied by an alternative account of what we really mean when we say that it is legally obligatory to φ. Drawing on Dworkin's recurring reference to how propositions of law are supposed to follow from practice-embedded principles of political morality,[54] I proposed the following truth condition: [it is legally obligatory to φ] is true *iff* a practice-consistent principle P requires that ψ and φ-ing is a way of ψ-ing. Consequently, the proposition expressed by the sentence 'it is legally obligatory to φ' is a generic content of the form 'the obligation to φ instantiates a principle of legal system S'. It thereby follows that by the view of a legal propositionalist, the truthmaker of the latter proposition must reflect what figures in the truth conditions of the sentence expressing it such that the proposition that φ-ing instantiates a principle P of legal system S is made true by the fact that P.

This is an interesting upshot as it illustrates a qualitative difference in Greenberg's and Dworkin's conception of what ontological commitments the content of the law of a legal system carries with it. The starting point is the fairly obvious thought that the content of the law consists of the totality of the truthmakers of legal propositions, which in their turn feature the entities to which a theory of legal content is ontologically committed. Provided that, according to Greenberg's moral impact theory of law, the truthmakers of legal propositions are facts about the obtaining of legal obligations, rights and powers, the total sum of legal content is just the set of normative facts about which legal obligations, rights and powers obtain in a given system. Consequently, a moral impact theorist is ontologically committed to things like legal obligations, rights and powers. In sharp contrast, according to the Dworkinian account of legal truth,

[54] There is a cryptic moment in Dworkin's deployment of his argument about what composes the content of the law. At some point, Dworkin seems to countenance the possibility of also including what instantiates principles of political morality into the content of the law. Greenberg notices this ambiguity when he observes that 'Dworkin sometimes formulates his theory to include in the content of the law not just the principles but also propositions that follow from them. He does not explicate the relevant notion of "following from", but presumably the idea is that the principles imply more specific propositions. For example, the principle that no one can benefit from his or her own wrong implies the proposition that one who murders a testator cannot inherit under the will' (Greenberg 2014: 1299–300). I believe that this ambiguity can be dispelled if we understand Dworkin's propositions of law as generic propositions about the instantiation of principles of political morality. If this interpretation merits our consideration, the type of proposition that becomes eligible for truthmaking is a proposition about the obtaining of the relation of instantiation. On pain of infinite regress, this relation is standardly understood as an internal relation such that predications of instantiation are made true by facts about the existence or the intrinsic properties of either one or both relata. In the present case, the proposition that a determinate obligation instantiates a principle is made true by the fact the principle exists in a given context by itself rather than by a combination of the contextually determined obligation and the principle. Given that the content of the law is composed of the set of truthmakers of legal propositions, we can safely assume that Dworkin's committed view features principles, but not their instantiations as parts of the content of the law.

propositions of law are made true by facts about which principles of political morality are operative in a particular legal system. It thereby follows that for Dworkin, the total sum of legal content is just the total sum of practice-embedded general principles of political morality rather than what instantiates or specifies these principles in a particular context.[55] This picture portrays an interpretivist as being ontologically committed to the existence of principles of political morality.[56]

At a more abstract level, our way of accounting for the relation of legal truth to the world is indicative of our way of accounting for what dictates our ontological commitments about law. Bearing in mind the commonality of presuming a pictorial relationship between truth conditions and truthmakers, we should be less alarmed by the fact that all four exemplary theories of law can be classified as more or less supportive of legal propositionalism. This remarkable convergence does not downplay the pervasive differences between these theories, but it serves to highlight a methodological possibility that seems to have been neglected so far. If my attribution of legal propositionalism to theories across the positivist-antipositivist spectrum holds, it would be a legitimate option to scrutinise all four theories from a common vantage point by questioning their shared meta-jurisprudential premise instead of trying to evaluate what this common premise entails for each theory separately.

As previously explained, the idea is that irrespective of how each of the four theories proceeds to defend a theory of truth conditions for legal statements, they all converge in the sense that the truthmakers of the propositions expressed by these statements must feature the entities that figure in these truth conditions. In random order, we have become acquainted with at least four eligible truthmakers for legal propositions: facts about the existence of legal norms (Raz),

[55] Greenberg acknowledges this crucial difference when he notes that '[the] Moral Impact Theory, like Dworkin's theory and unlike the Standard Picture, holds that the relation between legal practices and the law is a moral one. But, unlike Dworkin's theory, the Moral Impact Theory holds that the law is the moral *impact* or *effect* of certain actions of legal institutions – i.e., the moral obligations that obtain in light of those actions – rather than the set of principles that best justify them. To use a spatial metaphor, on the Moral Impact Theory (as on the Standard Picture), the law is *downstream* of the legal practices; on Dworkin's theory, by contrast, the law is *upstream* of the legal practices' (ibid 1301).

[56] Whereas Greenberg tends to affirm Dworkin's ontological commitment to general principles, he wonders whether Dworkin's incipient shift in *Justice for Hedgehogs* marks a clear departure from his robust commitments in *Law's Empire*. He remarks that '[near] the end of *Justice for Hedgehogs*, however, Dworkin briefly suggests that he now holds a very different view … The discussion is highly compressed, but one reading is that Dworkin's new position is that the content of the law is that part of the moral profile that is created by the actions of legal institutions *and* that the courts are morally obligated to enforce' (ibid 1300). In Greenberg (2017), this apparent shift is identified as the 'Judicial Enforcement Theory' (at 283–85). If this interpretation is correct, it follows that the truthmaker of a proposition of the form 'it is legally obligatory to φ in S' is made true by virtue of the fact that the obligation to φ is enforceable in S. This is not the place to evaluate Dworkin's emerging shift of opinion, mainly because the textual evidence is very limited to license any direct attribution of such an important change in Dworkin's theory of law. At any rate, if this view could be confirmed by further evidence, it would definitely affect other areas of Dworkin's thought, including his conception of how legal practices are distinguished.

facts about the existence of plans (Shapiro), facts about the obtaining of legal obligations, rights and powers (Greenberg) and facts about the obtaining of principles of political morality (Dworkin). All these kinds of fact feature among their constituents the entities that also figure in the truth conditions of the respective legal statements, which is precisely what the metaontological thesis of legal propositionalism predicts. The interesting upshot of this uniformity is that there seems to be no room for substantive metajurisprudential disagreement among these four candidates with respect to the question of what accounts for a theory's ontological commitments. They are all aboard the same metaontological 'ship'.

III. DISAGREEMENT OVER LEGAL GROUNDING

Up to this point, the varieties of jurisprudential and metajurisprudential disagreement we have encountered are intimately connected to the nature of legality in the sense that they regard either the nature of facts about legal content or the nature of its constituting materials, or the relationship between these two. In this last section, I will explore how theoretical disagreement about law manifests itself at the most fundamental level. Again, the scope of questions that may be asked at this level can accommodate disputes one could characterise as first-order or, to repeat the term coined in Chapter 3, intra-jurisprudential or second-order or, to repeat the term I also used in the same chapter, inter-jurisprudential depending on the degree of abstraction we allow.

The first level is the one that Dworkin reserved for use when he coined the term 'theoretical disagreement about law'. This is the level featuring the non-legal facts by virtue of which the truthmakers of legal propositions, be they legal facts or whatever these facts are reducible to, obtain. This is perhaps the only level at which the distinction between positivism and antipositivism is manifested in the least distorting way. Generally speaking, it is fairly obvious by now that unmediated appeals to this distinction fail to capture many questions about the metaphysics of legal content in a joint-carving, so to speak, way. For instance, we saw that a positivist like Raz and an antipositivist like Greenberg would most likely welcome the possibility of legal constitution. Moreover, it became less obvious whether antipositivists like Greenberg and Dworkin would converge in the object of their ontological commitment. That said, the positivist–antipositivist divide remains a useful device for making informative distinctions, provided that its applicability is restricted to the question of what grounds facts about legal content.

The second, more abstract level invites us to consider the possibility of whether and how facts about legal grounding – that is, facts about which facts ground legal facts (or their substitutes) – are themselves amenable to further grounding. This is precisely the instance wherein I purport to draw an analogy between the question of what in Greenberg's terms makes legal grounding rationally intelligible and the question of what grounds the non-categorical (modal and sortal) difference between abstractly or materially coincident objects. The latter question concerns the grounding of not just one but a variety of modal or sortal facts about constituting and constituted objects. Instead of employing this analogy across the spectrum of possible modal and sortal facts about legal content, I will confine my attention to one modal fact that corresponds to the first-order question raised above. The crucial question is what if anything grounds the fact that facts about legal content are grounded in non-legal facts. Like any fact about grounding, this fact is also modally nuanced in the sense that the obtaining of the *explanans* necessitates the obtaining of the *explanandum*.

If something could uniquely characterise my way of handling this aspect of jurisprudential disagreement, it is the fact that it purports to disassociate one's participation from her status as a legal positivist or antipositivist. As I critically remarked in Chapter 3, a major problem with how theoretical disagreement about law is understood is the fact that its operative principles are usurped and modelled in a way that can exclusively accommodate disagreement either about the descriptive grounds of legal content or about its normative grounds, but never about whether facts about legal content are grounded in social facts or also partly in normative facts. This is precisely the way in which both Dworkin and Shapiro attempt to model theoretical disagreement about law, each of them from the perspective of his own theory of law.

This restrictively idiosyncratic treatment of the concept of theoretical disagreement results in what I will call the *Absurdity Thesis*. According to the Absurdity Thesis, whereas a legal positivist and a legal antipositivist can qualify as engaging in meaningful philosophical disagreement about the *nature of law*, they cannot engage in meaningful theoretical disagreement about the *grounds of law*. In other words, the two sides are portrayed as being capable of disagreeing about whether the extension of legality is determined solely by descriptive or also by normative facts, but not as being equally capable of meaningfully disagreeing about whether a particular legal fact of the form 'it is legally obligatory to φ in S' is grounded exclusively in descriptive facts or also in normative facts. The latter type of disagreement turns out to be merely verbal as the two sides mean radically different things in their appeals to the notion of legal facts. Positivists like Raz and Shapiro take legal facts to be descriptive facts about the existence of legal norms or 'legal' plans respectively, whereas antipositivists like Dworkin and Greenberg regard legal facts as normative facts about the application of principles of political morality or about the obtaining of legal obligations, rights or powers respectively.

In a partial departure from the purely metalinguistic concerns I associated with legal positivists in Chapter 3, I shall now put forward the bolder claim that if we factor in their methodological and not simply metalinguistic premises, both parties to this debate turn out to be equally complicit with regard to the 'insular', so to speak, way of portraying theoretical disagreement about the grounds of law.

Although the focus of my exposition is the nature of theoretical disagreement about the grounds of law, I believe that the primary origin of this misconception can be traced back to the format of a different type of disagreement regarding the methodology of jurisprudence. The latter type of disagreement is traditionally instantiated by the dispute between proponents of descriptive and proponents of normative jurisprudence. Descriptivists argue that the task of analytic jurisprudence is to provide a description of law either by means of analysing law as a functional, normative or social kind or by means of analysing the concept of law by appealing to necessary and sufficient conditions for the identification of a social structure as a legal system. Both descriptivist approaches focus on the question of what law is as if it were a matter of descriptive rather than evaluative fact. On the other hand, normativists argue that the proper task of analytic jurisprudence is to provide a coherent moral justification of legal practice such that the pivotal question for analytic legal philosophers is what law ought to be or, more precisely, what makes law's demands on us morally legitimate.

Before evaluating the impact of this methodological controversy, it might be useful to depict the order of emergence of three distinct varieties of disagreement about law as they are commonly conceptualised.[57] The ordering I will present is a function of the degree of abstractness each type of disagreement allows in framing its questions. As a way of calibrating the degree of abstractness, I will use Dworkin's distinction between the sociological, the taxonomic and the doctrinal concepts of law. I should note that the conceptual vocabulary I purport to use is not meant to cast Dworkin's theory in a favourable light for two distinct reasons; first, I do not aim to present one concept of law as more pivotal than the rest; and, second, my illustrative use of Dworkin's suggested concepts does not strictly correspond to how Dworkin himself would prefer to allocate these concepts across the spectrum of legal disagreement. That said, I do believe that there is a strong correlation between these three different concepts of law and the three types of disagreement:

I. Disagreement about the Methodology of Jurisprudence
Sociological Descriptivism: what is a legal practice Sociological Normativism: what justifies a legal practice
II. Disagreement about the Nature of Law (Disagreement about Essence)
Taxonomic Positivism: morality does not determine the extension of Legality Taxonomic Antipositivism: morality determines the extension of Legality
III. Disagreement about the Grounds of Law (Theoretical Disagreement)
Descriptive Doctrinal Disagreement about the facts that ground legal facts Normative Doctrinal Disagreement about the facts that ground legal facts

[57] In their present formulation, all three types of disagreement are commonly perceived as meaningful by all participants precisely because they seem to employ the same concept of law at each level of disagreement.

At the methodological level, the crux of the controversy lies in the question of what use we are to make of the institutional social structure we call 'law'. This glibly corresponds to Dworkin's 'sociological concept of law',[58] which, more or less, purports to capture the identity criteria for classifying a general practice or institutional structure as a legal system. Traditionally, questions about whether Nazi law was really law or whether there can exist non-coercive legal systems fall within this conceptual domain.[59] In this sense, the descriptivist affirms that analytic jurisprudence proceeds to understand law by elucidating what individuates a legal practice as such.[60] Moreover, there are a host of nuanced subdivisions or, perhaps, competing conceptions of what it means to do descriptive jurisprudence. The spectrum is long enough to feature views ranging from a wholehearted espousal of a naturalistic epistemology that severely limits the role of a priori conceptual analysis in law to indirectly evaluative theories that aspire to make a case for a morally neutral legal theory that is nonetheless informed by non-moral, evaluative considerations.[61] In sharp contrast, the normativist retorts that this descriptive approach is dangerously close to licensing the absorption of legal philosophy by the sociology of law. In her dissenting opinion, what identifies legal philosophy as a distinct type of discourse is its preoccupation with the normative impact of legal practices.[62]

[58] Dworkin offers a description rather than a definition of different concepts of law. With regard to the sociological concept of law, he remarks that 'we use "law" to name a particular type of institutional social structure. We might ask, for instance, using that sociological concept, when law first appeared in primitive tribal societies, or whether commerce is possible without law' (Dworkin 2006: 3).

[59] Nigel Simmonds is perhaps an exception to this polarity. His Hegelian bent gives priority to how we reflect on the platitudinous actuality of concepts. He regards the divide between analytical and normative jurisprudence as a non-issue, noting that 'law is an intrinsically moral idea, and that inquiry into the nature of law is ultimately a moral inquiry; and it will be argued that system-specific debates about law's content can never wholly be separated from the philosophical inquiry into the nature of law as such' (Simmonds 2007: 6).

[60] Joseph Raz offers a concise formulation of this descriptivist approach to jurisprudential methodology when he points out that legal philosophers 'produce explanations of the law, and therefore also of the concept of law, the concept which singles out legal systems from other normative and social institutions and practices' (Raz 1998: 276). On another occasion, Raz notes that '[legal] philosophy has to be content with those few features which all legal systems necessarily possess' (Raz 2012: 105).

[61] Brian Leiter's 'naturalized jurisprudence' is a typical instance of a thoroughly empiricist descriptive methodology for law. Leiter suggests that a typical example of an all-the-way-down naturalistic jurisprudence is the mid-twentieth-century movement of Scandinavian Legal Realism, which sought reductive analyses for the use of normative terms in law in terms of empirical models for predicting official behaviour. For a global presentation of this line of thought, see Leiter (2007). At the opposite end of the descriptive spectrum, we encounter views like Julie Dickson's 'indirectly evaluative legal theory'. Dickson takes indirectly evaluative judgments to be '[j]udgments of which features of the law it is important and significant to explain … that neither entail nor require support from directly evaluative judgments such as whether and under what conditions law is morally justified or creates moral obligations to obey it' (Dickson 2004: 126). For an in-depth analysis of this approach, see also Dickson (2001: chs 2–3).

[62] It is worth emphasising that a legal antipositivist need not be committed to a normativist methodology as a matter of conceptual truth. Michael Moore is a typical representative of antipositivist descriptivism about legal methodology. He lucidly states this point when he remarks that 'ours is a

The type of disagreement that figures at the intermediate level between methodological and theoretical disagreement regards the nature of law in its most abstract sense and, as such, it invites us to consider what marks the essence of legality, irrespective of its circumstantial attribution to acts or norms or its casuistic interpretation by different legal practices. This is precisely the level at which the debate about the relationship between law and morality has reached its modal peak. Instead of asking whether and how morality is relevant in deciding what grounds legal facts, we are used to asking whether and how morality necessarily determines the extension of 'law'. Dworkin's coinage of the term 'taxonomic concept of law' appositely serves to illustrate this essentialist type of disagreement.[63] Taxonomic positivists argue that moral principles or facts about value cannot acquire a second-order attribute of being legal by virtue of their content or status as moral entities. Taxonomic antipositivists[64] reject this claim, mainly by way of advancing functionalist or constitutivist arguments. For instance, they may argue that law has a distinctly moral function such that anything that falls short of realising this function is defective *qua* law.[65] Alternatively, they may argue that it is part of what makes law essentially action-guiding that it purports to make law-conforming action morally intelligible.[66]

quest in descriptive general jurisprudence' (Moore 2000: 309). The descriptivist element in Moore's conception of jurisprudential methodology is attested by his constant invocation of the analogy he draws between the discovery by natural scientists of the underlying *structure* of natural kinds and the discovery of the underlying *function* of law and other artefactual kinds. Moore's moral realist convictions are manifestly prevalent in his jurisprudential writings, as evidenced by his oft-repeated claim that law's nature is to be found in its function rather than in its structure. He further associates this function with a 'true moral value' that 'can be served by law uniquely' (ibid 294).

[63] For an elucidation of Dworkin's use of the taxonomic concept of law, see Dworkin (2006: 26–30).

[64] Not every antipositivist would be willing to classify herself as a taxonomic antipositivist; thus, not every antipositivist would be willing to engage in a taxonomic disagreement about the nature of law. For instance, it is definitely the case that Dworkin would abhor such a label precisely because the nub of his argument against positivism consists in the case he sets out to make about the plausibility of doctrinal antipositivism and the absurdity of trying to tap into the nature of law as if it were a natural kind. I also believe that Greenberg would be equally unwilling to participate in this disagreement, as his moral impact theory of law derives its strength from the idea that normative facts make it rationally intelligible why facts about the moral impact of social facts constitute law.

[65] Mark Murphy is a proponent of this way of understanding what is commonly known as the 'Weak Natural Law Thesis'. According to this thesis, law's being a rational standard of conduct is not part of what it is to be a law, but part of what it is to be non-defective or good *qua* law. Murphy tries to render this thesis as comprehensive as possible by presenting it as a thesis about the identity conditions of law rather than as a thesis about the realisation conditions of law. The latter conditions are captured by what he refers to as the 'hypothetical necessity argument', which acknowledges the importance of attaching a set of realisation requirements on the constitutional ability of an object to perform its essential function. Whereas, as Murphy explains, being constitutionally capable of being a rational standard – as opposed to *actually* being a rational standard – is an essential property of law, it remains open 'for legal theorists to argue from this thesis about law's office to necessary conditions on being law that are either normative or non-normative' (Murphy 2013: 14).

[66] Lon Fuller develops a constitutivist argument in support of his thesis about the 'inner morality of law'. According to Fuller's antipositivist theory, law is the enterprise of guiding human conduct by subjecting it to governance by rules (see Fuller 1969: 106). His non-instrumental or constitutivist idea is that law is essentially such that it is part of what it is to be guided by legal rules that they

The Absurdity Thesis assumes prominence the moment we descend to the level of theoretical disagreement about the grounds of legal facts or, in my preferred terms, the grounds of the truthmakers of legal propositions. Dworkin has coined the term 'doctrinal' to describe jurisprudential debates on what the law of a specific jurisdiction requires. Whereas taxonomic disagreement about law enables, to a considerable degree, a meaningful confrontation of positivist and antipositivist views, doctrinal disagreement about law appears to be bifurcated between a descriptive and a normative strand of disagreement. This is clearly evidenced by Dworkin's distinction between analytic doctrinal positivism and political doctrinal positivism.[67] According to the standard picture, only the latter type of positivism can be meaningfully represented in normative doctrinal disputes about the grounds of law, whereas the former type figures exclusively in the descriptive version of doctrinal disagreement which Dworkin rejects as philosophically uninteresting. Dworkin associates the political genre of positivism with what is broadly known as 'normative positivism',[68] which seems to be more like a historically constructed continuum of views about the value of separating positive law from moral judgement rather than a particular account of the nature of law. The cluster of views falling under the generic name 'normative positivism' is impressively comprehensive, ranging from historically embedded political accounts of the value of positive law-making[69] and jurisprudential accounts of why moral grounds of legal truth are conceptually possible but morally problematic,[70] to methodological bridging arguments about the

instantiate the rule of law principles. It is not that these principles are conducive to making legal guidance good or valuable; rather, they are part of what makes legal guidance possible as such. For a comprehensive defence of Fullerian constitutivism, see Bennett (2011).

[67] Dworkin (2006: 26–32). In *Law's Empire*, Dworkin describes the same notion of evaluative positivism as 'legal conventionalism'. His position is aptly given by his comment in the latter book that: 'The heart of any positive conception of law is its answer to the question why past politics is decisive of present rights … Past political decisions justify coercion because, and therefore only when, they give fair warning by making the occasions of coercion depend on plain facts available to all rather than on fresh judgments of political morality, which different judges might make differently' (Dworkin 1986: 117).

[68] For an explication of the standard notion of descriptive or analytic positivism, see Coleman (1982). Coleman presents what he takes to be the dominant conception of legal positivism as a 'conceptual or analytic claim about law, and that claim should not be confused with programmatic or normative interests certain positivists, especially Bentham, might have had' (ibid 147).

[69] Varieties of this strand of normative positivism hail back to seminal criticisms of the natural law tradition by philosophers of the Enlightenment, like Jeremy Bentham and Immanuel Kant. Despite their radically different philosophical bents, they both sought to challenge natural law's inflationary metaphysical foundations on empiricist and rationalist grounds respectively. Martin Stone showcases the informative convergence of utilitarian and deontological theories of law by defining the scope of their contrast. In his words: 'Kant is effectively ad idem with Bentham (against the earlier "natural law" theorist) in saying (in Bentham's words) that "there are no rights without law – no rights contrary to law – no rights anterior to the law". But the grounds upon which Kant and Bentham affirm the same conclusion are quite different' (Stone 2010: 30).

[70] Despite the lack of taxonomical consensus, it is at least plausible to associate the spirit of contemporary normative positivism as defended in Waldron (2001) and Dyzenhaus (2000) with the Kantian tradition of legal thought. Waldron's appreciation of the Kantian conception of positive

connection between normative political theory and analytic jurisprudence.[71] According to this picture, what supports the accusation of absurdity is not the fact that legal positivism is never confronted with legal antipositivism at the level of the grounds of legal facts, but the fact that the normative version under which it figures in this dispute is not recognised by the majority of positivist philosophers as a primary or even genuine version of analytic positivism. The result is that the doctrinal dispute about the grounds of legal facts cannot inherit the inclusiveness of the genuine taxonomic dispute about the nature of law. The former is genuine only among political variants of positivist and antipositivist views or among analytic variants of legal positivism.

I would now like to supplement my motivation for labelling this result as absurd with an explanatory claim. What I am about to argue is that we can remain excusably blind to the absurdity of this outcome for as long as it remains cloaked under the current methodological divide between descriptive and normative jurisprudence. As noted at the beginning of this section, the dispute between analytic (descriptive) positivism and antipositivism about the grounds of legal facts appears to be merely verbal precisely because the parties to this debate hold radically different views about the nature of legal facts. Whereas the former take them to be purely descriptive facts about the existence of legal norms or the existence of whatever these norms are reducible to, the latter regard them as more determinate variants of the broader family of normative facts. Fortunately, the verbalness of this dispute is not irreversible. There is still room to argue that positivists and antipositivists can meaningfully disagree about the grounds of legal facts, provided that we reconsider the way in which the divide between descriptive and normative jurisprudence is conceptualised.

law is evidenced by the utility he attributes to it in his own long-lasting preoccupation with the question of political disagreement (Waldron 1996: 1537–38). By contrast, other normative positivists like Campbell (1996), Postema (1986) and MacCormick (1985) are closer to the Benthamite, consequentialist strand of normative positivism. MacCormick, for instance, notes with regard to the intricacies of determining the content of the law that: 'There is a spectrum which ranges from the obviously simple to the highly contestable, and across that spectrum it could never be judged more than vaguely at what point some doubt as to "relevancy" or "interpretation" or "classification" could be raised so as to clear the way for exploiting consequentialist arguments and arguments of principle or analogy' (MacCormick 1994: 230). In a similar rule-consequentialist vein, Campbell claims that: 'The factors that turn rationales for having rules into rationales for having laws relate mainly to the seriousness of the purposes the rules serve and the extent to which general conformity to precise and agreed rules is a precondition of their effectiveness' (Campbell 2004: 36).

[71] Stephen Perry's defence of the *value-of-intentionality condition* on legitimate political authority is a combined task marshalling arguments from both political and legal philosophy. According to Perry's view, the value of intentionally changing another person's normative condition by one's say-so points to the inner morality of positive law. In his words: 'Jurisprudence is related to political philosophy in many ways, but the one with which I am concerned here is the close relationship which clearly exists between the concept of authority and the concept of law. I would like to conclude with the perhaps overly bold suggestion that the value-based conception of a moral power is the conceptual core and, perhaps, – depending on one's views about descriptive versus normative jurisprudence – also the moral core both of jurisprudence and of law itself' (Perry 2013: 72). For a contrastive elaboration of this view with traditional accounts of legal positivism, see Perry (2009).

Whereas very little has been said about the structural similarity of this divide with other neighbouring divides such as the one between ideal and descriptive political theory, or between metaethics and normative ethics, we can safely infer a common pattern in the way in which these cognate divisions are constructed.

The building pattern I have in mind is informed by a mutually recognised principle of theoretical neutrality[72] governing the relationship between overlapping domains of discourse marked by different levels of abstraction. Adjusted to the present context, this principle holds that a metajurisprudential theory remains neutral so long as it does not *entail* a certain jurisprudential thesis. The formulation of this principle is strictly chosen in order to exclude another association of metatheoretical discourse with neutrality. This is the view that what makes a metatheory neutral is that it has no direct implications for the *methodology* of substantive theories.[73] In view of the way in which the taxonomical controversy between descriptivist and normativist approaches to jurisprudential methodology has been articulated, I would dare to suggest that the fact that the current division of opinion more or less overtly sustains the Absurdity Thesis is partly explained by an unpronounced assumption on the part of jurisprudential descriptivists that the methodology of normative jurisprudence violates the neutrality of metajurisprudential inquiry and hence cannot qualify as a proper metatheoretical thesis precisely because it has direct normative implications for the methodology of first-order theoretical disagreement about the grounds of law. On this assumption, there can be no genuine disagreement about the nature of the grounds of legal facts between descriptivist and normativist theorists because the former would consider themselves as violating what they *take to be* a properly neutral metajurisprudence.

In response to this misconception, I would like to suggest a truce that preserves the insularity between first-order instances of descriptive and normative doctrinal disagreement on the grounds of legal facts, whilst allowing the possibility of a second-order instance of disagreement not about the grounds (descriptive or normative) of legal facts, but about the *nature* of legal grounding. This latter type of disagreement respects the neutral character of its degree of abstractness in the sense that it does not *entail* a certain jurisprudential view like exclusive legal positivism, plan positivism or interpretivism. At the same time, it has implications for the methodology of general jurisprudence precisely

[72] This quest for neutrality can be traced back to AJ Ayer's alarming remark that metaethics is or should stay neutral vis-a-vis substantive normative theories. In his words, metatheoretical work on ethics can 'make no ethical pronouncements' (Ayer 1946: 103).

[73] I owe this distinction and the argument that follows from it to Tristram McPherson's account of unity in moral theorising. Keeping analogies in sight, McPherson's idea is that '[t]he best way to pursue the project of normative ethical theorizing involves integrating that theorizing with metaethical theorizing' (McPherson 2012: 524). He contrasts his Unity Thesis with traditional conceptions of metaethical neutrality that try to insulate the progress made in the domain of metaethical inquiry from infiltrating normative debates. In this regard, he singles out the Rawlsian method of reflective equilibrium as a solid token of a tradition of thought that seeks to guard the methodological independence of normative ethical inquiry against metaethical argument.

in the sense that this type of metajurisprudential disagreement can be conducive to choosing correctly between contrasting views on legal epistemology,[74] which can in turn have implications for our assessment of the explanatory potency of competing theories of law.

To see how the metaphysically oriented second-order or inter-jurisprudential disagreement about the nature of legal grounding can be relevant for choosing among competing epistemological theories of legal content and, consequently, how the latter choice can also affect our assessment of substantive theories of law, I will have to unpack a bit further the precise meaning I intend to attribute to the concept of (the nature of) legal grounding. A nascent concern among philosophers working in metaphysics and epistemology regards the question of whether facts about grounding – namely, facts about what grounds what – can themselves be grounded in other facts or whether they are fundamental and, if so, why.[75] Occasionally, there are philosophers who believe that the same question should be cast in epistemological terms as a question about what makes it intelligible or rationally accessible that certain facts ground certain other facts. In other words, they invite us to ask what makes facts about grounding epistemically accessible rather than what makes them hold.[76] The ambivalence with respect to the categorisation of this question as purely metaphysical or as mainly epistemological is indicative of a more general concern about the extent to which the epistemological foundations of a theory can also track the theory's metaphysical commitments. This is a debate I would like to forgo, mainly because I lack the necessary insight and expertise to pass judgement on the plurality of its aspects. Regardless of its proper resolution, I believe that the controversy I have just described reveals the importance of disagreement about the nature of grounding for the assessment of a theory's epistemic scrutability. At the same time, a theory's epistemic accessibility is crucial for evaluating the explanatory force of its content. For instance, a positive answer to the question of whether virtue ethics can explain how we can know what course of action is morally recommendable for a situation inviting the exercise of conflicting virtues is a first but very important victory of the theory's general explanatory

[74] By legal epistemology, I mean nothing more than what a proper theory or method of legal interpretation would consider to be the proper standards for ascertaining the content of the law from law practices.

[75] For an overview of this debate, see Trogdon (2013).

[76] An example is offered by Louis deRosset, who takes the case of a disjunctive fact of the form P v Q. Evidently, this fact is partly grounded in the fact that P. His premise then is that when explaining why P grounds P v Q, any reference to the rules of disjunctive inference will only help to make this explanation epistemically accessible to a given audience. In his words: 'The facts one must cite to render the explanatory relation between and Beijing's cityhood is merely ancillary material. Indeed, the point of inserting ancillary material into the explanatory story is to deliver the relevant epistemic payoff – intelligibility – to one's audience. In this respect, it is analogous to an appeal to inference rules in an explanatory story backing the proposal to explain a disjunctive fact by appeal to one of its disjuncts' (deRosset 2013: 22).

capacity, which may have interesting implications for its capacity to explain why atomic moral facts are grounded in facts about virtue.

Transposing this debate to the jurisprudential domain, we may similarly ask whether exclusive legal positivism can explain how we can know that a particular legal norm exists by virtue of a fact about the issuance of an authoritative pronouncement, or whether interpretivism can explain how we can know that facts about the instantiation of principles of political morality both justify and are triggered by aspects of law practices. In what follows, I will try to introduce some formal distinctions that are already applicable in debates in general metaphysics, in the hope that I can demonstrate how these distinctions could animate a metajurisprudential disagreement about the grounds of facts about legal grounding. The upshot will be that an interpretivist or a moral impact theorist can be genuinely engaged in a second-order dispute with positivist theories about the grounds of legal facts. This second-order dispute remains neutral with regard to the first-order insular disagreements about the descriptive or normative grounds of legal facts respectively, in the sense that it does not directly entail a certain thesis about the content of these grounds. That said, this more abstract type of dispute can legitimately reclaim its relevance for the methodology of descriptive or normative doctrinal disagreement precisely because it can affect both the way in which we should epistemically access facts about legal grounding and the way in which different candidate grounds (descriptive or normative) can explain the resolution of conflicts between different aspects of law practices or the resolution of problems of legal indeterminacy.

To the best of my knowledge, our first acquaintance with the importance of making sense of the relation of grounding and concomitantly of the relation of legal grounding can be found in Mark Greenberg's notion of intelligibility-enabling facts. In Greenberg's own words:

> The A facts rationally determine the B facts just in case the A facts metaphysically determine the B facts *and* the obtaining of the A facts makes intelligible or rationally explains the B facts' obtaining. Thus, L is the conjunction of two doctrines, a *metaphysical-determination doctrine* and a *rational-relation doctrine*.[77]

By way of this conjunction, it seems that according to Greenberg's own understanding of the rational determination relation, intelligibility-enabling facts and non-legal facts operate at the same level of first-order grounding, namely they jointly ground legal facts.[78] Whereas I will continue to treat Greenberg's rational determination thesis as a compass for how the broader debate on grounding

[77] Greenberg (2004: 163). For a critical elaboration of Greenberg's idea, see Chilovi and Pavlakos (2019).

[78] For a corroboration of this understanding of rational determination, see also Plunkett (2012). Plunkett remarks that 'in cases of rational grounding, where one set of facts rationally grounds another set of facts, the grounding-relationship facts are always intelligible to us. Moreover, this is no accident. For in cases of rational grounding, the fact of intelligibility is itself among the grounds of B facts' (ibid 156).

can be transposed to our local discussion about the nature of legal grounding, I will also introduce two important reasons for making the structure of his thesis more abstract.

First, locating the grounds of legal facts and their intelligibility-enabling facts on the same level of explanation imposes an unnecessary constraint on how we can make sense of our disagreement about the latter with respect to the former. In other words, if, for instance, the fact that a moral obligation brought about by the actions of legal institutions makes the moral situation better *and* the fact that the actions of legal institutions owe their impact to considerations of democracy operate *on the same level of explanation*,[79] it will be more difficult to make sense of how Greenberg could intelligibly disagree with a positivist claiming that the intelligibility-enabling facts are conceptual rather than normative facts. The reason is that it will be impossible to provisionally bracket the primary grounds of each theory in a principled way. By 'primary grounds', I mean the case-specific grounds that figure in each explanation, namely the normative fact that a moral obligation brought about by the actions of legal institutions makes the moral situation better (Greenberg) and, for instance, the descriptive fact that a given 'legal' plan is authorised by the system's master plan (Shapiro).

Moreover, by introducing this amendment, I purport to obviate a plausible objection to Greenberg's invocation of facts about value as intelligibility enablers. The objection is roughly as follows: if legal facts are grounded partly in descriptive facts about the activities of legal officials *and* partly in the fact that X enables us *qua* rational beings to make sense of the precise relationship that exists between non-legal facts and legal facts, X merely assumes an *epistemic* rather than a robustly metaphysical (or grounding) role. X cannot figure *qua* metaphysical ground at the same level of grounding with non-legal facts. This is so because the following hypothesis does not hold: if we assume that the set of non-legal facts that are needed for the grounding of a legal fact currently does not exist, the fact X that makes the grounding impact of these non-legal facts intelligible cannot exist either simply because there is nothing to make sense of! But this is an absurd result if we take partial grounding at face value; it is part of the concept of what it is for X to be a partial (as opposed to a full) ground that X can exist and yet not ground Z because the other partial ground Y is missing.

In the light of these caveats, I would like to suggest that we consider the possibility of treating these intelligibility-enabling facts as facts that operate at the level of grounding or explain facts about the grounding of facts by other facts. In the legal case, this regimentation will deliver the following definition: an intelligibility-enabling fact is a fact that grounds the fact that a non-legal fact grounds a legal fact. I believe that this qualification remains in harmony with

[79] By 'same level of explanation', I refer to the level of what grounds legal facts, as opposed to the level of what grounds the fact that some non-legal facts ground some legal facts.

the spirit of Greenberg's apposite remarks about the necessity of making sense of legal grounding itself. That said, there can be at least four distinct routes to affirming or denying the existence or purpose of the grounds of grounding facts. One position which I intend to associate with Greenberg's attribution to Raz of the so-called explanatory directness thesis is that facts about the grounding of legal facts by non-legal facts are not fundamental facts *because there are no fundamental facts*. Another position which I intend to associate with Dworkin's conception of the virtuous circularity of legal grounding is that the grounds of facts about legal grounding are iterated in the sense that that <[*p*] is grounded in [*q*]> is grounded in [*q*], <[*p*] is grounded in [*q*] is grounded in [*q*]> is grounded in [*q*], and so on. A third position is the one Greenberg seems to endorse for his own theory of law, which holds that it is normative facts about the value of democracy, fairness or other substantive moral values that ground facts about legal grounding. Finally, a fourth view, which is actually an internal variant of the first, anti-fundamentalist view, can be associated with a conceptualist reading of Shapiro's claims about the function of legal institutions and legal norms. According to this approach, what grounds facts about legal grounding are conceptual truths of this sort.

Perhaps the most challenging aspect of the above distinctions concerns a problem about the relation of grounding facts to the notion of fundamentality. A common description of this problem is provided by Ted Sider's gloss on what he calls *Collapse*.[80] *Collapse* is a problem that emerges as soon as we take grounding claims to be claims to the effect that reality has a layered structure. Suppose that [p] is immediately grounded in [q], construed as a claim about what is more fundamental than what [q] is more fundamental than [p]. By virtue of the claim about fundamentality, *the fact that [p] is grounded in [q]* is also fundamental. But if that is the case, then [p] will figure in any complete description of the more fundamental layer such that all layers collapse into one.

Collapse becomes an imminent threat for anyone who wishes to understand how to ground facts about grounding explanations. One possible explanation is the one summarised by the concept of iterated ground. Philosophers like Louis deRosset[81] and Karen Bennett[82] try to solve this puzzle by advancing the idea that a grounding explanation is directly grounded in its explanans such that <[*p*] is grounded in [*q*]> is grounded in [*q*], <[*p*] is grounded in [*q*] is grounded in [*q*]> is grounded in [*q*], and so on. To illustrate his case, deRosset takes as an exemplary explanation the statement that Beijing is a city because ψ. His suggestion is that [Beijing is a city because ψ] because ψ for three reasons: first, appealing to both relata does not avoid the *Collapse*; second, appealing to Beijing's cityhood or to some other fact involving neither relata trivialises the explanatory relevance of ψ; and, third, postulating ψ as the explanans of

[80] Sider (2011: §§7.2, 8.2.1).
[81] DeRosset (2013).
[82] Bennett (2011).

[Beijing is a city because ψ] meets the requirement of upward necessitation, namely the principle that in order for an explanation to be complete, its explanans must necessitate its explanandum.

To see how this line of argument applies to the hypothesis about Dworkin's metajurisprudential conception of legal grounding, we need only replace the variables in the explanation [A is grounded in B]. Because of *Collapse*, it would follow that the fact that facts about law practices ground legal facts is also fundamental, thus enabling legal facts to figure every time at the fundamental level of explanation. The alternative interpretation which fits Dworkin's fusion of the dimension of fit with the dimension of justification would entail that the facts about principled consistency with past political practices operate as iterated grounds. On the level of grounding, the fact that a given obligation justifies the consistency with which the practice has been enforcing past demands grounds the fact that this obligation is a proper instantiation of the principles of political morality embodied within a given political community. On the level of what grounds this grounding fact, it would be the same fact about principled consistency that is supposed to ground the fact that a fact about about legal content is grounded by a fact about principled consistency. Despite the formal oddity of this solution, it remains a valid option that glibly corresponds to Dworkin's elaborated view that there is no distinct explanatory role reserved for brute pre-interpretive data about a legal practice. On the contrary, legal practices are such that they are individuated by reference to their normative impact.

The hypothesis that facts about principled consistency operate as iterated grounds can be corroborated by appeal to deRosset's and Bennett's claim that the postulation of a third fact that involves neither the grounded fact nor the grounding fact trivialises the explanatory relevance of the grounding facts. In Dworkin's case, this claim can be translated into the more familiar claim that appeal to practice-independent normative facts would assign to morality the role of a normative filter. This could play out in two ways: either morality would filter out any parts of past political practice that are inconsistent with what it now requires; or it would filter out those aspects of the practice the moral objectionability of which exceeds some threshold of moral acceptability.[83] At any rate, I believe that Dworkin would be happy to recognise at least an aspect of the rationale of his own view within the rationale of the theory of iterated grounds. The reason is that despite differences in their degree of abstractness and practical import, both views take the trivialisation of the explanatory role of the primary grounds to be an unwanted consequence of postulating a *tertium quid* as an explanation of why facts A ground facts B.

[83] Greenberg rejects this understanding of intelligibility-enabling facts by introducing a relevance limitation. On this qualification, the *sub specie aeternitatis* moral goodness of some state of affairs will figure as an intelligibility enabler 'only to the extent that its goodness contributes to making it intelligible that an aspect of a particular law practice has one bearing rather than another on the content of the law' (Greenberg 2004: 195).

That said, I cannot be oblivious to the certainty of Dworkin's aversion to the metajurisprudential coating of his original view about the ineliminable normative relevance of legal practices. This is the reason why it would be unfair to take the iterated grounds thesis as an interpretive expansion or elaboration of Dworkin's view. At the same time, however, this is not an argument against the availability of this more abstract level of voicing Dworkin's point about the indistinguishability of 'fit' from 'justification'. Moreover, Dworkin's first-order or normative version of this view is not an argument against the intelligibility of its metajurisprudential version precisely because the latter takes iteration to be a feature of grounding explanations in general rather than as a feature of specific grounds.

An alternative approach to grounding explanations seeks to terminate an iterative circuit of grounds by making the distinction between grounding and grounded facts a little more fine-grained. Philosophers who object to the type of reasoning that deRosset employs in his attempt to address the *Collapse* problem typically suggest that besides facts about what grounds what, there also exist certain groundless facts concerning the essences of the entities that stand in the primary relation of grounding. This qualification yields the tripartite scheme on which this alternative view is premised. For the sake of convenience, I will adopt the term 'trialism'[84] in order to refer to this position.

A characteristic defence of trialism is exemplified by Shamik Dasgupta's argument in favour of the existence of what he calls *autonomous* facts.[85] To briefly illustrate his line of reasoning, we may suppose that the fact that action A is wrong is grounded in the fact that A fails to maximise utility. For Dasgupta, this explanatory fact is grounded in: (i) the fact that part of what it is to be a wrong action is that if an action fails to maximise utility, that action is wrong; and (ii) A failed to maximise utility. Dasgupta's way of eluding *Collapse* is to posit the existence of facts that are autonomous or basic, but not grounding. It is autonomous or basic facts that are fundamental in the sense that they figure in the specification of fundamental reality. By contrast, grounding facts are taken to be a *tertium quid* which are neither fundamental nor basic, but that together with basic facts can explain the obtaining of derivative or non-fundamental facts. So, in the present example, the fact that part of what it is to be a wrong action is that if an action fails to maximise utility, that action is wrong is not itself a grounding fact, but together with the grounding fact that A failed to maximise utility it explains the full array of facts. In Dasgupta's own words, an autonomous fact is not a brute fact, it is just that 'it is not apt

[84] I owe this term to Louis deRosset. In his words, 'all basic facts are fundamental: they do not obtain in virtue of any further facts. But the converse is not guaranteed: some fundamental facts – in particular, those fundamental facts concerning what grounds what – may fail to be basic. Thus, according to trialism, we need to distinguish two different kinds of fundamental fact: the basic facts and the fundamental grounding facts' (deRosset 2013: 17).

[85] Dasgupta (2014).

for being grounded in the first place, if the question of why it obtains does not legitimately arise'.[86]

In what follows, I would like to explore the way in which Dasgupta's insight could serve the explanatory ambitions of two different ways of unpacking Greenberg's notion of intelligibility-enabling facts. As expected, the first way is envisaged by Greenberg himself when he proposes that 'value facts are well suited to determining the relevance of law practices, for value facts include facts about the relevance of descriptive facts'.[87] Greenberg takes this view to be the correct response to the fact that descriptive facts about law practices cannot determine their own contribution to the content of the law. As it stands, Greenberg's formulation of the rational determination relation is not directly equivalent with the way in which philosophers like Dasgupta would prefer to regiment an example of legal grounding. The reason is that, in the light of this formulation, value facts and descriptive facts about law practices must operate on the same level as partial grounds of legal facts on pain of uncharitably distorting Greenberg's view. A coarse-grained translation of this claim into a two-level claim would entail the absurd result that according to the moral impact theory of law legal facts are fully grounded in descriptive facts and that what explains this grounding fact are facts about value. Obviously, this is not Greenberg's view, but this provisional failure to reparse his claim should not dissuade us from pursuing a more charitable avenue. This, of course, will require an interpretive initiative on my part, which I think is worth the effort.

The primer for decoding Greenberg's rational determination thesis lies in his own remarks about the legally proper way of changing the moral profile. Despite the fact that, as Greenberg himself confesses, this is still a concept under elaboration,[88] he also acknowledges that the core of this concept is already available in the claim that 'in order for a change in the moral profile to come about in the legally proper way, it must be the result of action by a legal institution that, by its nature, is supposed to improve the moral situation'.[89] This claim can thus be used to enrich the content of the moral impact thesis as follows:

> The content of law is that part of the moral profile created by the actions of legal institutions in the legally proper way ↔ The content of the law is that part of the moral profile created by the actions of legal institutions in a way that makes the moral situation better.

With this adjustment, we may return to our initial concern about the proper level of abstraction at which facts about value figure in Greenberg's explanatory

[86] ibid 5.

[87] Greenberg (2004: 187).

[88] In his words, 'we can use our understanding of what law and legal systems are supposed to do to explain which ways of generating obligations are legally proper – and therefore which obligations are *legal*. But I do not have a complete account of the legally proper way; further work is needed' (Greenberg 2014: 1322–23).

[89] ibid 1324.

model. I believe that the added complexity that might ensue from this reconstruction is outweighed by the obviation of the concerns I expressed earlier on the co-presence of descriptive facts about law practices and facts about the value of democracy or fairness at the same level of grounding explanation.

The emerging alternative would be to say that, strictly speaking, the fact that a particular legal obligation obtains is grounded in the fact that particular aspects of the activity of legal institutions have changed the moral profile in a way that makes the moral situation better. On this alternative reading, this grounding fact is not basic or autonomous. The autonomous fact in this case will be the fact that values such as democracy, fairness and procedural justice *essentially* figure in the explanation of how certain aspects of the activity of legal institutions change the moral situation for the better. This latter fact is not in itself a grounding fact, but *together with* the grounding fact that a particular legal obligation obtains because particular aspects of the activity of legal institutions have changed the moral profile in a way that makes the moral situation better, they generate the derivative or non-fundamental fact that a particular legal obligation obtains. The following table provides an illustration of this more elaborate view:

Grounding fact	**Legal fact**
The fact that it is legally obligatory to φ in S is grounded in the fact that particular aspects of the activity of legal institutions in S have changed the moral profile in a way that makes the moral situation better.	It is legally obligatory to φ.
Autonomous or basic fact	
Values such as democracy, fairness and procedural justice *essentially* figure in the explanation of how certain aspects of the activity of legal institutions change the moral situation for the better.	

According to this view, although *both* facts about what grounds what and basic or autonomous facts are needed in order to account for the obtaining of derivative facts, only the latter figure in the specification of fundamental reality. In our local case, it is only the fact about the essential explanatory association of the legally proper way of changing the moral profile with value facts about democracy, fairness and the like that should properly be taken as a fundamental normative fact.

Another metajurisprudential application of trialism can be found in Shapiro's conceptual argument about the relationship between legal institutions and legal norms. This is not a novel interpretation. David Plunkett[90] was the first to advance an interpretive enhancement of Shapiro's theory against Greenberg's doubts about the possibility of making legal grounding intelligible by appealing to non-normative facts. The only difference between Plunkett's reading of

[90] See Plunkett (2012).

Shapiro and my interpretive move is that he abides by the formal structure of Greenberg's rational determination thesis without distinguishing between the levels of abstraction at which descriptive facts about the planning activity of legal officials and intelligibility-enabling facts perform their explanatory role. That said, it is important to notice that the view I am about to associate with Shapiro's planning theory of law can serve as an autonomous entry in a hypothetical episode of metajurisprudential disagreement about the nature of legal grounding. The only substantive difference compared to Greenberg's potential use of the same view is that for Shapiro, it is not normative or value facts that assume the role of autonomous or basic facts in generating legal content, but conceptual facts about the nature of legal institutions and legal norms. Before attempting to flesh out this idea, it is worth noting that Greenberg himself leaves open the possibility of conceptual intelligibility-enablers.[91]

In what follows, I shall rely heavily on Plunkett's ingenious reconstruction of Shapiro's remarks about the logic of legal planning with a view to injecting an additional refinement associated with the trialist conception of grounding. Plunkett takes as his starting point Greenberg's refined version of conceptual truth, according to which a robust conceptual truth 'is not determined by consensus about the use of words and is not determined by our law practices'[92] and at the same time does not depend or include moral facts. Greenberg's suspicion about the prospect of associating legal grounding with conceptual truths is that conceptual and moral universal facts are so much alike in terms of their structure and explanatory function that it is highly unlikely that purported conceptual truths about law are not necessary moral truths in disguise.[93]

[91] As Greenberg concedes: 'It might be suggested that an appeal to conceptual truth offers a way to avoid the conclusion that the content of the law depends on value facts. The idea would be that the concept of law (or some other legal concept), rather than substantive value facts, determines that some models are better than others. As noted above, conceptual truth is the kind of consideration that could provide reasons of the necessary sort. The question is whether conceptual truth does so in the case of law' (Greenberg 2004: 187).

[92] ibid 188.

[93] In response to Greenberg's concern, Plunkett observes that there is no epistemic barrier to assuming that although Shapiro's theory of law is prominently a metaphysical account of law, it is supplemented by a panoply of revelatory concepts that could inform a positivist solution to the rational determination requirement. The distinction between revelatory and non-revelatory concepts is raised by David Chalmers in his defence of the relevance of a priori reflection. In short, for Chalmers, a concept C about a property P is a *revelatory concept* when a subject's possessing the concept C puts that subject in a position to know (through a priori reflection) what the property P is. To this effect, Plunkett draws on the work of philosophers like David Chalmers and Frank Jackson in order to showcase the relevance of a priori reflection both philosophers advocate for our understanding of abstract reality. In Plunkett's words, 'on Chalmers and Jackson's view, there is a sort of *intelligibility* that is produced when one makes progress in conceptual analysis. Namely, one finds it more intelligible why true claims about the world that are made in one vocabulary (e.g., the vocabulary of the social sciences) necessarily determine true claims about the world that are made in some other vocabulary (e.g., the vocabulary of legal content)' (Plunkett 2012: 184). Plunkett's hypothesis is thus that if legal concepts like 'legal institution' and 'legal norm' are revelatory concepts, 'then possession of those concepts puts one in a position to have a *constitutive* understanding of what the relevant properties are, and not just a constitutive understanding of the conceptual content of the

A beginning of an answer to Greenberg's worry might involve the 'strengthening' of a second-order definition I have already attributed to Shapiro's account of legality as a property. The idea would be to say that the following definition possesses the status of a conceptual truth:

> Being legal just is the property of having some other properties P in B such that R(P), where R specifies a condition on members of B which is satisfied just by those properties in B that allow their bearers to be represented as serving a moral aim.

Building on Plunkett's understanding of the role of moral aims in Shapiro's theory of law, I tend to believe that there is strong evidence in Shapiro's analysis in favour of treating his treatment of legality as the second-order property of legal institutions and legal norms having other properties, the possession of which enables their bearers to be represented as serving (legal institution) or realising (legal norm) a moral aim. At this point, I will not repeat my remarks about the importance of preserving the notion of representation within this definition. It will suffice to repeat that the relation of property instances like 'a legal institution is a compulsory institution' to the necessity of solving contentious moral problems is representational rather than explanatory. In other words, it is not because the law has a moral aim that legal institutions must be compulsory institutions in order to serve it properly. Instead, the claim is that because the law is represented by planning officials as having a moral aim, the compulsoriness of its institutions is also represented as being in the service of these aims. That said, we may expand the previous definition into a version that corresponds to the ambit of Shapiro's possible conceptual claim:

> It is a conceptual truth that being legal just is the property of being a shared, official, institutional, compulsory, self-certifying activity and/or norm of social planning in B such that R(P), where R specifies a condition on members of B which is satisfied just by those properties in B that allow their bearers to be represented as serving a moral aim.

This definition purports to specify the exact content of Shapiro's basic conceptual premise. That this is indeed his position is further corroborated by his own remarks about what he calls the 'logic of planning'. The logic of planning is a set of conceptual claims about the determination of the existence and content of legal plans which are presented as following on from Shapiro's main cluster of claims that legal institutions are institutions of social planning of a certain kind and that the content of the law is just the content of a set of shared plans. Provided that by virtue of the above definition, legal norms (much like the general activity that produces them) are shared, official, institutional, compulsory and

given concepts. In turn, it is then reasonable to hold that such conceptual facts, in illuminating the constitutive nature of these properties, are capable of illuminating something important about their grounding and, in particular, are capable of illuminating the fact that certain facts ground the legal facts' (ibid 186).

self-certified plans that are represented as serving a moral aim, 'then it follows', Shapiro remarks:

> [That their] existence and content cannot be determined by facts whose existence the law aims to settle. For if the existence or content of the law were determined in such a manner, then the proper way to ascertain its existence or content would be to deliberate about the merits of different courses of action. But the point of having plans is to obviate this very activity.[94]

Shapiro calls this claim the 'Simple Logic of Planning' (SLOP). My own suggestion will then be that the conceptual fact that could play the role of an autonomous or basic fact in the spirit of Dasgupta's argument is precisely this fact about the logic of legal planning.[95] According to this picture, conceptual facts about the logic of planning will help to explain why facts about the shared acceptance of a master plan ground the existence of plans.[96] As an illustration of how Shapiro would see this reconstruction as a reply to Greenberg's doubts about the explanatory relevance of conceptual facts, we may also notice that he explicitly presents SLOP as a rival to the idea that moral facts can determine the relevance of descriptive facts about law practices. He notes that:

> According to the Planning Theory, however, moral facts *never* determine the content of the law. As we saw in connection with the Simple Logic of Planning argument of the last chapter, the content of plans cannot be determined by facts whose very existence the plans are supposed to settle. Since laws are plans that are supposed to settle moral questions, moral facts cannot be grounds of law.[97]

This may be better portrayed in a figure that is structurally similar to the one associated with the reconstruction of Greenberg's normative version of trialism.

<table>
<tr><td>Grounding fact
The fact that a plan to φ in S exists is grounded in the fact that it is authorised by the shared acceptance of S's Master Plan.</td><td rowspan="2">Legal fact
A plan of S to the effect that φ-ing is required exists.</td></tr>
<tr><td>Autonomous or basic fact
The existence and content of a plan cannot be determined by facts the existence of which the plan aims to settle.</td></tr>
</table>

[94] Shapiro (2011: 275).

[95] Plunkett makes a brief reference to Shapiro's use of this term and tries instead to articulate the social fact thesis as a conceptual thesis by breaking down Shapiro's argument into four conceptual propositions: (i) legal institutions are planning organisations of a certain specified kind; (ii) legal norms are norms that are produced by or endorsed by legal institutions in a particular way; (iii) legal content is equivalent to a set of shared plans; and (iv) the content of plans rests on social facts alone (Plunkett 2012: 199).

[96] Whereas I take Shapiro's purportedly conceptual claim about the logic of planning as a figuring in a metaphysical explanation of why social facts ground legal facts, Plunkett leaves it an open question as to whether the role of these conceptual facts is metaphysical or epistemic. Revealingly, he notes that: 'This is not to say that these conceptual facts ground the fact that such-and-such facts ground the legal facts. Rather, it is to claim that grasping the conceptual facts (in cases of revelatory concepts) can help us gain epistemic access to such facts about ground and thereby make intelligible what needs to be made intelligible on the rational-relation requirement' (ibid 186).

[97] Shapiro (2011: 302).

In what remains of this chapter, I will try to offer an outline of how Raz's account of exclusive legal positivism could feature in a similar episode of metajurisprudential disagreement about the nature of legal grounding. Unfortunately, there is no solid textual evidence as to how Raz would prefer to deploy the terms of his participation in such a dispute. This is not because he would in principle object to the relevance of metatheoretical disagreement about law, but mainly because his comments on the nature of legal grounding are explanatorily subordinate to his account of the authoritative production of legal norms. In other words, it seems unlikely that Raz would like to add anything more about the grounding of legal facts in social facts beyond his claim that facts about the existence of legal norms are grounded in social facts about the exercise of legal authority. As we already saw in section I.A above on the relevance of the notion of legal constitution for Raz's concept of a legal directive, his core idea – as I tried to regiment it – is that legal claims are claims about the constitution of legal norms by authoritative directives. These are claims about the relationship between a non-legal (authoritative directive) and a legal (valid legal norm) abstract object.

The same claim could also be reconfigured in terms of facts about the existence of legal norms and facts about the existence or issuance of an authoritative directive. In this regard, instead of talking about the constitution of legal facts by authoritative facts, it is conceptually more accurate to talk about the grounding of facts about the existence of legal norms in facts about the issuance of authoritative directives. What is interesting in this case is that Raz's account would most likely welcome the hypothesis that this particular instance of grounding seems to inherit a property that is peculiar to relations of material of abstract constitution. I will adopt Karen Bennett's use of the term 'determinative' in describing a cluster of relations that do not seem to unify or gather together a multiplicity as in the case of composition. Bennett includes constitution in this cluster of 'building' relations, noting that:

> [S]ome of the relations seem to involve a certain kind of wrapping up into one, and others do not. That is, some unify, or gather together a multiplicity, in a way that others do not. This is a difference in logical form: some of the relations are many-one, and others are not. Composition, for example, pulls several smaller things together to make a single larger thing. Similarly for microbased determination, the process by which properties of a thing's parts come together to determine the properties of the whole. But realisation and constitution – one–one relations both – do not do this. They are determinative rather than aggregative; there is little sense of 'bringing together' involved.[98]

What would it mean then to say that the way in which an authoritative directive is related to a legal norm is (among other things) determinative? It would certainly mean that legal norms do not have parts of authoritative directives as their parts. This seems a natural precisification of what it is for an *abstract*

[98] Bennett (2011: 86).

object to constitute another abstract object. But this is not the most salient feature of this relation instance. My suggestion is that we could associate the determinative aspect of abstract constitution with what Mark Greenberg refers to as the explanatory directness by which authoritative pronouncements constitute legal norms. Greenberg takes this idea to be a constitutive element of what he calls the Standard Picture of legal content, which he further associates with traditional positivist accounts of law-making. According to him, this idea can be unpacked as follows:

> There are no explanatory intermediaries between the authoritative pronouncement's being made and the norm's obtaining ... An explanatory intermediary between A and B is something that a) is explained (at least in part) by A; and b) explains (at least in part) B. Therefore, to say that the making of an authoritative pronouncement explains a norm's legal validity *without* explanatory intermediaries is to say that the making of an authoritative pronouncement explains a norm's legal validity, and that it does so *not* by explaining something else, which then explains the norm's legal validity.[99]

Greenberg is careful to distinguish between the explanation of legal authority itself and the fact that the product of its exercise can by itself directly explain the obtaining of a legal norm. As he notes, 'the fact that authoritativeness itself can be explained in no way introduces an explanatory intermediary between the authoritativeness of a pronouncement and its impact on the law. (The explanation of authoritativeness is by definition upstream of the pronouncement's authoritativeness)'.[100] With these conceptual clarifications in mind, we may easily diagnose the connection between Greenberg's attribution of explanatory directness to standard positivist accounts[101] and what would amount to a wholesale acceptance of *Collapse*. As we may recall, both the iterated ground approach and the trialist approach to grounding explanations aim by design to escape the problem of *Collapse*. This is a problem that emerges as soon as we take grounding claims to be claims to the effect that reality has a layered structure.

[99] Greenberg (2011: 44).

[100] ibid 45.

[101] This means to exclude Shapiro's planning account of law. As Greenberg himself acknowledges, Shapiro's account of legal content does not seem to take on board the thesis that the pronouncements of a planning authority constitute the content of 'legal' plans without explanatory intermediaries. It should be noted that this is not a counter-indication to my attribution to Shapiro of the idea that the rational requirements bearing upon legal officials constitute 'legal' plans. The reason is that in my version of the constitutive relation in work, it is not authoritative pronouncements but wide-scope requirements of planning rationality that constitute the content of specific 'legal plans'. Whereas the latter do seem to operate as direct explanations of the content of 'legal' plans, they do not also operate as the grounds of the existence of particular plans. The latter fact (about the existence of a plan) can only be explained by an equally contingent fact rather than a rational necessity. In Shapiro's case, we saw that this is a fact about the shared acceptance of an authorising master plan, which, as we just saw, does not directly explain the existence of a plan, except by virtue of its combination with conceptual truths about the logic of planning.

In the present case, this could be represented in the following way: suppose that [existence of legal norm] is immediately grounded in [existence of authoritative directive]. Construed as a claim about what is more fundamental than what, [existence of authoritative directive] is more fundamental than [existence of legal norm]. By virtue of the claim about fundamentality, *the fact that [existence of legal norm] is grounded in [existence of authoritative directive]* is also fundamental. But if that is the case, then [existence of legal norm] will figure in any complete description of the more fundamental layer such that all layers collapse into one.

The upshot of this association is that Raz's hypothetical participation in a disagreement about the nature of legal grounding would lead him to bear the brunt of explaining away *Collapse*. This is not a hopeless task so long as one is willing to argue against a basic premise of the *Collapse* argument, which is that there are fundamental facts in the sense that there are facts that are not explained by any other fact. This is not an orthodoxy in metaphysics, as evidenced by the recent work on the notion of fundamentality. A major contributor to this alternative way of thinking about existence and fundamentality is Jonathan Schaffer, whose view about the possibility of drawing an infinite descending hierarchy of levels of reality does not seem to necessitate the existence of a fundamental level. Rather, as he notes, there is no solid evidence in favour of this view and for that reason, he invites us to consider the possibility that all entities are equally real.[102] This is not an unpalatable assumption, but I would also hesitate to even hypothetically associate Raz's ontological commitments with such a concrete position. At any rate, it is worth noting that there is a way to engage a proponent of the Standard Picture in second-order disputes about the nature of legal grounding without unfairly exposing her to the charge of being incapable of escaping the *Collapse*.

[102] Schaffer (2003: 498).

5

Resisting Ordinary Reasons Imperialism

THERE IS LITTLE doubt that what dominates contemporary philosophical prose on practical normativity is cast, at least partly, in terms of what gives someone a reason for something. The concept of a reason has proven much promising in meeting the demand for parsimony in normative metaphysics, whilst preserving our most-cherished intuitions about what is normative. There is nothing bizarre in this outcome, as the three-place relation of something's being a reason for someone to take an action or adopt an attitude is apt enough to cover a wide span of normatively challenging phenomena, including instances of practical reasoning, epistemic evaluation and pragmatic inference.

The versatility of reasons is precisely what makes them philosophically appealing. It is commonly said that reasons can favour, entice or even categorically demand our responsiveness to them; they can be invoked both in the context of explaining intentional action and justifying prospective decisions;[1] some of them can enter into additive, comparative or defeasibility relations to other reasons, whereas there is a growing consensus that reasons serve as the reduction base of second-order thin evaluative properties like goodness. In addition to this enumeration, I would dare to suggest that the most prominent advantage of parsing normative claims in terms of reasons is that reason

[1] Those familiar with the lore about the way in which reasons come to bear on action cannot resist being engaged at some point in the debate on the relevance of the distinction between motivating and normative reasons. Motivating reasons are related to actions or attitudes by means of their providing an explanation thereof, whereas our appeal to normative reasons aims at providing a justification of the same type of events. During this discussion, issues of normativity arise only with respect to the concept of normative reasons, even though for the sake of simplicity, the attribute 'normative' is usually omitted, but is implied in the way in which reason ascriptions are employed in philosophical argument. What is crucially important is that in both cases, the explanandum is *described* as an obtaining state of affairs or event involving an agent and the performance of an action or the adoption of an attitude. Thus, we habitually say that there is a reason for someone to act or behave in a particular way and we are also used to providing explanations in terms of the reason why someone acted or behaved in a particular way. Nevertheless, subscribing to the importance of the distinction between explanatory and normative reasons is only the beginning of a breakdown into cases of normativity that call for philosophical scrutiny. For an illuminating exposition on this topic, see, among others, Heuer (2004) and Mantel (2014).

ascriptions may contain an implicit or explicit argument position for an agent variable. This vindicates the notion of the first-personal authority or the deliberative standpoint that figures in most philosophical accounts of normativity. Even the staunchest normative realist who denies that the possibility of motivation or practical endorsement is constitutively linked to normative truth will not hesitate to accept that normative demands apply *to* agents irrespective of whether it is the nature of agency itself, a fact about one's ideal motivational set or some mind-independent fact that ascribes normative status to an action or attitude.

There is no doubt in my best understanding that reasons – of whatever sort – occupy centre stage in the burgeoning literature on philosophy of normativity for an array of compelling reasons. Consequently, the arguments I will try to advance will not serve the purpose of disconfirming the relevance of reasons for our understanding of normativity. The idea that motivates the ensuing exposition is that the quest for an 'accurate razor' in normative metaphysics moulded and cast in terms of 'reasons' is far from over. My central objection to taking 'reason-giving' as all that matters with regard to practical requirements and their explanation is that whereas reasons assist us in regimenting our disputes about the considerations that direct our response to practical problems, practical normativity as such seems to include questions beyond the realm of acting for ordinary reasons. By 'ordinary reasons', I mean the family of considerations that, under epistemically felicitous conditions, can simultaneously bear upon a particular response, enable that response to be reflective of the agent's rational profile, prudence or moral character, and make the occurrence of that response normatively intelligible.[2]

As will become evident immediately below, this chapter ventures a digression from the core of analytical debates about the normativity of law. Very little in this chapter will hinge on anything specific about how law operates as a source of reasons for action. The following analysis will be generously inclusive with respect to the potential sources of practical normativity, making particular reference to requirements of rational consistency and coherence, as well as to the gamut of social practices that invite the use of thick evaluative terms like 'courageous' or 'civil'. This digression is not an ad hoc addition of the metaethical background that usually informs discussions about the normative force of legal requirements. As I will aim to show, it is a necessary step in demonstrating that the fluidity of appeals to the normativity of legal facts as reason-givers is not an insular phenomenon that characterises the jurisprudential treatment of normative reasons.

For a non-negligible class of jurisprudential theories, law much like rationality and thick evaluation is a normative domain that provides compelling testimony

[2] In ch 6, I will replace talk of ordinary or 'full-fledged' reasons with Joseph Raz's talk of *Nexus* reasons. The difference is purely terminological, but the use of the latter term must wait until I outline the background that informs the simultaneous performance of what I will be referring to as the influential ('bearing-upon'), evaluative and explanatory role of normative reasons.

to the need to partly extricate talk of practical normativity from exclusive talk of practical guidance or direction by ordinary reasons. Whereas the latter talk forms a major part of what is actually at stake in thinking about the former, there remains a significant portion of normative discourse whose orientation is not teleological or 'intentional' in the narrower than usual sense that practical normativity is about explaining the act- or attitude-directionality of certain considerations. Some considerations are normative without being only or mainly *about* or *for* action or any other type of cognitive, conative or affective response. Depending on one's jurisprudential allegiances, law as a normative domain may be described in non-teleological or directional terms. This chapter is dedicated to canvassing a model of representing two partly deviant domains of practical normativity – rationality and social practices involving the attribution of thick evaluative properties – in a way that also accommodates the ordinary role of normative reasons as response-directing considerations. The reason why I take the articulation of this more general model to be a necessary prelude to the following two focally jurisprudential chapters is that the latter are nothing more than straight applications of this model to two distinctly jurisprudential queries: the metanormative commitments of jurisprudential theories and the intelligibility of theoretical disagreement about the normative force of the law.

I. AXES OF NORMATIVE RELEVANCE

My way of subjecting the elasticity of the concept of a normative reason to a 'strain test' is to venture to introduce a two-dimensional model that can account for the different ways in which descriptive facts about the world and/or normative facts can felicitously figure in our practical deliberation without *necessarily* operating as ordinary reasons in the previously specified sense. The model will be hospitable enough to accommodate two cases of 'non-ordinary' reasons. What is peculiar about these reasons is that they operate in the presence of *independent* considerations, which can neither intensify or attenuate the weight of these reasons nor disable or enable their applicability. These are considerations that either constrain the ways of responding to ordinary reasons (what I will be referring to as cases of response-constraint) or take over their role as evaluators of agents (what I will be referring to as cases of constitutive impact). The upshot of this supplementation will be a more 'democratic' assembly of considerations where the imperial status of ordinary reasons as the linchpin of practical normativity gives way to a merely majoritarian status.

More precisely, what I aim to sketch will feature two distinct, albeit interconnected, axes of normative relevance on which facts, agents and agential responses (actions or attitudes) interact. In very broad terms, the first axis purports to represent a spectrum of normative import or, as I will prefer to call it, *normative salience* ranging from strict constraints on action or combinations of attitudes to robust attitude- or action-direction. The axis of salience purports to represent two different ways (response-directing and response-constraining) in which facts of any sort bear upon our actions or attitudes. The second axis purports to represent a spectrum of normative self-understanding or, as I will prefer to call it, *normative impact* ranging from counterfactual to actual reflections of ourselves *qua* agents in or as a result of our actions or attitudinal responses. The axis of impact purports to represent two different ways in which the facts that operate on the axis of normative salience can also impact our agency by enabling our responses (actions or attitudes) to serve as reflections of our qualitative profiles *qua* agents (rational, prudent, moral, immoral, courageous, cruel etc). In what follows, I will provide a more detailed account of how this two-dimensional scheme is supposed to work, with a view to ultimately associating it in the next two chapters with competing conceptions of legal normativity.

With regard to the first axis of normative salience, the idea is that a fact or consideration can be action-directing if and only if *one and the same* fact or consideration can stand in a relation of *bearing upon* (influencing) an act-type or attitude-type *and* also figure in the normative *explanation* of actual occurrences of acting for reasons. By 'normative explanation', I mean the type of relation that showcases why a particular occurrence is normatively intelligible as an instance of acting for a reason. For the sake of remaining flexible about the extension of the predicate 'normative', I will be treating it as a determinable concept whose determinates can be moral, rational, prudential, aesthetic or evidential considerations. For instance, in certain circumstances, the event of my giving money to charity is made morally intelligible by the fact that helping people in need is morally good, whereas the event of my supplementing my diet with some vitamins is made prudentially intelligible by the fact that boosting my immune system is good for my health or personal welfare. As will become evident later on, the identity of the *influential*[3] fact that favours a particular type of responses with the *explanatory* fact that makes a response-token normatively intelligible is the grounding thought behind the ordinary association of reasons with *direction* of actions or attitudes.[4] Normative direction *is just* the fusion of

[3] Henceforth, I will use the term 'influential' as the adjectival counterpart of the verbal phrase 'to bear upon' in order to refer in the most non-committal way possible to the way in which a consideration relates to a certain type of response. It is worth emphasising that I will *not* be using this term to convey a causal relation of any sort. The relation at hand is *normative* through and through. Accordingly, both action-directing and action-constraining considerations will be classified as normatively influential considerations, their difference consisting in the fact that the former (action-directing) considerations are such that one and the same consideration plays both the influencing role and the explanatory role.

[4] See Hieronymi (2011). Hieronymi attributes the original worry about the dissociation of the normative bearing or influence of reasons from their explanatory relevance to Thomas Nagel's worry about explaining action by appeal to psychological states. In her words: 'Nagel here suggests that if the reasons that explain action bear no clear relation to that which might count in favour of action – if, to use Nagel's term, the explanation of action does not "touch" the question of whether there was adequate reason (in the standard normative sense) to act – then it can seem that 'we don't

influence and *intelligibility*. Accordingly, this is a variant of normative salience which I plan to refer to as *normative action (or attitude)-direction*.

What I aim to challenge is not the veracity of this formal rendition of normative direction, but its explanatory scope. What I will be ultimately aspiring to do by providing a formal account of the relationship between practical normativity and normative direction is to make a plausible case about the possibility of expanding the available 'normative space' to cases of what I shall term *normative action (or attitude)-constraint*, where the normatively influential fact and the explanatory or intelligible-making fact diverge in a 'benign' or normatively felicitous, so to speak, way. In cases of normatively salient constraining – as opposed to directional – considerations, the locus of normative pressure is not what needs to be made manifest in one's thought and action – namely, to act in a particular way or to exercise one's rational capacity in a particular way – but what needs to remain absent or unmanifest – namely, to *avoid Φ-ing while* Ψ-ing or X-ing.

Crucially, what is meant by the disjunction 'Ψ-ing or X-ing' is that what will eventually determine whether Ψ-ing or X-ing is the all things considered optimal response to a certain situation is not settled by what determines why Φ-ing should not take place in the course of either Ψ-ing or X-ing. The facts that bear upon the omission of an action (Φ-ing) or attitude *in the course of* performing other actions or adopting other attitudes (Ψ-ing or X-ing) cannot also figure in the *explanation* of why someone Ψ'ed or X'ed. The latter explanation will rely on *separate* explanatory considerations that favoured Ψ-ing instead of X-ing, or X-ing instead of Ψ-ing. The idea then is that in certain contexts, what really matters in a normative sense is not what is present in one's actual conduct, but what remains absent as a result of one's heeding to a given constraint. Such absences[5] are not explanatory in the robust sense in which ordinary reasons for action are portrayed as explanatorily potent. As I aim to explain further below, the importance of such absences is evident in the domain of rational requirements of coherence and consistency among our practical and/or epistemic attitudes.

The second axis of normative impact will present cases of convergence and divergence between the explanatory facts or considerations that render our responses normatively (morally, rationally or prudentially) intelligible and the evaluative facts to which we appeal in order to appraise the way in which the

really act for reasons at all … Nagel draws our attention to a different gap – between that which explains an action and reasons in the standard normative sense' (at 415).

[5] In Aristotelian terms, a response-constraining consideration is explanatory of a specific response only in a formal sense (formal cause), whereas a response-directing consideration is explanatory in a final sense (final cause). I am inclined to believe that, despite a general reluctance to 'teleologise' the debate, the contemporary discussion about the normative explanation of action by appeal to reasons is centred on a modern, perhaps deflationary understanding of 'final causation' in the sense that locutions of the form 'she Ψ'ed because X' where X is a reason for action and not simply an efficient cause can be reparsed as 'she Ψ'ed for the sake of X'. For the latter view, see Schueler (2003: 56–87).

moral worth of our actions is reflective of ourselves as bearers of agency.[6] On this axis, nothing about the normative influence of any fact or consideration plays any substantive role precisely because the *influential* facts that favour or require a particular response (action or omission) do not figure in the relations of normatively impactful convergence or divergence; only *evaluative* (standards of appraisal) and *explanatory* facts do. This is not to say, of course, that one and the same fact or consideration cannot perform all three roles (influential, evaluative and explanatory) in certain circumstances;[7] it is just that this overlap is not a necessary ingredient of the taxonomy I am trying to articulate here.

To illustrate this distinction, take the example of John's visiting his friend at the hospital as a result of his taking his friend's sickness to be a reason to visit him. In that case, the fact that *actually* renders John's action morally intelligible – that his friend is sick at the hospital – has also been *actually* treated by him as a reason for action. The actual performance of both the explanatory and the evaluative role by the same fact or consideration results in his being evaluatively reflected or, as I will prefer to say, *depicted* in his action as a reasons-responsive agent. Accordingly, I will be referring to this variant of normative impact as *depictive impact*. Normative depiction *is just* the fusion of *evaluation* and *intelligibility*.

The second instance of normative impact is the most challenging one precisely because the fact that bears upon the evaluation of an agent's moral or rational profile assumes its role *counterfactually*, whereas *another* fact may assume the role of rendering normatively intelligible what has *actually* happened. In this latter case, an agent may not be evaluatively depicted in what she does, but rather evaluatively *constituted* by what she does; in other words, she *counts as* being good in some respect by virtue of the counterfactual second-order fact that she *could have treated* a first-order consideration as a reason to act. My choice of term for this variant of normative impact will be *constitutive impact*. Later on, I will show why I take social-norm-governed activities[8] of attributing

[6] Hieronymi (2011) associates such cases of divergence and convergence with Jonathan Dancy's preoccupation with the relationship 'between the agent's own (operative) reasons and the psychology that purportedly explains action (the motivating reasons)' (at 415).

[7] In Chapter 6, I will associate this case with what Joseph Raz describes as an instance of *Nexus* reasons. This is roughly the thesis that in order for a fact to qualify as reason-giving, it must be capable of both justifying and explaining a person's actions when she acts for that reason. The idea behind this unified approach is that the person's recognition of the reason or her treating a fact as a reason for action is crucial to the quality of normative explanation involved in actions done for reasons; see Raz (2011: ch 5). More precisely, I will invoke this case as a standard of appraisal by virtue of which competing theories of legal normativity can be evaluated with respect to their normative robustness. The *Nexus* model will serve as a mediating element between the general model of normative salience and normative impact I have been developing in this chapter and its application to theories of legal normativity in the next chapter.

[8] It is worth noting that it is the *social practice* dimension of thick evaluation that invites the label of 'constitutive impact' rather than simply the exemplification of evaluative properties. The latter may be also modelled in the likeness of ordinary reasons for action, in the sense that it is always possible to assume that someone's generosity or civility is also a function of whether she *actually*

thick characteristics to persons to be an illuminating manifestation of this type of normative phenomenon.

II. NORMATIVE ROLES

The main contrast I wish to draw with the standard picture advocated by proponents of the normative 'ubiquity' of reasons[9] boils down to the fact that for the latter, any divergence between the facts that acquire normative relevance in a given case is alarming or normatively suboptimal in the sense that it is indicative of a defect either in the subject's behaviour or in one's theory that can only be amended either by deflating it or by subdividing the case at stake in such a way that different facts fully explain different cases. Cases where, necessarily, the facts that emerge as normatively relevant fail to provide reasons that are response-directing and depictive of an agent's deliberative profile or character are treated as an opportunity to introduce internal distinctions between different *types* of reasons (subjective and objective), whose content may concur or diverge depending on extra-normative contingencies such as the epistemic profile of an agent.[10]

In response to these corrective strategies, I will suggest that our haste to classify cases whose disambiguation is at face value recalcitrant to the model of reasons as response-directing considerations is driven by an unpronounced tendency to suppress aspects of normativity that are not directional in any robust sense. More precisely, the idea will be that there are three distinct roles – influential, evaluative and explanatory – by virtue of which different types of facts can flesh out their normative relevance. To see how this more fine-grained approach is supposed to work, I suggest we take an ordinary descriptive fact like

treats the descriptive features of generous or courteous acts as reasons to act accordingly. This is the verdict that a virtue-ethical accommodation of thick concepts would endorse, but the domain of virtue is not the only domain where these concepts are fit for use. Social practices (rituals, etiquette or other norm- or code-governed activities) also rely heavily on the use of many evaluative concepts in a way that does not make that use *aretaic* in any robust sense.

[9] This ubiquity can be defended in terms of the metaphysical primacy of normative reasons or in terms of their explanatory primacy, or in terms of both. For an elaboration of this distinction, see Väyrynen (2011: 188–90).

[10] Space constraints do not allow an extensive digression into the casuistry accompanying the debate on how something's being a reason for someone to do something can radically diverge from someone's having a reason to do something. However, what deserves to be mentioned is that the central case for instances of this type of divergence is that of epistemic error, as when I am standing around at a cocktail party asking for a glass that I believe to contain gin and tonic, whereas in fact it is full of petrol. Under such circumstances, there seems to be a reason that favours my not drinking its contents, while at the same time this reason cannot be ascribed to me for the purposes of rational evaluation. Mark Schroeder defends the view that the impasse we encounter whenever the reasons that exist as a matter of fact and the reasons we actually have diverge can be overcome by accepting that there are two cross-cutting reason relations at stake: the objective reason relation and the subjective reason relation. See Schroeder (2008).

the fact that John's friend is sick at the hospital as what could be appropriate to perform all three roles of normative relevance.

First off, there is a sense in which the fact that John's friend is sick at the hospital *bears upon* John's act of visiting him.[11] This relation could be easily reparsed as the claim that the fact that John's friend is sick at the hospital *is a reason* for John to visit him. A 'reason to' is a consideration that is normatively influential with respect to particular type of response. Once again, I would like to reiterate that my use of the notion of *influence* is technical, in the sense that it pertains to a normative rather than a causal relationship between reasons and actions or attitudes. To put it in figurative terms, the influential role of normatively relevant facts is where our world acquires normative shape. This is perhaps the most prominent role associated not just with ordinary descriptive reason-giving facts, but also with other types of normative fact like thin deontic facts or thick evaluative facts. On some theoretical accounts, facts about the possession of thick evaluative properties like generosity, politeness and cruelty can also stand in normatively influential relations to act-types or attitudes.[12] Moreover, facts about the possession of thin deontic properties – that is, facts about what is right or wrong – are also regarded by some philosophers as suitable for exerting a distinct normative influence in the sense that their influence is not reducible to the normative influence of the respective right-making or wrong-making properties of actions.[13]

A second role that is frequently assigned to normatively relevant facts is that of serving as a standard of evaluation for agents. In this context, it is common to imply the evaluative use of reasons by portraying them as *being possessed*, so to speak, by agents. The standard metaethical vocabulary for this role uses the expressions *having a reason*[14] or *treating* a (putative) fact *as a reason* to act

[11] Hieronymi (2011) reserves the locution 'bears upon' for the relation that holds between considerations and practical *questions* rather than *actions*. This is a further refinement I would like to forgo here, as nothing in the ensuing analysis crucially depends on keeping this distinction salient.

[12] Facts about the possession of thin evaluative properties have been recently subjected to severe scrutiny resulting in their reduction to facts about the reasons provided by a set of descriptive properties of the bearers of thin value. Buck-passing analyses of properties are standardly treated as reductive. See Heuer (2006).

[13] I should note at this point that by including normative facts – that is, facts about what ought to be the case or facts about what is good or bad in some respect – in the pool of normatively relevant facts is not a tautological statement. It is perfectly possible for a normative fact to figure either in further metaphysical relations to actions or attitudes (for example, facts about wrongness are, arguably, themselves reason-giving) or in explanatory relations (for example, the same type of facts about wrongness can ground normative facts about why there is an all-things-considered reason not to act in a particular way). My choice to keep the distinction between reason-giving and right-making facts alive through my analysis merely serves an illustrative purpose and is not meant to disclose any inclination in favour of preserving the irreducibility of facts about rightness or wrongness to reason-giving facts.

[14] To be more precise, the locution 'A has a reason to φ' is not always treated as paraphrasable into the expression 'A treats R as a reason to φ'. The literature is replete with uses of this locution in a metaphysical rather than an evaluative sense. Mark Schroeder's talk of *having* a reason in the subjective or the objective sense is one such instance; see Schroeder (2008).

in a particular manner. Holding our exemplary fact about John's friend fixed, we also wish to ask what it is for John to treat the fact that his friend is sick at the hospital as a reason for him to visit him. What is distinctive about this kind of practical possession relation is that an agent that *has* a reason to act[15] is also thought as having a certain amount of a certain kind of control over an action favoured by a reason in the directional sense. Actually *treating* or being counterfactually capable of *treating* something as being normatively relevant in some way is a psychological fact about one's actual or counterfactual motivational stance, but it falls short of illustrating how facts 'possessed' by agents can have any normative implication.[16]

My suggestion with regard to how to fully capture the normative importance of this agent-related aspect of facts is to inquire into the evaluative connotation of the deliberative control assumed by a 'fact-possessing' agent over her action. Instead of thinking of control in terms of ability conditions, we can enrich our conception by advancing the idea that in order for it to be the case that an agent is in deliberative control of her action, it must be the case that her action becomes *evaluatively* reflective of her in the sense that she can be characterised as being *responsive to reasons* or *praiseworthy* in a more robust sense on the basis of the facts she *treated as* counting in favour of acting.[17] According to

[15] According to a standard approach, for it to be the case that one *has* a reason to φ is for it to be the case that there *is* a reason to φ that one *has*. At first sight, this looks more like an epistemic rather than a practical relation that an agent bears to facts that favour φ-ing, but its practical relevance can become immediately apparent as soon as we seek to explain instances of acting for a reason. Instances of acting for a reason seem to be logically explained as instances of exercising one's *capacity* to act for a particular reason. The latter capacity is conditional on one's actually having the reason in question, in the sense of *being aware* of the facts that are reasons in the metaphysical sense for favouring a particular action. Acting for a reason R asymmetrically entails that one is in a *position* to act for R, which in turn entails that one *has* R.

[16] I am deliberately omitting the complications arising in cases of epistemic error with regard to what facts actually exist. This is a puzzle of its own, but suffice it to say that *necessarily*, given the appropriate background conditions, reasons in the normatively influential or metaphysical sense *can be* – even though they need not always be – reasons in the practical and consequently in the explanatory sense. For two alternative approaches to the problem of falsely believed facts, see Schroeder (2008) and Hieronymi (2011).

[17] Thomas Scanlon articulates this evaluative dimension of reasons in terms of the *meaning* or *significance* they bestow upon actions or attitudes. As he notes: 'My call to a sick relative has a different meaning for the recipient (and hence also for me), depending on the reason for which I call. It is one thing if I call because I am genuinely concerned about his welfare, another if I am indifferent to his welfare but want to please my wealthy grandfather by appearing to be concerned about my relatives' (Scanlon 2008: 52). Scanlon's primary concern is cases of *depictive impact*, which he articulates in terms of the relevance of considerations that are *actually* treated as reasons, for the permissibility of actions. Although he does not further elaborate on the other half of the axis of normative impact (constitutive impact), he explicitly portrays its significance when he notes that: 'The meaning of an action in the sense I am concerned with should be distinguished from a different sense in which the meaning of an action is determined by the reactions of others (or by the ways it would be reasonable for them to react). For example, if the only family in the neighborhood that was not invited to the block party is also the only black family in the neighborhood, then that family may reasonably take this as a sign of prejudice, even if they were left out by mistake, or because only people with children were invited and they have none. Effects like their reaction are important

this approach, to actually or counterfactually have a reason or, equivalently, to actually or counterfactually treat some facts as reasons makes a fact normatively relevant, in the sense that it can serve as a standard of appraisal of an agent's profile or character for what she has done or failed to do *precisely in respect of* the fact(s) – that is, the reason-giving facts – she had or could have factored in her practical thoughts.[18] Returning to John's example, his actually *treating* the fact that his friend is sick at the hospital as a reason to visit entails that he is properly responsive to the existence of normative reasons. One and the same fact about his friend's condition has so far served as a normatively influential consideration that bears upon acting in a particular way and as a standard for evaluating John's profile *qua* moral agent.

The third role that can be assumed by a normatively relevant fact is a composition of the other two. The question pertaining to this role is usually cast in metaphysical terms, but its nature is such that it ultimately reveals a more elaborate way of thinking of how normativity figures into practical reason. The intuition behind this manifestation of normative relevance is that we do not only care to justify our actions or attitudes and evaluate ourselves as agents, but we also care to explain a series of event types like acting for a normative reason[19] or instantiating (through one's actions) a normative practice, satisfying a requirement of rationality or acting in conformity with the law. Supposing that the fact that John's friend is sick at the hospital is the case and that John treats this fact as a reason in the evaluative sense explained above, then this same fact, apart from standing in a relation of normative influence to John's act of visiting his friend and in a relation of evaluative possession by John, will also stand in an *explanatory* relation to the act-token of 'John's having visited his friend at the hospital on Thursday evening'.

and can affect the permissibility of an action. Meaning in this broader sense is not a function of the agent's actual reasons. It is, rather, a matter of what others reasonably or unreasonably take those reasons to be' (at 53). Where Scanlon talks about the meaning of an action as determined by an agent's actual reasons, I talk about *depictive* impact. Where Scanlon talks about the meaning of an action as determined by the (reasonable) reactions of others, I talk about *constitutive* impact.

[18] An important caveat is in order here: throughout this exposition, I intend to associate the normative relevance of the actual or counterfactual possession of facts qua reasons for action with the *evaluative* question of how agents are reflected in their actions, not with the *metaphysical* question of whether in order for it to be the case that R is a reason for A to Φ, it is necessary that A be actually or counterfactually motivated by the normative force of R. The latter question is a substantive one; for instance, there are roughly two versions of reasons-internalism. According to the actualist version, if something is a reason for someone to act in a particular way, then it follows by necessity that she *actually* is somewhat motivated to do *A*. Counterfactual versions make the weaker claim that if there a reason for someone to do something, then it follows by necessity that she *would* be motivated to some degree under some ideal conditions. Both versions regard the relevance of facts about one's actual or counterfactual motivation for the grounding of claims about the existence of normative reasons. For alternative specifications of these ideal conditions, see Finlay and Schroeder (2012).

[19] For two competing treatments of this question, see Hieronymi (2011) and Korsgaard (2008: 207–32).

Again, there arises the question of how this explanatory role assumed by facts is normative in any informative sense. To adopt the view that facts can causally explain an action is to go back to a point where a conception of facts *as* reasons for action is dispensable, unless one is willing to re-conceptualise the normative pressure exercised by reasons as a type of causation. In order to preserve the normative relevance of facts, we need to accept that they can operate as *normative grounds* of atomic facts about what one did, thought or felt. According to this approach, the same facts that bear upon a prospective action can rationalise and make morally, rationally or prudentially intelligible actual instances of acting for reasons such that the link between the actual acting and the question of whether the action was called for in the first place remains unsevered.

Anyone who is willing to take on board the idea that a fact can display its normative relevance in three distinct ways (influential, evaluative and explanatory) can also entertain a further hypothesis as to why reason-giving facts take pride of place in so many recent theories of normativity. The hypothesis I have in mind is fact-convergence or synchronicity; the same descriptive fact that bore upon John's visiting his sick friend and served as a standard of his appraisal as a reasons-responsive agent is also the fact that occupies the position of the explanans in the question of why John went to the hospital on that particular day and time. Under favourable conditions, a reason-giving fact seems to be such that it can perform all three roles and this convergence undoubtedly attests to the versatility of the concept of a normative reason.

However, the problem begins as soon as we take this fact convergence as evidence of how anything that qualifies as normatively felicitous is supposed to function. The tendency to frame discussions about practical normativity in more or less reasons-based terms bears testimony to a failure to see that there can exist instances of *one and the same* normative phenomenon where the fact that plays the (a) influential role is *not identical* with the fact that plays the (b) explanatory role. The convergence of these two roles corresponds to the variant of normative salience I have termed *normative action (or attitude)-direction*, whereas their divergence corresponds to the variant of normative salience I have termed *normative action (or attitude)-constraint*. Normative direction is the variant of normative salience that is individuated as an instance of identity or convergence between the normative considerations that play the influential and the explanatory role. Conversely, normative constraint is the variant of normative salience that is individuated as an instance of difference or divergence between the normative considerations that play the influential role and the explanatory role.

At the same time, the alternative model I have sketched is also well suited to anticipate instances of *one and the same* normative phenomenon, where the fact that plays (c) the evaluative role is not identical to the fact that plays (d) the explanatory role. Moving to the other axis of normative self-understanding or impact, I will associate the convergence of these two roles with our actual depiction *qua* agents *in* our actions (what I have labelled *depictive impact*) and their divergence with our counterfactual constitution *qua* agents *by* our actions (what I have labelled *constitutive impact*). My interim conclusion will be that the standard approach to practical normativity is blind to the possibility of there being 'benign', so to speak, divergences either between the facts that bear upon our responses and the facts that explain their actual instances[20] (response-constraint) or between the facts that serve as standards of our evaluation *qua* agents and the facts that explain our actual conduct (constitutive impact).[21] Accordingly, both response-constraint and constitutive impact will only point to *benign* cases of divergence rather than cases where an epistemic or moral error deprives response-constraining or constitutive considerations of their normative 'punch'.

More precisely, I shall argue that the standard approach correctly predicts that what is distinctive of reason-giving facts is that in ideal conditions, all three roles of normative relevance are performed by the *same* reason-giving fact and under the same *actual* circumstances. Returning to my previous remark, the problem begins the moment that friends of the standard 'imperialist' model of ordinary normative reasons are called upon to evaluate the nature and scope of potential divergences either among facts or among the modal profiles of the circumstances of their use. According to the standard approach, any divergence between what occupies each role-position is treated either as an indication of a normative defect in how an agent deliberates or as evidence of the need to be ontologically expansive in our use of the concept of a normative reason. At any rate, what undergirds this approach is an effort to solve any normative inconsistency *within* the conceptual realm of reasons, even if this necessitates a moralistic understanding (non-defective and defective reasons) or inflationary ontology (objective and subjective reasons) of *reasons*.

At this stage, I will not regurgitate any further stipulative claims as they may add more confusion or justify disbelief in the worth of suggesting an alternative taxonomy. Instead, I will venture a short digression in the hope that it will facilitate our understanding of how this alternative conceptual scheme can do better work both in terms of explanatory neatness and metaphysical parsimony. An instructive way to verify this hypothesis is to test whether this new scheme can help elucidate two persisting problems plaguing those who remain sceptical about the pride of place that the directional status of normative reasons should enjoy. The first question regards the prospect of vindicating the robustness of normative requirements that fail to operate as full-fledged response-directing reasons. The second question regards the reducibility of thick evaluative concepts into concepts involving only thin evaluation plus some descriptive criteria. The latter question is crucially related to the putative

[20] Pamela Hieronymi portrays such cases as exhibiting a 'Nagel's gap' (Hieronymi (2011: 415).
[21] Pamela Hieronymi portrays such cases as exhibiting a 'Dancy's gap' (ibid 414).

primacy of directional reasons precisely because if the reductive hypothesis proves correct, thin evaluative concepts like good or bad are particularly vulnerable to objections of metaphysical dispensability, so reasons of the directional kind will assume the role of explaining the normative appeal of thick evaluative concepts.

My idea is that what should motivate and legitimise the choice to reconsider the explanatory virtues of available taxonomies of normative concepts is the justified belief that one's available normative concepts *in the precise pattern on which* they are tabulated cannot sufficiently account for *all* types of normatively felicitous cases. Domains of normative activity like law, social practices involving the attribution of thick evaluative traits to agents and their actions as well as rationality are most probably – as I intend to argue – the primary collateral 'victims' of available normative taxonomies, in the sense that attempts to model their normative function or dysfunction on the template of directional reasons as commonly understood fail to showcase what is precisely at stake when their requirements are being transgressed. In what follows, I will provisionally bracket the way in which law falls into this picture and will instead focus on the more familiar cases of thick evaluation and requirements of rationality that have come to ascendancy lately and are still avidly disputed.[22] As already explained, the application of this alternative model to the law will be a separate topic of discussion in the following chapter.

In the remainder of this chapter, I will try to demonstrate how the two most controversial aspects of this alternative model of 'salience-cum-impact' – namely, the concepts of response-constraint (as opposed to response-direction) and constitutive impact (as opposed to depictive impact) – can explain in non-reductive terms the tension between our responsiveness to directional reasons and ascriptions of rationality and thick evaluative properties. On the one hand, the normativity of requirements of rationality is commonly questioned on the grounds that rational requirements seem to tolerate a kind of normative asymmetry between the different ways in which they can be satisfied. In other words, in a given context, not all ways of satisfying a rational requirement are such that they can guarantee the rational justifiability of someone's response.

On the other hand, there is growing suspicion that thick evaluative properties like being generous or cruel cannot by themselves ground the truth of claims of global evaluation of a person's character or behaviour precisely because their descriptive component is always revisable in the light of goodness *simpliciter* or (for friends of reasons-reductivism) of reasons, all things considered. In what

[22] Niko Kolodny, for instance, argues that the normativity of requirements of rational coherence is only apparent and can be easily deflated by semantic means; see Kolodny (2005: 557–60). Mark Schroeder appeals to a distinction between objective reasons based on facts and subjective reasons based on beliefs, and proceeds to analyse the latter in terms of the former. In this reductive scheme, the normativity of rational requirements is represented as piggybacking on the normativity of objective reasons; see Schroeder (2009). For a reconciliatory approach, see Lord (2014).

follows, I will offer a 'benign' explanation of these cases whilst preserving the intuitive appeal of the objections just described. The first task will involve an explanation of the normative asymmetry of rational requirements in terms of attributing to them a response-constraining rather than response-directing function. The second task will employ the concept of constitutive impact in order to explain how the practice of thick evaluation is itself partly constitutive of the normativity of thick properties.

At the risk of sounding unnervingly repetitive, I will make one final point about the potential payoffs of this digression. Besides the need to guard this alternative taxonomy against the obvious objection of solely serving the purposes of an eventual argument about legal normativity, there is a further reason that dictates this detour. In the preceding paragraph, I committed myself to unpacking the connection between what is generally regarded as a peculiarity about rational requirements and thick evaluation with what I take to be the most controversial aspects of my alternative taxonomy, in the hope that this association will prove mutually beneficial for proponents of the irreducibility of some domains of normativity to reasons as well as for the purpose of vindicating the general explanatory force of this alternative taxonomy.

III. RATIONAL REQUIREMENTS, ASYMMETRY AND RESPONSE-CONSTRAINT

The question which I will attempt to associate with the issue of the normative robustness of rational requirements is as follows: what goes wrong if a rational requirement of coherence or consistency is violated? The only (widely accepted) premise of this question is that *if* there are normative requirements of any kind, it must be possible to violate them or, to put it another way, it must be possible to act or behave otherwise. At a later stage, I will be in a better position to show how this question about the wrongness, disvalue or grounds for reasonable criticism associated with the violation of a normative requirement dovetails with the question of whether there is any need to inject new distinctions within an already-convoluted normative universe.

At first sight, we could ask whether there can be a distinct class of normative requirements on action or attitudes such that the wrongness of their violation does not analytically entail a standing to hold someone accountable and/or address demands with respect to what counts as a way of failing to *satisfy* a normative requirement, but with respect to what counts as a way of making the obtaining of an intrinsically valuable kind of agency *normatively impossible*. The latter case is not a cryptic reparsing of a standard association of moral responsibility with moral obligation, as one may reasonably infer from the apparent imputability of an act of making the satisfaction of a normative requirement impossible. To see why this is not the case, I will take the liberty of making a short detour into the intricacies of rational requirements.

More precisely, I will try to illustrate the distinctness of the latter case by resorting to a topic frequently brought up in discussions on the normativity of rationality. It is customary to say that rationality requires us not to believe contradictions, to intend the means necessary to our intended ends, to have transitive preferences and to preserve a specific mode of coherence between our intentions and our normative beliefs. For ease of exposition, I will single out the so-called 'enkratic' requirement of rationality,[23] which in its most simplistic form is represented by the following schema:

Rationality requires of you that you intend to φ if you believe you ought to φ.

What is particularly interesting in the case of requirements of rationality in general is that sorting out their normative status crucially depends on sorting out their precise logical form. More specifically, philosophers who are sympathetic to the possibility of there being robustly normative requirements of rationality take it that the proper logical form of such requirements allows deontic modals to range over entire conditionals rather than mere consequents. The upshot of this wide-scope approach is that it allows a novel distinction between what is required of us by rationality and what counts as a way of *actually* satisfying this requirement. Even more surprisingly, the same requirement cannot settle what actually counts as the appropriate way to satisfy it in a given circumstance.

This leaves us with a conundrum: some requirements of rationality can be 'silent' on their optimal satisfaction, yet remain stringent with regard to the irrationality of their possible violation. Take the example of the enkratic requirement. Suppose that A holds a patently immoral belief. From the point of view of enkratic rationality, she is required not to *jointly* hold that belief and not intend to act on it. Both intending to act on a normative belief and revising/dropping it equally count as *pro tanto* legitimate ways of satisfying the requirement at hand such that *there is no violation* of the enkratic requirement as long as A chooses to respond in *either* of the two ways mentioned. But it is certainly the case that something goes wrong if in A's example, she chooses to intend to act on her immoral belief instead of dropping it. The latter normative asymmetry cannot be captured by what makes the enkratic requirement itself stringent. In other words, there seems to be a divergence between what accounts for what makes akratic behaviour as such normatively suboptimal and what accounts for what makes a *pro tanto* rational response to the enkratic requirement inappropriate *all things considered*.[24] Whereas it is always the case that jointly holding

[23] The term 'enkrasia' was coined by John Broome. For a concise presentation of his argument on the semantics of the enkratic requirement, see Broome (2010: 283–92).

[24] The same point has been expressed in slightly different terms by Way (2011). Granting that only a wide-scope reading of coherence requirements of rationality can accommodate a robust reading of their normative force, Way remarks that the wide-scope view on requirements of rationality 'maintains that local irrationalities are irrational as such. They are not irrational only because they involve independently irrational attitudes ... The distinctive Wide-Scope claim is that local irrationalities are irrational even if none of the elements constituting them is irrational. The problem is *in the combination*' (at 230, emphasis added).

a normative belief and failing to acquire a corresponding intention counts as a violation of the enkratic requirement, it can be the case that an *actual* intention to act on that normative belief or an *actual* revision/rejection of the same belief counts as an instance of irrationality all things considered.

Keeping this example in mind, it is an opportune moment to reflect on the informative value of the distinction I ventured to draw earlier between holding someone accountable and/or addressing demands with respect to what counts as a way of failing to *satisfy* a normative requirement all things considered, and holding her accountable with respect to what counts as a way of making a particular type of *agency* normatively impossible. If we suppose that in the case of the akratic agent, the content of her normative belief is morally opprobrious and that she actually holds that belief and at the same time lacks the intention to act on it, a possible ground on which we would blame her for being akratic is not that she holds a morally unacceptable belief, but that, for instance, as a result of her holding a normative belief that is unaccompanied by an a corresponding intention, she fails to be a self-governed agent or deliberator.[25] This is not to say that we will not *also* blame her for the content of her belief, but the grounds we will invoke are not co-extensive with our reasons for taking issue with akratic behaviour! The same point can be made by remarking that for a class of normative requirements, there is no symmetrical relationship between the normative consequences of their violation and their satisfaction, or, as Jonathan Way puts it, '[wide-scope] requirements are importantly asymmetrical: you are necessarily irrational if you violate a requirement, but not necessarily rational if you comply with a requirement'.[26]

That said, I would like to invite the reader to provisionally take on board the idea that the normativity of non-response-directing normative requirements is a function of their making a type of intrinsically valuable agency normatively possible rather than of their requiring a particular response (action or attitude). The bridging element that can explain why the dimension of normative salience is not limited to the case of convergence between the facts that normatively influence or bear upon a response and the facts that normatively explain its occurrence is the fact that it is a *separate* normative question which of the ways of realising an intrinsically valuable type of agency is normatively appropriate in a given context. By talking about separation, I do not intend to downplay the importance of ultimately resolving our problems of rational choice in the normatively optimal way; all I am trying to say is that the resolution of this problem is perfectly compatible with the response-constraining role of requirements

[25] This is the justificatory ground employed by Bratman (2009) in his defence of the normative robustness of requirements of rational coherence and consistency. It does not matter for our current purposes whether this idea about the intrinsic value of self-governance is the best vehicle to guard wide-scopers against the heap of objections to the normative robustness of rational requirements. What is of relevance is the fact that self-governance points to a multiply realisable type of agency that can supervene on concrete deliberative choices, actions or adopted attitudes.

[26] Way (2011: 230).

of rational coherence and consistency.[27] The latter serve to limit the scope of our rational responses to a domain of options that make an intrinsically valuable type of agency like self-governance normatively possible, irrespective of what the specific context will deliver as the best choice in a given situation. According to this picture, the divergence between the facts that bear upon the obtaining of a given conditional and the facts that normatively explain its satisfaction accurately overlaps with the distinction between the intrinsic value of a multiply realisable form of agency and the *separate* value of its actual occurrences.

IV. THICK EVALUATION, GLOBAL JUDGEMENT AND CONSTITUTIVE IMPACT

Moving to the second case, I intend to use the same contrastive example about John and his friend in order to illustrate how constitutive impact manifests itself in a way that lends support to the normative 'autonomy' of social practices of thick evaluation. For the sake of simplicity, let us assume again that the first fact is that John's friend is sick at the hospital and let us contrast this fact with the fact that John's taking the first bite at the beginning of a dinner he is hosting is polite in a context where an etiquette code E applies. The first fact is the same ordinary descriptive fact that also figured in the previous case. However, the second fact is a fact involving the practice-based attribution of a thick evaluative property which for the sake brevity I will refer to as a 'thick evaluative fact'.[28] Now suppose that in a given context C, John actually *treats* the fact that his friend is sick at the hospital as a reason to visit him. Acting in recognition of the reason-giving property of this fact serves as a depiction of John's actual responsiveness to reasons.[29] In other words, the fact that simultaneously serves

[27] Jonathan Way makes a similar point when he remarks that rational requirements are always supplemented by 'basing principles'. The facts about the latter principles assume the role of normative explanation of occurrences that satisfy requirements of rationality. In Way's words: 'Basing principles specify whether an attitude, or set of attitudes, is an appropriate basis for another attitude … Wide-Scope requirements are not directly concerned with basing, and so need to be supplemented with independent basing principles. But then we can expect those principles to explain this type of asymmetry' (ibid 231).

[28] Strictly speaking, the type of fact about thick value that I will associate with reasons for *action* is dispositional by nature, in the sense that it is about the disposition of certain *act-types* to be socially evaluated as having thick value. Conversely, facts about the possession of thick value by *act-tokens* will provide reasons for certain types of *attitudes*, like admiration, commendation, indignation and condemnation. I have decided to suppress this difference for two reasons: first, this distinction requires some additional premises and it is not a received view about the structure of general facts about thick value; and, second, the topic of this section is the evaluation of agents for what they have done rather than the direction of their prospective actions.

[29] This is how Joseph Raz encodes the meaning of one's rational capacity to respond to reasons; see Raz (2011: ch 5). This is not the only available way to understand how our actions or responses can be evaluatively reflective of who we are. More robust approaches may appeal to an evaluative aspect of responsibility rather than mere responsiveness to reasons, such that to act out of awareness that a particular fact is a reason for action entails one's status as a rationally, morally or prudentially

as a standard of his appraisal as a being responsive to reasons and as an explanation of John's conduct is such that John is actually aware of its relevance. We can now contrast this example with the case where in a given context C – where a particular set of etiquette rules applies – the fact that it is a token of politeness that the dinner host takes the first bite is a reason for John *qua* host to take the first bite. In this case, nothing compels John to treat the fact that taking the first bite is polite as a reason to act accordingly, because nothing about what can serve as a standard of appraising his behaviour as a polite host depends on what actually motivates him to take the first bite. To put it more graphically, the route to explaining John's actual behaviour might have a surprising end. For instance, John might have taken the fact that he is excruciatingly hungry as a reason to take the first bite, but even if that were the case, he would still count as polite *from the point of view* of etiquette. By contrast, if John had not acted as he did for the reason that his friend was sick at the hospital – for instance, he might have wanted to uphold his esteem as a caring friend among his peers – his act would fail to reflect him as being responsive to reasons.[30]

Interestingly, this contrast can be structurally reflected in the modal contexts in which these two facts figure as normatively relevant. In the first case, the fact that serves to evaluate John's response to the situation is also the fact that explains his actual response precisely because this same fact is actually treated by John as a reason to visit his friend. This is precisely a case of *depictive impact*, where one and the same fact plays both the evaluative role and the explanatory role. By contrast, in the second case, the fact that serves as a standard of appraisal of John's performance as a host – eg, the fact that he felt very hungry – is not identical to the fact that explains John's actual conduct![31] This is a case

praiseworthy agent. David Shoemaker (2011) describes this dimension of (moral) responsibility as attributability. An even more robust account can appeal to the value of freedom or personhood. There are various strands of thought in this ballpark, all of which converge in a Kantian conception of rational action *qua* realisation of freedom. According to this view, acting out of awareness that a particular fact is a reason for action involves a normatively relevant mode of self-understanding. In acting for reasons, we represent ourselves as free agents or persons such that facts about actions done for reasons are registered in our agential profiles as moments of being free or a person; for this more robust view, see Julius (2017).

[30] It is worth noting that both examples are constructed in such a way that the role of an underlying social practice is portrayed as being actively conducive to the explanation of the situation only in the case of John's being a host, but not in the case of his being a good friend. This is a stipulation that serves an illustrative purpose. Nothing prevents us from enriching the context of John's friendly conduct in a way that the social norms governing friendship in a given community are also operative. In such a case, John's visit would not be analysed as an ordinary instance of being responsive to action-directing reasons; rather, it would be treated as an instance of socially conditioned conduct where the standards of appraisal apply that are mediated by facts about how the *practice* governing the evaluation of friendship becomes *in and of itself* morally relevant.

[31] Space constraints compel me to omit some aspects of this phenomenon. An important premise is that in the case of depictive impact, reason-giving facts will be non-normative, non-evaluative facts about the world. This qualification is not meant as a stipulation, but as a leap of metaphysical parsimony. With regard to the exclusion of non-normative facts like facts about what is right or wrong, all things considered, there seems to be an instance of 'double-counting' for the reason that, as Dancy explains, 'what there is overall reason to do (and note that "reason" in this phrase is not a

of *constitutive impact*. The evaluative fact is a fact about John's counterfactual treatment of – namely, the fact that, in the present circumstances, he *could* have treated – a norm of etiquette as reason-giving, whereas the explanatory fact that renders John's conduct prudentially intelligible is the physiological fact that he is hungry.

This divergence is neither accidental nor normatively infelicitous, but is a telling indication of how social-norm-governed thick evaluations impinge upon our counterfactual rather than our actual agential profiles. Whereas in the first case, treating a fact as reason-giving serves to measure the actual degree of our responsiveness to reasons, in the second case, it is not our actual responsiveness to reason-giving facts that matters for our appraisal, but the counterfactual fact that our actual behaviour that falls within the extension of the description *associated by a given practice* with an evaluation of some sort *could be* informed by a recognition of the reason-giving force of a thick evaluative fact – eg, that taking the first bite is polite.

The contrast between the depiction of our actual selves *in* our actions and the constitution of an ideal self *by* our actions is not meant to serve as a figurative device. Instead, it purports to motivate an explanatory shift in our understanding of thick evaluation in the context of norm-governed activities. To see how this shift can be achieved, it is worth giving a general picture of what is at stake in debates about the notion of evaluative thickness. Standard defences[32] of thick evaluative concepts point in one way or another to the fact that the descriptive and the evaluative components of these concepts are so intricately entangled that the former do not suffice to determine their extension without the input of some evaluative judgement that applies to *the whole* concept. On the other hand, a forceful objection is advanced by proponents of reductivism, who are willing to grant that evaluation is an indispensable determinant of the extension of thick concepts, but also argue that this premise can be easily accommodated by reductive analysis.[33] The upshot of this controversy is that the thickness of

count noun) is to talk about where the contributory reasons come down – on this side or on that … These verdicts do not themselves specify further reasons (of an overall sort), on pain of changing the very situation on which they pass verdict. So there are no overall reasons' (Dancy 2004: 16). On the other hand, the buck-passing controversy about thin value is heated enough to justify a preliminary exclusion of facts embedding thin evaluations about what is good or bad in some way. That said, nothing about the way normative depiction is supposed to work turns on whether thin evaluative truths are themselves reason-giving or just report the instantiation of a higher-order property of goodness by a reasons-relation holding between other descriptive or thick evaluative properties and actions or attitudes.

[32] The force of arguments proffered in support of the irreducibility of thick concepts varies from focused appeals to ideas about the uncodifiability and inseparability of thick evaluation to a more global defence of the metaphysical primacy of thick evaluative properties vis-a-vis their thin cognates. For the former view, see McDowell (1979), Williams (1985) and Dancy (1996). For the latter approach, see Tappolet (2004).

[33] This strategy proceeds by way of analysing thick concepts in terms of not just one but two thin evaluative components: one that applies to the object of evaluation globally ('x is good') and one that is embedded in the descriptive part of the concept. According to this picture, a thick attribution

evaluation is measured by reference to whether it necessitates only one type of evaluation that applies to a concept as a whole (thick global evaluation). If one can successfully demonstrate that the latter type of evaluation can be broken down into a pair of thin global evaluation ('x is good') and thin embedded evaluation ('for the sake of good goals'), the guise of thickness disappears.

An unexplored way of bypassing this controversy is indicated by the previous brief exposition of constitutive impact. The beginning of wisdom is to consider whether this controversy has been taking place in the wrong dimension. A possible explanation of the persistence of this dispute is that both parties converge in their assumption that what is at stake in the (ir)reducibility of thick evaluation is its capacity to operate as an independent source of normative *direction*. In other words, friends of thick evaluation want to insist, whereas reductivists want to deny, that facts about the possession of thick value are genuinely reason-giving in the sense that they can *provide* reasons for action (or attitudes) rather than be *reductively explained* in terms of the latter.[34] Reductivists want to deny this possibility for a host of reasons, one of which is that many of these thick evaluative concepts can be morally objectionable.[35] On the other hand, defenders of thick evaluation aim to preserve the irreducibility of a cluster of thick evaluative properties in the hope that this can be used as valid evidence against a sweeping reduction of value into reasons.[36] For instance, if it turns out that the fact that Φ-ing is courageous cannot be reduced to the fact that Φ-ing involves accepting harm or the risk of harm for a superior goal and Φ-ing is good in this way, thick evaluative facts can escape the buck-passing fate of their thin cognates.[37] In that way, they can operate as sources of reasons without also being themselves explicable in terms of reasons.

Introducing a second axis of normative relevance (normative impact) invites us to consider the possibility that the crux of controversy about thick evaluative

of the form 'x is C' is analysable into something like '(i) x is good, (ii) there is a set of determinable properties X, Y, Z it is good to have in some determinate respect such that if x exemplifies those properties, x is good'. Goodness figures in this analysis in two different roles, first as an attribute of 'x' and, second, as an attribute of the determinable properties X, Y, Z. To illustrate this analysis, we may replace C with the property being courageous. According to this reductive method, 'x is courageous' in analysed into 'x is good and x involves accepting certain risks of harm for the sake of good goals'. The crucial step in this analysis is that the embedded evaluation (the goodness of certain goals) holds independently of whether accepting harm or the risk of harm for the sake of good goals is good in a certain way. The latter global type of evaluation is the only one recognised by non-reductionists. For a detailed illustration of this view, see Elstein and Hurka (2009).

[34] I leave aside buck-passers about thin value, as their participation in this debate is only epiphenomenal in the sense that the whole controversy about whether thick evaluation is reducible to thin evaluation is a non-starter for the globally reductionist project of buck-passing.

[35] For instance, thick attributes like *chaste* or *lewd*, or slur words like *faggot* or *Kraut* embody values that really ought not to be endorsed, thus rendering the very truth-aptness of sentences embedding them problematic. A non-cognitivist use of this line of reasoning has been forcefully advanced by Blackburn (1992). For a comprehensive review of the relevant literature, see Väyrynen (2012).

[36] Ulrike Heuer has consistently pursued this line of argument; see Heuer (2006).

[37] ibid 235.

facts lies not – primarily, at least – in their capacity to be action-directing (axis of salience), but in their capacity to affect our evaluation *qua* agents independently of whether we *actually* treat them as reasons for action and, consequently, of whether they can normatively explain our actual conduct. In the latter sense, it is misguided to try to locate the thickness of evaluation in the inseparability of description from the evaluation of action; rather, our quest for the essence of evaluative thickness should find its destination in the inseparability of description from the evaluation of *agents qua members of a social practice*. This is to say that defenders of thick evaluation should consider downplaying their worries about the possibility of analysing thick evaluative properties in terms of (a cluster of) thin evaluative ones or, even more, in terms of normative reasons and should redirect the force of their objection towards the possibility of conditioning the possession of thick evaluative traits by agents not just on how their actions fit a certain description, *however this is ultimately determined*, but also on whether it would be possible to treat the fact that acting in a thus-determined way is courageous or generous[38] as a reason to perform an action.

This reconfiguration of the site of our metanormative disagreement about the indispensability of thick evaluation associates the latter with the possibility of the counterfactual or constitutive (as opposed to actual or depictive) evaluation of agents rather than of their actions. This claim calls for some further unpacking. The general idea is that, as we navigate through the thin–thick spectrum, moving from its thin end towards its thick territories, the role of practices and more specifically the role of the practice of attributing thick evaluative traits to persons by partial reference to some descriptive standards acquires a distinct moral importance that cannot be captured in terms of thin value or perfectionist considerations. That said, I should caution that this shift in normative relevance does not mark a difference in kind between, say, ordinary reason-giving facts and thick evaluative facts, but a difference in degree. As stated earlier, the idea is that if there is a sense of inseparability that the defender of thick evaluation should take on board, it is the inseparability of descriptive content from our actual social, norm-governed practice of valuing that content in distinct ways.

To see how this argumentative shift might work, let us recall what the most pressing version of the reductivist argument claims. The objection is that we can

[38] If we take the path of reduction, the same objection would be directed either to a conjunction of thin evaluative facts or, if we also decide to pass the buck, to a fact about the reasons provided by a cluster of descriptive facts. To dispel some of the complexity of this long road to ultimate reduction, take the fact that Φ-ing is courageous. A non-buck-passer reductionist will take on board a composite fact of the form 'the fact that one accepts harm or the risk of harm for the sake of a superiorly good goal and the fact that this acceptance is good'. Furthermore, a buck-passer reductionist will argue in favour of a fact like 'the fact that a goal's instantiating a set of descriptive properties X, Y, Z is a reason to pursue it and the fact that accepting harm or the risk of harm for the sake of this reason-giving goal is a way of achieving it'. In the former case, it is the conjunction of thin evaluative facts that provides a reason to act accordingly, whereas in the latter case, it is the conjunction of a fact about reasons and a descriptive fact that provides a reason to act accordingly.

perfectly well make sense of thick evaluation by reducing it into a pair of thinly evaluative components, one of which – the descriptive component – embeds a thin evaluative judgement, whereas the other is a pure thin evaluation of the form 'x is good'. As Daniel Elstein and Thomas Hurka note, this embedded thin evaluation introduces a standard that holds *independently of the practice* of attributing thick traits to agents. In their words, 'many and even all virtues and vices involve a relation to some *independently given* moral consideration, often (though not always) an independent good or evil' (emphasis added).[39] For them, it is precisely this practice-independent standard that dissolves the 'argument from disentanglement',[40] as it allows evaluation to drive the extension of the concept as thinly construed.

The introduction of the axis of normative impact and more specifically its counterfactual half (constitutive impact) serves to highlight why this reductive account fails. Shifting our talk from actions to agents, we may focus on a reductive analysis of the concept of being courageous. According to the reductivists' view, to say that A is courageous is to roughly say that A accepts harm or the risk of harm for the sake of a superior good goal and that A is good in this respect.[41] According to this argument, it follows that A's goodness of character is settled as soon as we settle the *independent* evaluative question of what makes a goal good and how the goodness of this goal contributes to the goodness of accepting harm or the risk of harm for its sake. But this manoeuvre misses the evaluative point of the practice of attributing courageousness. The reason is that it fails to see the distinct moral value in regimenting the scope of thick evaluation by reference to our actual practice of attributing courageousness to the same agent or different agents across different times and contexts. Social history and societal context matter here, and so does its relevance for calibrating our appraisal of people's actions and attitudes. If we focus our disagreement on what it means to subject *actions* to thick evaluation all things considered – or, in more archaic prose, *sub specie aeternitatis* – we miss the chance to acquaint ourselves with the unique moral intricacies of consistently *treating agents qua practice participants* as the subjects of positive or negative thick evaluation. The latter aspect can only become visible if that we are willing to provisionally abandon our preoccupation with valuable individual actions and put ourselves *qua* practice participants at the centre of this controversy.

The moment we decide to shift our perspective in the way suggested above, we will see that substituting a practice of thick evaluation for a practice of thin evaluation all things considered would instantly deprive us of our ability to distinguish between various instances of evaluation. To give just one example, take the case of the values of beneficence and friendship. As Pekka Väyrynen

[39] Elstein and Hurka (2009: 527).

[40] McDowell (1981: 144).

[41] One may replace 'good in this respect' with fitting-attitude predicates like 'admirable', 'laudable' etc.

remarks, 'the pre-theoretical data about welfare and friendship are consistent with the idea that we should respond to welfare subjects as if they were friends. Pre-theoretically, however, the properties that provide reasons of welfare and reasons of friendship do seem similar enough not to distinguish the two properties'.[42]

Pre-theoretically – that is, prior to the identification of a historically embedded practice of attributing thick evaluative traits – the descriptive properties that would figure in a reductive analysis of both concepts would seem to overlap to a degree nearing total coincidence. Roughly, both concepts would involve a disposition to benefit others out of sympathy for their ends or person. Embedding a thin evaluative judgement in the latter description like 'out of sympathy for the goodness of their ends or person' would add nothing in the service of affording a more fine-grained explanation of why beneficence and friendship evoke distinct evaluative responses. The farthest point such an analysis would take us is to qualify someone's overall goodness in terms of a practice-independent conception of what makes others' ends or character merit our responsiveness.

Advocating for the inseparability of some privileged description of virtuous activity from the way it should be evaluated acquires significant force the moment we allow ourselves to consider the distinct moral importance of our actual practices of thick evaluation. According to this alternative view, to which, as I am about to show, the notion of constitutive impact adds significant explanatory depth, these practices are morally important not for how closely they emulate the moral truth all things considered – as thin evaluation suggests – but because they the way we have been treating past instances of courageous, generous, cruel or polite behaviour make morally intelligible, as well as the way we proceed to treat current or future instances of such behaviour.[43] Under this scheme, the question we should be asking is not how to fit available descriptions into an all-things-considered conception of the good *simpliciter*, but how to define the societal conditions under which the actual past instances of attributing thick evaluative traits to agents can be justifiably invoked as guides for evaluating agents in the present or the future.

This is precisely the moment that the relevance of normative impact *qua* ideal constitution becomes visible. As I previously noted, the difference between our actual selves being evaluatively depicted in our actions and our ideal selves being constituted by our actions in the context of a social practice lies in the fact that in the latter but not the former case, our actual actions enable our

[42] Väyrynen (2006: 319).

[43] I owe the general layout of this argument to Ronald Dworkin's broader understanding of the value of integrity; see Dworkin (1986: 176–224). His idea is not strictly confined to the case of law, as he explicitly remarks that integrity can serve as a template-value for different kinds of regulative or constitutive practices. Whereas the restrictive effect of the practice of thick evaluation pales in comparison to the coercive impact of legal enforcement, it is nonetheless directive of people's behaviour in a way that diminishes their capacity to exit the practice or remain psychologically or practically immune to the application of its norms.

evaluation irrespective of how actually sensitive we are to the evaluative point of the practice, that is, irrespective of whether we actually treat facts about thick value as reasons for action.[44] The idea is roughly that practices of thick evaluation take place within the context of our imperfect, socially and culturally overdetermined lives and less than ideal institutional or collective arrangements. The domain of social practices is not simply an 'arena' where human excellence is tested and promoted. If we practised perfect virtue, it would make no sense to try to distinguish instances of the value of beneficence from instances of the value of friendship, as every possible action or form of behaviour would immediately fall under a concept of absolute, unqualified goodness. However, in our imperfect world, there are reasons to want to supplement what we ought to do with privileged, socially determined descriptions of how things are in a certain respect.

This is the need that thick evaluation purports to serve in a way that thin evaluation cannot accommodate. Socially or culturally privileged descriptions in the relevant sense will be descriptions that the principles that inform a given practice can sufficiently justify. In this non-ideal setting, we want to ask who *counts as*[45] courageous, cruel or polite for the purposes of social evaluation. The answer that the theoretical viewpoint of constitutive impact offers is that a courageous person is one whose actual behaviour would satisfy a certain description if *in light of a given practice of attributing courageousness*, she could have treated the fact that this type of behaviour is courageous as a reason for action. This definition can help explain why being courageous is not a matter of acting for the right kind of reasons[46] whose rightness is determined independently of how courage is actually being predicated of people *here or there*. As long as a morally fallible person acts in compliance with the descriptive standards that a given practice showcases as evaluatively relevant, it does not matter whether she actually treats this evaluation as a reason for action. The reason is that this evaluation is not presented as an evaluative fact that has an independent normative appeal that everyone should be able to recognise *irrespective of the existence of a practice* – that is, to act in recognition of its all-things-considered importance. It matters only to the extent that it makes the practice of thick evaluation of members of that practice morally intelligible as such.

[44] The reason is that thick evaluative facts are not facts about evaluative truth *simpliciter*, but their obtaining is sensitive to the point of the practice of employing these facts as standards for evaluating agents and, concomitantly, their actions.

[45] I deliberately use the expression 'counts as' as syntactic evidence for the relevance of the notion of constitution in the case of practice-instantiating actions.

[46] In the contemporary literature, the term 'wrong kind of reason(s)' has also acquired a technical sense. In this sense, it purports to describe cases where the desirability of something seems to provide the wrong kind of reason to determine whether that thing is good or not. This problem is closely associated with a set of account aspiring to explain value in terms of fitting ('reasons-induced') attitudes. For an approach that makes the normative-relevance of the right kind of reasons practice-dependent, see Schroeder (2010).

The latter point with which I intend to conclude this digression serves to safeguard practices of thick evaluation from the charge of sweeping moral relativism. It cannot be denied that it would be a great loss of explanatory force if we allowed simply any kind of practice of thick evaluation to count as being able to constitute our ideal selves by our actions. A limiting principle or set of principles must be available that makes the moral intelligibility of these practices attainable for both their members and non-members in a unified way. This would be the only way to make our normative judgements sensitive to the difference between a practice that withholds attributions of cruelty to cases of female mutilation and a practice situated in the nineteenth century when no general anaesthesia was medically available that declined to characterise surgeons of that time as cruel. An idea that has been lurking in this area for quite a long time is that any practice involving the attribution of thick evaluative traits to people should be informed by a principle of egalitarian distribution, the latter being about the 'distribution' or allocation of virtues and vices *within a given community*.

As such, this suggested principle cannot be purely formal in the sense that it ought to be capable of making distributions of evaluative traits themselves morally intelligible. This could be attained if we decided to qualify this principle by hedging its content with a clause to the effect that any egalitarian distribution of evaluative traits across different times and contexts must reflect equal respect and concern for all its addressees, irrespective of their congenital or situational advantages or strengths. In the latter case, our evaluative task is driven by a thickly egalitarian principle rather than a principle of personal desert. Our public practices seem to direct us to evaluate personal conduct in the same way we would evaluate the same actual conduct had it taken place under ideal conditions, which in the relevant case is partly determined by reference to the practice's own past.

6

The Metric Approach to Legal Normativity

FOLLOWING THE LENGTHY digression in Chapter 5, I will resume the progress of my argument and focus on the way in which contemporary accounts of legal normativity – both antipositivist and positivist – tend to measure their robustness by reference to how closely they can afford to associate their metaphysical account of legal facts with what could qualify as an ideal relationship between normative reasons and the explanation of intentional action. Even for legal philosophers who favour a very thin account of legal normativity, the grounds of their deflationary approach are a function of their distance from the region of normative space where one and the same consideration can be normatively influential, evaluatively relevant and explanatorily potent.

I will associate this ideal standard of normative agency with what Joseph Raz has aptly described as the normative/explanatory *Nexus*.[1] More precisely, I will try to demonstrate how the *Nexus*, instead of mapping the entire domain of practical normativity, points to a specific region of normative space whose 'gravitational pull' attracts theories of legal normativity which postulate the existence of legal facts[2] atop a stratified ontology featuring moral and/or social facts in its lower strata. To codify my argument, I will be referring to this tendency as the *metric approach* precisely with a view to accentuating the role of the *Nexus* as a comparative standard of normative robustness. The metric approach will be presented as a *metanormative* thesis about the determinants of a legal theory's normative robustness.

Joseph Raz's account of the *Nexus* is a remarkable leap forward thanks to the switch he endeavours from talk about the dependence of normativity on our beliefs about reasons to talk about *Reason* or, equivalently, our capacities *qua* rational agents. By allowing this switch, Raz replaces the challenge of accounting for the mind-dependence of reasons with the challenge of accounting for the dependence of reasons on our rational functioning. It is precisely in the

[1] For the original elaboration of this notion, see Raz (2011: ch 2).

[2] For the sake of consistency with my previous analysis, I should be talking about the truthmakers of legal propositions rather than legal facts. Occasional lapses into this more familiar expression are simply meant to economise on the use of lengthy jargon.

context of this switch that Raz's concept of the normative/explanatory *Nexus* becomes operative. Whereas traditional externalists about reasons affirm and internalists deny that there is always a reason to do what would in some respect be *right*,[3] Raz's *Nexus* provides a negative answer to the question of whether there is always a reason to do what would in some respect be *good*.[4] Reasons, according to Raz, must be capable of guiding us, but not every fact that would make our actions good in a certain respect is a reason to act, because there are values that we may not be able to recognise or respond to.

The *Nexus* is presented as an explanation of the occasional mismatch between response-dependent reasons and response-independent values by operating as a filter on what could count as a reason: reasons are such that they are capable of guiding our actions by virtue of our awareness of them. In Raz's words: 'The point is that normative reasons must be capable of providing an explanation of an action: If that R is a reason to φ then it must be possible that people φ for the reason R and when they do, that explains (is part of an explanation of) their action.'[5] The concepts of normative bearing, (the exercise of our) rational capacity and explanation of intentional action are the three components of the *Nexus* which I plan to recast in functional terms for the sake of rendering more intelligible their methodological relevance for a theory's normative robustness.

To illustrate the specificity of the region of normative space occupied by *Nexus* reasons, I will provide an anatomy of *Nexus* reasons by mapping their components onto the three normative roles (influential, evaluative and explanatory) I detailed in Chapter 5. These roles will also provide the metrics of normative robustness of a theory of normativity. A genuine *Nexus* reason-giving fact will be further analysed as a fact that performs all three roles in a given context. In the language of Chapter 5, this triple function of *Nexus* reasons can also be described as a case where a reason-giving fact is *response-directing* (axis of normative salience) and *depictively impactful* (axis of normative impact). In other words, such facts are apt for guiding our responses to practical problems, and their actual treatment by agents as normatively influential is evaluatively reflective (depictive) of the good or proper exercise of our rational capacity.

[3] The crux of the relevant controversy lies in identifying the relevance of facts about our actual or counterfactual motivational states for the grounding of facts about what reasons we have or what reasons exist. Despite their strikingly conflicting internal divisions, internalists hold that part of what it is for something to be a reason for action is that it must bear some relation to a motivational fact, whereas externalists model their position on the rejection of this schematic premise.

[4] In contrast to the possibility of motivation, the possibility of correctly exercising our rational powers does not track but rather limits the extension of the concept of a normative reason. Our rational capacities perform this limiting task by way of indicating which values are apt for serving as a standard of our appraisal *qua* agents. For an elucidation of Raz's departure from a standard internalist conception of the normativity of reasons, see Heuer (2012).

[5] Raz (2011: 27).

Consequently, a theory of normativity will be maximally robust when and because the facts it identifies as normatively relevant are genuine *Nexus* reasons. Raising awareness about the 'demandingness' of the *Nexus* as a habitat for competing metanormative theories will serve as the background for making better sense of how and why the available theories of legal normativity can be classified as thinner or more robust by reference to their approximation of the *Nexus* entanglement between normative bearing, evaluation and normative explanation.

It should be noted from the beginning that the attractive force of the *Nexus* does not necessarily lead to the espousal of an account of legal facts as *Nexus* reasons. What I intend to argue instead is that legal philosophers who choose to resist the idea that law provides reasons in the same way that interpersonal morality or prudence does tend to present their decision as a partial departure from what would count as an instance of robust practical normativity. The *Nexus* purports to be a theory about what makes something robustly normative; it does so by serving as a plausible case about the combined possibility of an agent's being directed by reasons and being evaluatively depicted in her action by virtue of her actually treating those same reasons as favouring or requiring her action.

In response to the concern that legal normativity can retain its status as a worthwhile topic only by appeal to its proximity to normative reasons, there has been an incremental recognition of the relevance of metaethical inquiry in addressing this problem. Fortunately, there is not just one way of rescuing legal normativity from the jaws of eliminative reduction. A variety of strategies have been offered to combat the spectrum of deflationist or quietist approaches to the question of whether law is normative. What is most important is the fact that the most robust defences of legal normativity draw upon the insights of metaethical theories of practical normativity marshalling arguments from classical teleology and philosophy of action,[6] constitutivism about agency[7] or a combination of the

[6] Veronica Rodriguez-Blanco develops her own teleological account of legal normativity by investigating what she describes as a paradox, namely how autonomous persons can allow the guidance of their actions by legal rules without compromising their autonomy. Her way of solving this puzzle is to model action governed by legal rules in the likeness of a particular conception of intentional actions as taken in, and because of, a belief that there is some good in them. The extension of the 'guise of the good' argument to law proceeds in two steps: first, she defends the broadly Aristotelian premise that reasons for action can in general be viewed as good-making characteristics of intentional actions and, consequently, she ventures to apply this idea to the case of following a legal rule. On this approach, acting on a legal rule is an action that is explicable in terms of the good-making characteristics (reasons) of more basic actions that serve as core instantiations of what it is to follow a legal rule. For a more detailed description of this view, see Rodriguez-Blanco (2012) and (2014).

[7] See Bertea (2009). Bertea aspires to draw a continuous line from the nature of human agency, through the domain of practical reason, to legal normativity. In his words, 'the essential features of the normativity of law, as well as of its obligatory force, can be arrived at by considering the normativity of the activity of which law is a special case, namely, practical reason. This is to say that, just as the normativity of practical reason is grounded in human agency, so is the normativity of law, and hence its obligatory force' (at 218). A non-Kantian version of the same constitutivist strategy is developed by Roversi (2011).

insights from theories of moral constructivism and discourse ethics.[8] Whereas there is little room for doubt that the prospect of marginalising normative nihilism about law is much safer now thanks to these contributions, there is a parallel concern I would like to raise with regard to the metanormative focus of these defences on the relationship between law and action-direction. What I intend to argue is that the platform of discussion about the normative import of law remains unwarrantedly narrow, mainly because most parties to this debate tend to measure the robustness of accounts of legal normativity by assessing their proximity to an ideal relationship between normative reasons and the explanation of intentional action. Even for legal philosophers who favour a very thin account of legal normativity, the grounds for their deflationary approach are a function of proximity to this region of perfect synergy between normative bearing, evaluation and explanation.

For the purposes of my exposition, I will single out Joseph Raz's account of authoritative reasons and Mark Greenberg's account of binding legal obligations as informative examples of how the *Nexus* model can be applied to a pair of radically opposed jurisprudential theories. At the same time, it would be totally misleading to suppose that all legal philosophers who pledge ontological commitment to legal facts are willing to make all the necessary concessions in order to model the normative force of legal facts in the likeness of ordinary reason-giving facts. In Chapter 7, I plan to defend the claim that, for an array of diverse reasons, Ronald Dworkin's principle-based account of legal obligation and Scott Shapiro's argument about the inner rationality of law are not fitting instances of the *Nexus* model. More precisely, the idea I aim to put forward is that the 'natural habitat' for Dworkin's conception of legal obligations as instantiations of principles of political morality is the quadrant featuring thick evaluation as its main occupant, whereas Shapiro's argument about the rationality of legal planning is unambiguously eligible for membership of the quadrant that also features wide-scope requirements of rationality.

If my intuition that the current debate on legal normativity is a local version of the standard treatment of the *Nexus* as a measure of normative success proves correct, I will be in a position to invoke this claim in the service of advancing my argument that legal philosophers who more or less explicitly subscribe to the metric approach are driven by the concern that any divergence in the identity or modal profile between the facts that bear upon, evaluatively test and

[8] Sylvie Delacroix is a major representative of this approach. She labels her account as 'genealogical' in the sense that it purports to explore the socio-culturally embedded conditions of its possibility. On this understanding, law's normativity gains in being understood 'dynamically'. In Delacroix's words, 'the normative dimension of law cannot ever be taken as a 'given' established once and for all, provided the officials' minimal commitment condition is verified. Understood dynamically, law's normativity may be said to be brought about everyday. Each time an individual is led to assess law's normative claims in the light of morality's demands, each time a judge is led to re-articulate what we want law for: these cases contribute to shaping the "fabric" enabling law's normativity' (see Delacroix 2009: 130).

explain legal conduct commits them to a thinner or more modest account of legal normativity. The ascription of this concern is not meant as an attempt at exegesis. For reasons that are structurally similar to those that have favoured the ascription of the metaontological view of legal propositionalism, I will also try to present this hypothesis as an attempt to charitably reconstruct the metanormative commitments of these theories. The purpose of this reconstruction is not to display any fatal inconsistencies in their reasoning about the normativity of law, but to alert the parties to this debate that its thorough adjudication requires full engagement in metanormative inquiry.

By virtue of their common metanormative background, I shall argue that Raz's *Normal Justification Thesis* and Greenberg's *Bindingness Hypothesis* can be meaningfully juxtaposed as competing first-order accounts about the determinants of the reasons for action provided by the legal facts.[9] In the light of these qualifications, the convergence I have attributed to my exemplary cases should not be considered as a sign of doubt about the extent to which legal positivism actually departs from the basic tenets that define antipositivist theories like interpretivism, moral impact theories or different versions of natural law theory. This is an evident truth I have no intention of refuting, precisely because I take it to be fairly uncontroversial that a legal positivist and a legal antipositivist do engage in a substantive and deep disagreement about the nature of law.

I. THE LIMITS OF THE METRIC APPROACH

As it turns out, my reconstruction cannot proceed on the mere assumption that my case theories are implicitly committed to the *Nexus* as a standard of normative robustness. The reason is that any putative appeal to this standard is evaluative, not constitutive, in the sense that it serves to measure the explanatory ambition of a theory of legal normativity rather than to dictate or pre-empt its metanormative commitments. The latter would be the case only if a given theory not only referred to the *Nexus* as a standard of robustness but also as a standard of correctness. On this hypothesis, legal facts would be normative if and only if they could emulate the normative function of ordinary reason-giving facts, that is, only if they could simultaneously require, evaluate and explain conformity with law. Since I am not willing to shoulder this much stronger presupposition, I am compelled to venture this reconstruction by introducing an internal division.

The explanatory role I have chosen to reserve for the metric approach is analogous to the role I assigned to legal propositionalism as a general thesis about

[9] It is not coincidental that the same pair of jurisprudential theories also figured in a first-order metaphysical dispute about the constituents of law. In ch 4, I argued at length that both Raz and Greenberg converge in their general acceptance of the possibility of legal constitution, yet they differ with respect to its 'materials'. Their metatheoretical affinity is, I tend to believe, a feature that is manifest across the board.

how the truthmakers of legal propositions are thought to be derived from the truth conditions of legal statements. In Chapter 2, legal propositionalism was presented as a *metaontological* thesis about the determinants of a theory's ontological commitments. In this chapter, the metric approach will be presented as a *metanormative* thesis about the determinants of a theory's normative robustness. In the same spirit in which non-reductivist (Greenberg and Raz), reductivist (Shapiro) and error-theoretical (Dworkin) approaches to the possibility of legal constitution were presented as different ways of implementing the basic rationale of legal propositionalism, I will also venture to offer three variants of the metric approach that track a similar pattern of division.

As one might easily guess, the defining feature of each variant will be a function of its proximity to the *Nexus* model of reasons. As a result, the first variant of the metric approach will be a direct application of the *Nexus* model to the legal case. Likening legal normativity to the *Nexus* presupposes that legal facts are such that they simultaneously operate as decisive or *pro tanto* considerations, as standards of appraisal for law-conforming agents and as normative explanations of instances of law-conforming behaviour. In section II, I will present Joseph Raz's account of authoritative legal directives and Mark Greenberg's account of binding legal obligations as two exemplary cases (one positivist and one antipositivist) of the *Nexus* conception of legal normativity.

As expected, the other two variants of the metric approach will deviate from the *Nexus* model to the extent that (and because) they take legal normativity to be less robust in certain respects. Their full elaboration will have to wait until Chapter 7, where I will spell out in contrastive terms the emerging metanormative disagreement between *Nexus* theories of legal normativity and their discontents (positivist and antipositivist). In anticipation of how these two remaining variants can be modelled as thinner versions of the *Nexus* model, we should bear in mind that the three prominent features of *Nexus*-consistent facts are their capacity to serve as reasons for action, their role as standards for appraising the actual ways in which we exercise our rational capacity and their role as normative explanantia of occurrences that can be described as acting for reasons. Consequently, attempts to mitigate the robustness or aspirational force of law as a source of *Nexus reasons* will feature legal facts either as lacking the capacity to independently serve as a standard for actual evaluation or as lacking the capacity to independently provide normative direction.

In this regard, there will emerge two routes of (partial) departure from the *Nexus* model which I plan to discuss in the next chapter. According to the first route, legal facts turn out to be moderately normative[10] in the sense that

[10] My use of the term 'moderately normative' is strictly associated with the fact that according to the metric approach, anything that falls short of emulating the model of *Nexus* reasons also falls short of operating as a robust normative standard.

they preserve their response-directive salience, but lack depictive impact – or, conversely, they are constitutively impactful. According to the second route, legal facts are moderately normative in the sense that they preserve their depictive impact, but lack the capacity to provide reasons for action – namely, to be response-directing. On this alternative picture, legal facts will play the role of response-constraining attitudinal facts that give rise to wide-scope rational requirements.

The first moderate variant seeks to downsize the scope of distinctly legal reasons to *institutional* reasons on the broadly Kantian basis that, as Arthur Ripstein puts it, law does not purport to answer 'the moral philosopher's familiar question of how people *ought* to treat each other, but the distinctively political question of how they may legitimately be *forced* to treat each other'.[11] According to this view, legal facts are also normative reasons, but their institutional character is such that it renders their evaluative impact *constitutive* rather than depictive. In what follows, I will specifically associate this position with Ronald Dworkin's account of the 'force of law' by suggesting that according to his theory of law as integrity, legal facts literally provide reasons for *enforcement on demand* rather than direct reasons for *action*. Despite appearances, *reasons of integrity*, as I would prefer to call them, are not exclusively addressable to legal officials, but, as Dworkin explicitly says, apply to all members of a community or forum of principle (legislatures, executives, judges and citizens). Each and every member of such a community is invited to take a globally reflective or 'protestant', in Dworkin's words, attitude towards the responsibilities of government vis-a-vis its citizens. The latter attitude is taken to be essential to a people 'united in community but divided in project, interest, and conviction'.[12]

According to this approach, to assume an interpretive stance towards the content of the law is to make a plausible case about the obtaining legal facts that justify the enforcement of rights and duties on demand. In this regard, reasons of integrity are less robust in the sense that despite their being full-fledged normative reasons, the evaluative impact of their possession need not be reducible to a psychological fact about an agent's actual attitudes. An agent can act on the basis of reasons of integrity and thus be evaluated as showing equal concern and respect for all members of the community on a counterfactual basis. As Dworkin remarks, the evaluative property of displaying equal concern and respect towards our fellow citizens 'is an interpretive property of the group's practices of asserting and acknowledging responsibilities … not a psychological property of some fixed number of the actual members'.[13]

[11] Ripstein (2004: 6).

[12] Dworkin (1986: 413). Gerald Postema believes that Dworkin's 'protestantism' goes far beyond this reflective viewpoint that every citizen should be urged to take in interpreting what the content of the law requires in particular circumstances; see Postema (1987).

[13] Dworkin (1986: 201).

The second moderate approach seeks to reverse the priority of action-direction over consistency in action by denying that legal facts or whatever these facts are reducible to provide reasons for action while retaining the component of depictive impact as what marks the model's proximity to the *Nexus* quadrant. As I plan to argue, Shapiro's argument about the inner rationality of law is a typical instance of this mitigating approach. According to this alternative view, legal facts impose rational constraints on the combination of attitudes that legal officials are allowed to adopt towards future legal planning. In that sense, their normative salience is not manifested as a compass for choosing the morally, rationally or prudentially best master plan, but as a constraint on what those who accept a legal system's master plan can further intend with regard to its implementation, preservation or modification.

Inevitably, the scope of planning normativity is more limited than the normative scope of the previous variants of the metric approach, as it is mainly addressed at legal officials or, more generally, those who are institutionally involved in the production, implementation and preservation of legal plans. The way in which this second thinner variant retains its affinity with the *Nexus* paradigm is not by providing reasons of a limited sort, but by evaluating the instrumental rationality of legal officials as they are actually (instead of counterfactually) depicted in their plan-following activities. In this regard, it remains crucial that according to this approach, legal officials remain rationally criticisable for failing to obey legal authorities.[14]

II. LEGAL FACTS AS *NEXUS* REASONS

Perhaps the most common platitude is that *if law is robustly normative*, the relevant reason-giving facts are legal facts or whatever these facts are reducible to. Of course, no legal positivist will endorse the further premise that legal facts are themselves normative facts. This is not a problem for friends of the metric approach, as it is perfectly possible for ordinary descriptive facts to figure in relations of 'being a reason for' precisely because what is normative is the relation itself and not (necessarily) its relata. In other words, unless one wishes to subscribe to an idiosyncratic version of the metric approach that treats certain classes of fact as intrinsically reason-giving, there is no theoretical pressure to explain how a legal positivist can even think of treating legal facts as eligible reason-giving facts.

By contrast, I would hazard to guess that most antipositivist theorists would be willing to accept that legal facts are at least capable of qualifying as

[14] As Shapiro remarks: 'The inner rationality of law, of course, is a limited set of constraints because the rational norms of planning only apply to those who accept plans. The bad man, therefore, cannot be rationally criticisable for failing to obey legal authorities insofar as he does not accept the law. On the other hand, since most officials do accept the master legal plan, they are criticisable for disobeying the law absent a compelling reason to do so' (Shapiro 2011: 183).

normative facts, given some further premises. It is a further question whether on an antipositivist picture, a legal fact is extrinsically normative (by virtue of more basic moral facts) or generically normative *qua* instance of a generic or universal fact (a fact about the essential properties of legal norms or a principle). For example, an antipositivist could argue that a fact cannot qualify as a legal fact unless it is capable of providing rational guidance according to a set of moral criteria or, alternatively, she could argue that there can be instances of defective legal facts, that is, legal facts that fail to provide rational guidance precisely because they fail to felicitously instantiate the criteria that establish their reason-giving capacity.

In what follows, I will employ the tripartite distinction between the influential, the evaluative and the explanatory role of normatively relevant facts in order to give a general description of how, in light of the metric approach, legal facts would manage to function in the likeness of ordinary *Nexus*-type reasons for action. More precisely, I will suggest that what explains the eligibility of *Nexus* reasons for serving as a marker of normative robustness is the fact that *Nexus* cases are those where one and the same reason-giving fact manages to simultaneously perform three distinct metanormative roles, each one corresponding to the three elements noted above: normative influence (the influential role), the evaluation of the exercise of our reasoning capacities (the evaluative role) and the explanation of actions done for reasons (the explanatory role).

Consequently, I will suggest that to say that a theory of legal normativity is robust with respect to the *Nexus* standards of reasonhood is to say that law-given reasons are such that they figure, within a given context, in three distinct metanormative claims about the performance of each role: (a) a practical claim about which facts bear upon a particular response; (b) an evaluative claim about which facts serve as standards for appraising an agent's exercise of her rational capacities; and (c) an explanatory claim about which facts make an event of intentional action normatively intelligible.

Putting the formal similarities of positivist and natural law theories aside, the most attractive part of the story consists in their nuanced divergence with respect to how legal facts can be simultaneously operative on all three axes of normative relevance. The contrast I would like to showcase is more illustrative than exegetical in the sense that one can plausibly encounter interesting variations within each jurisprudential camp. Moreover, it goes without saying that my target theories do not offer any explicit remarks that verify their espousal of the taxonomical model I am trying to defend. As a result, my intention of suggesting an informative map of available accounts of legal normativity is modest enough to welcome the possibility of there being alternative routes to introducing the same theoretical distinctions. That said, there is an informative, internal distinction to be drawn among theories of law that tend to favour in more or less explicit ways an account of legal normativity that emulates or purports to emulate the robustness of *Nexus* reasons. This distinction is visible from all three perspectives (influential, evaluative and explanatory) on the role of normatively relevant facts. I would venture to claim that this distinction roughly corresponds to a very broad sketch of the positivist–antipositivist divide, at least, in the sense that it tracks the pattern of relevance of moral facts for law.

The reason why I insist on labelling this correspondence as rough is that in contrast with what determines legal content, questions of legal normativity are answerable by recourse to normative facts either as direct determinants of the content of legal reasons for action and/or as determinants of the normative truth that a given legal fact *is* a reason for action. In other words, whereas for a legal positivist, normative facts can never figure as determinants of legal facts, it is inevitable that they will figure in one way or another as determinants of the normativity of descriptive legal facts. Fortunately, this is not a contradiction in terms as it is perfectly intelligible to submit that much in the same way as ordinary descriptive facts are not intrinsically reason-giving but can nevertheless figure in reason-giving relations to actions or attitudes, legal facts are not intrinsically reason-giving facts. According to this assumption, it is possible to assume that the normative fact(s) that will determine the degree of normative pressure or force exerted by legal facts will not also be constitutively implicated in the determination of the facts themselves. As a result, it remains an open line of reasoning for the legal positivist to construct her account of legal normativity in such a way that the premises of the latter will not contradict with the metaphysical premises of her account of what determinates the content of the law.

Keeping this caveat in mind, we can return to the question of how the divide between legal positivism and legal antipositivism can be 'inherited' by accounts of legal normativity. As noted earlier, this distinction supervenes on a general background agreement with regard to what counts as robustly normative and, as such, it is not a distinction that merits a meticulous treatment similar to how we would treat matters marked by deep disagreement. Nevertheless, it serves the purpose of rendering the espousal of the metric approach more fine-grained.

The first aspect of this distinction regards the way in which positivist and antipositivist accounts of legal normativity diverge in their assessment of the role of legal *content* as such in normative action-direction. Normally, the more irrelevant the invocation of the content of a legal fact is for assessing its reason-giving capacity, the closer we get to a positivist understanding of legal normativity, whereas if the reverse is true, it is safer to assume that by and large, our theory will favour a more substantive role for normative facts not only with respect to the normativity of law but also with respect to its metaphysics. The second aspect of this distinction regards the sources of evaluation of legal agents appealed to by positivist and antipositivist supporters of the *Nexus* variant. Positivist accounts tend to appraise actions done for legal reasons as being depictive of people's degree of rationality, whereas antipositivist accounts are more prone to appeal to the virtue of law-abidance as the leading evaluative concept. Finally, I shall argue that whereas both positivist and antipositivist simulations of the *Nexus* model are committed to a subsumptive or nomological model of normative explanation, they differ with respect to how they define the counterfactual 'tenacity' of legal facts. Positivist accounts are more compatible with a systematic appeal to a legal system's disposition of being generally efficacious, whereas antipositivist accounts are more charitably interpretable as appealing to the normative notion of defect in their treatment of perturbing counterfactuals involving justified law-breaking behaviour.

A. The Influential Role of Legal Facts

In this section, I will apply the idea of normative influence to legal facts by way of associating it with two variants of legal reasons for action: *content-independent*, as the legal jargon goes, and *generic* legal reasons for action. Beginning with the concept of content-independence,[15] it should be noted that it has acquired the shell of a technical term used by analytic legal philosophers to describe the broadly positivist claim that the obtaining of a reason-giving relation between a legal fact and an act-type is independent of the directive's specific content and/or consequences. At the risk of absurdity, this claim does not entail the further claim that the obtaining of this relation is independent of the obtaining of any normative fact whatsoever. The only constraint it imposes is that *the normative fact* that a legal (descriptive) fact is a reason to φ is grounded in normative facts that are not about the *content* or the *essential function* of legal norms.[16] According to this construal, the fact that that it is legally required to φ is a content-independent reason to φ in the sense that the reason why this fact and not another one is normatively salient has nothing to do with its constituent parts – that is, with the moral merit of φ-ing or the consequences of its being authoritatively prescribed.[17]

[15] The term was coined by HLA Hart; see Hart (1958: 102) and Hart (1982: 254–55). For a critical discussion of this notion, see Markwick (2000) and Sciaraffa (2009).

[16] Mark Greenberg refers to content-independence as a necessary but not sufficient condition for the constitution of legal norms. He notes that: 'Even if a command has the effect of creating an obligation to do as commanded for a reason independent of the content of the command, it doesn't follow that the explanation is simply that it was so commanded. There might still be explanatory intermediaries – e.g., the explanation might be that *because of the command* – not because of its content – it is fair to do as commanded. The property that is needed is the one I have spelled out in the Explanatory Directness Thesis. Content independence is necessary but not sufficient for Explanatory Directness' (Greenberg 2011: 47). I believe that Greenberg's reasons for associating content-independence with explanatory directness are ill-founded. The latter is a metaphysical thesis about how legal norms are created, not about how legal reasons are created. As a result, authoritative pronouncements may very well create (or constitute) legal norms without explanatory intermediaries, but this has no bearing on how facts about the existence of legal norms provide reasons for action. Facts about the provision of reasons for action by legal facts are, par excellence, normative facts. The only qualification that the content-independence thesis imposes is that the facts that ground these normative facts are not about the merits of the content of legal norms.

[17] I have deliberately chosen to avoid scholarly variations of the term 'content-independent reason' with a view to showcasing the core idea on which competing positivist theories seem to converge. For instance, in Raz's account of legal positivism, the 'exegetical' analogue of content-independence

Joseph Raz explicitly embraces content-independence as a prominent feature of the way in which legal facts – that is, facts about the existence of legal norms – mandate action. At the same time, he is cautious enough to add that it is not a distinctive feature of guidance by legal reasons, mainly because there are other groups of concepts like promises and vows, offers and threats or requests and commands that also operate on the model of content-independence.[18] Provided that legal authority is not the only type of authority capable of providing external guidance, Raz associates the generic notion of practical authority – that is, the normative power of a person or institution to impose duties on others[19] – with content-independent reasons precisely because their bindingness or, alternatively, the fact that they favour or require action is not grounded in the value of the content of these reasons, but on the fact that they are proper manifestations of the exercise of one's practical authority.

would be the *first-order* component of a protected reason. In Raz's own unpacking of the term, '[r]ules and commitments are what I call protected reasons, i.e. a systematic combination of a reason to perform the act one has undertaken to perform, or the one required by the rule, and an exclusionary reason not to act for certain reasons' (Raz 1999b: 191). My emphasis on excluding the second-order component – also known as 'exclusionary reason' – is well-thought-out in the sense that I reserve a distinct position for the concept of an exclusionary reason on the second, evaluative role of legal facts. My idea is that it would ultimately be in the service of Raz's point to resist registering exclusionary reasons as an ontological addition to an already-layered ontology of reasons for action. The notion of an exclusionary 'reason' can be better accounted for as a figurative allusion to the evaluative dimension of norm-guidance in the sense that compliance with an exclusionary reason can be logically understood as the attribution of the evaluative property of rationality to an agent that chooses not to act on competing first-order reasons.

[18] Raz (1986: 35–37).

[19] Whereas it is intuitively possible to accept that practical authority is definable as the normative power to impose duties on others, things get murkier if we try to extend this definition to the case of political or legal authority. The reason is that it is not conceptually clear whether political or legal authority is more like a normative power rather than, say, justified coercion or the right to rule. The latter notion is distinctly Kantian in its origin as it emphasises the relational character of political authority. In this regard, I would hazard to claim that despite appearances, it is wrong to reductively interpret the Kantian model of political authority as a model for justifying state coercion. For Kant, the permissibility of state coercion is conceptually entailed by the right of a civil state to rule over its citizens rather than vice versa. In this regard, the exercise of state coercion is non-instrumentally linked to political authority by virtue of its being a manifestation of the latter rather than a means of achieving an end that holds independently of the relationship between the rulers and the ruled. By contrast, a more genuine emphasis on the notion of justified coercion can be found in the work of more contemporary political philosophers like John Rawls and Thomas Nagel, who, despite their markedly Kantian bent, have developed their ideas on an original or emancipatory rather than exegetical or scholarly basis. Both stand in favour of a liberal principle of political legitimacy that is triggered by the coercive practices of modern states. Rawls frames the pivotal question as 'in the light of what reasons and values … can citizens legitimately exercise … coercive power over one another?' with a view to advancing as a solution the claim that 'political power is legitimate only when it is exercised in accordance with a constitution (written or unwritten) the essentials of which all citizens, as reasonable and rational, can endorse in the light of their common human reason' (Rawls 2001: 41). In a similar vein, Thomas Nagel argues that 'it is this complex fact – that we are both putative joint authors of the coercively imposed system, and subject to its norms … that creates the special presumption against arbitrary inequalities in our treatment by the system … This request for justification has moral weight even if we have in practice no choice but to live under the existing regime' (Nagel 2005: 128–29).

That said, Raz proceeds to incorporate the notion of content-independence into his theory of authority by noting that:

> [A] reason is content-independent if there is no direct connection between the reason and the action for which it is a reason. The reason is in the apparently 'extraneous' fact that someone in authority has said so, and within certain limits his saying so would be reason for any number of actions, including (in typical cases) for contradictory ones. A certain authority may command me to leave the room or to stay in it. Either way, its command will be a reason. This marks authoritative reasons as content-independent. By this feature they can be distinguished from many reasons, including various other kinds of utterances that are reasons.[20]

By contrast, a generic reason is not a term I would hazard to directly attribute to any legal philosopher, but, nonetheless, I consider it apposite to the spirit of many antipositivist accounts of legal normativity. For instance, the concept of defect as it is usually employed by defenders of the *Weak Natural Law Thesis* is standardly associated with the failure of a law to be a rational standard of conduct.[21] On this approach, a legal fact is generically reason-giving in the sense that its failure to provide a reason for action is indicative of its being a defective instance of a normative kind, so to speak. Employing Judith Jarvis Thomson's normative analysis of directives,[22] we could reparse this claim as a proposition to the effect that:

> If L is a legal fact, then for it to be the case that L is a reason for A to φ is for it to be the case that there is a directive kind K (LAW) such that L is an instance of K and if a K doesn't provide a reason for action, then it is a defective K.

Legal facts are, then, *generically* reason-giving precisely in the sense that they are reason-giving *qua* instances of a normative kind rather than reason-giving *simpliciter*. Taking the above formulation as a template of how legal facts could operate as generic reasons, I would like to go a step further and expand the applicability of this concept to antipositivist theories that cannot be classified as belonging to the classical natural law tradition of legal thought. In this regard, I would like to try to extrapolate Mark Greenberg's view on legal normativity from his elaboration of what he calls the 'bindingness hypothesis'.

According to Greenberg, the bindingness hypothesis is a hypothesis about the way in which legal obligations are related to all things considered moral obligations. He proceeds to formulate this hypothesis by remarking that 'a legal system is supposed to operate by arranging matters in such a way as to reliably

[20] Raz (1986: 35).

[21] Mark Murphy's more apposite formulation states that 'necessarily, law is a rational standard for conduct. It is of the nature of law to provide a set of standards that rational agents should take as a guide to their conduct' (Murphy 2003: 244).

[22] Thomson (2008: 207 ff).

ensure that its legal obligations are all-things-considered morally binding (or, equivalently, that a legal system is *defective* to the extent that it does not so operate)' (emphasis added).[23] Greenberg attempts to illustrate this claim by offering the example of the relationship between the legal obligations about tax payment and the moral obligations about the redistribution of resources. If, in a particular legal system, there is a legal obligation to pay tax on one's income in accordance with a certain scheme, the legal system will be morally defective to the extent that it remains morally permissible not to pay the income tax. Greenberg explicitly associates this remark with legal normativity when he clarifies that: 'An intuitive way of putting the point is that the law is supposed to be binding, where that means genuinely binding all things considered – not just legally binding (which the law trivially is).'[24]

Keeping this connection in mind, we can see how his theory of legal normativity can be read as carrying a generic[25] claim about the way in which facts about the obtaining of legal obligations are normatively influential. The crucial link in this analysis is to be found in Greenberg's choice to disassociate his own account of bindingness from general accounts of political legitimacy that purport to explain how we come to acquire a general moral obligation to obey the laws of our political community. Greenberg acknowledges that the bindingness hypothesis is amenable to an alternative formulation that features in its antecedent the possession of legitimate authority and a general moral obligation to obey the law (political obligation) in its consequent. To avoid this route, he draws a distinction between two putative ways in which the operations of legal systems can change the content of our moral reasons.

According to the first approach which Greenberg explicitly associates with authority-based theories of law, legal systems achieve bindingness by possessing legitimate authority – that is, by arranging matters so that citizens have a general moral obligation to obey legally authoritative pronouncements. This approach does not endow legal facts *themselves* with the power of generating particular reasons for action, but rather switches their role into that of merely enabling conditions for the instantiation of a general moral obligation to obey what becomes part of the content of the law of a given system. By contrast, Greenberg's favoured approach purports to turn bindingness into a property of legal facts themselves in the sense that a legal system operates properly when the actions of its institutions change the circumstances that, in combination with the most fundamental moral truths or principles, determine the content of our moral obligations. On this understanding, legal facts *are just* the moral significance of these new circumstances.

[23] Greenberg (2011: 85).

[24] ibid.

[25] Genericity is used in the technical sense of denoting the cluster of properties associated with instances of a *kind* (natural, social, normative etc).

With this distinction in mind, we can proceed to reformulate the above-mentioned formula about generic reasons in a way that closely resembles Greenberg's conception of bindingness:

> If L is a legal fact, then for it to be the case that L is a reason for A to φ is for it to be the case that there is a directive kind K (Legal System) such that L is part of the normative content of K and if a K doesn't arrange matters so that the constituent parts of its normative content do not provide reasons for action, then it is a defective K.[26]

B. The Evaluative Role of Legal Facts

Moving to the second evaluative standard for measuring a theory's responsiveness to the *Nexus* standards, the question to be asked is how agents are evaluatively reflected in their law-conforming behaviour. As evidenced by the relevant literature, the most appealing option for the legal positivist is to associate one's treating a legal fact as a reason for action with one's being (locally) *rational* in following a legal directive. Arguments about the inner rationality of law or the rationality of being guided by authoritative rules are commonly used by positivist philosophers who want to keep their normative vocabulary free of thick moral terms (like being law-abiding) or thinner moral terms (like being morally praiseworthy). At the other end of the spectrum, antipositivist appeals to the virtue of law-abidance or the moral praiseworthiness of giving weight to how the actions of legal institutions affect what we ought to do are, as expected, more apposite to the role assigned to morality by antipositivist theories of law. In what follows, I will apply the same pattern of exposition by illustrating how the same two exemplary instances of legal positivism and legal antipositivism converge in their metanormative commitment to legal facts as standards of agential evaluation.

Joseph Raz's revisionist approach[27] to rule-guided behaviour is the main source of information as to how he prefers to model the evaluative impact of

[26] In this more specific formulation, bindingness and the concomitant notion of defect are strictly speaking properties of legal systems rather than of legal obligations or, more precisely, of facts about the obtaining of legal obligations (legal facts).

[27] I borrow this term from Edward McClennen's taxonomy of theories of rule-based rationality. According to McClennen: 'The revisionist agrees with the compatibilist that rule-guided behaviour does have a real place within an instrumental theory of justification, but one that forces us to revise the standard account of practical reasoning. The revisionist, then, denies that if the rule gives the wrong result it would be irrational to follow it' (McClennen 2004: 225). He then immediately proceeds to classify Raz as a paradigmatic revisionist by noting that revisionism has attracted a significant following in recent years. One can trace this, to a large extent, to the influence of Joseph Raz, who argued that it might be rational to act in ways that are not recommended by the balance of reasons. According to Raz, 'rules can constitute 'second-order reasons' – *exclusionary* reasons – not to act on certain first-order reasons, where the latter are the sorts of reasons that lend themselves to the balancing approach. When an exclusionary reason applies, the first-order reasons that are

legal facts – that is, of facts about the existence of legal norms. The gist of this approach is that under certain conditions, it is rational to follow a rule even if on balance, the reasons suggests otherwise. This general idea about how rules impact our practical reason is further specified by Raz's notion authoritative *pre-emption*. In Raz's words, this model states that an authoritative directive is not simply one reason to be added to the balancing of reasons in determining how to act, but 'should exclude and take the place of some of them'.[28] Reparsed as a principle of rationality pre-emption can be also understood as saying that it is irrational not to see the directive as excluding certain first-order reasons[29] from the process of balancing because this would amount to counting the reasons behind the directed action twice: once in the balancing done by the agent herself and again in establishing the reason backing the authoritative directive.[30]

My reconstructive intervention consists in my proposing an understanding of Raz's notion of pre-emption and the auxiliary concept of an exclusionary reason as elements of an evaluative account of what it is to be 'legally' rational, rather than as elements of a metaphysical account of how legal reasons exclude other reasons by virtue of their kind and not by virtue of their weight. There is an abundant secondary literature that purports to make sense of how reasons of authority are endowed with this exceptional capacity of excluding other reasons from being part of the case for an action. Part of the difficulty of positioning Raz's pre-emption thesis within the broader family of exclusive positivist theories is that there is a persistent ambivalence in Raz's writings about the conception of exclusion between a metaphysical, so to speak, understanding of exclusion as a distinct *property* of authoritative reasons and a psychological understanding of exclusion as a *way* of reasoning or being practically rational in contexts of authoritative guidance.[31]

On many occasions, Raz seems to endorse the latter view, for instance, when he notes that: 'The only proper way to acknowledge the arbitrator's authority

excluded by it are completely removed from the balance of reasons. Thus, it would be possible that a balance of first-order reasons recommends an action but that the existence of an exclusionary reason requires the agent to disregard that recommendation and act in a different manner' (ibid).

[28] Raz (1986; 58).

[29] There has been a gradual shift in Raz's view about the type of first-order reasons that are subject to exclusion. In the second edition of *Practical Reason and Norms*, Raz suggests that 'one ought to exclude all the reasons both for and against [the prescribed act] which were within the jurisdiction of the authority' (Raz 1999b: 191; see also Raz 1989: 1194). In his later work, he confines the scope of exclusion to first-order reasons against an act prescribed by a rule claiming that '[t]he service conception [of authority] expresses that thought by the thesis that authoritative directives preempt those reasons against the conduct they require that the authority was meant to take into account in deciding to issue its directives' (Raz 2006: 1018). For a critical account of Raz's oscillation with regard to the scope of exclusion, see Essert (2012).

[30] Raz (1986: 58).

[31] Kenneth Ehrenberg locates the same ambivalence when he remarks that, strictly speaking, authoritative directives purport to track the *reasons* that apply to those subject to legal authority rather than the *reasoning* that leads an agent to act in conformity with those reasons. Ehrenberg frames this distinction as holding between law's claiming authority and law's demanding that we treat authoritative directives as pre-emptive; see Ehrenberg (2013).

is to *take* it to be a reason for action which replaces the reasons on the basis of which he was meant to decide' (emphasis added).[32] However, this subjective language is frequently replaced by a more objective, so to speak, language that portrays legal norms or, more precisely, facts about the existence of legal norms as defeating other reasons not by virtue of outweighing or overriding them, but by virtue of removing them from deliberation. Raz identifies this unique property of reasons produced by the say-so of an authority with the second-order property of being an exclusionary reason. According to this metaphysical approach, exclusionary reasons are second-order reasons not to act on first-order reasons. For instance, in this rather metaphysical tone, Raz observes that: 'Every legal rule requiring the performance of an action (or its omission) is a reason for the performance (or omission) of that act and also an exclusionary reason for not acting on conflicting reasons which are not themselves either legal norms or legally recognized reasons.'[33]

Despite these conflicting formulations, it is worth proceeding on the charitable assumption that Raz would not accept an inflationary treatment of the concept of pre-emption such that both interpretations are taken to convey different aspects of the same idea. A promising way to see that, despite his occasionally ambiguous prose, Raz actually treats exclusionary reasons not as an addition to the metaphysical inventory of normative entities, but as a evaluatively laden description of what it is to reason *well* with rules is to focus on his distinction between the behaviour of *conforming* and the behaviour of *complying* with a reason. In the postscript to the second edition of *Practical Reason and Norms*, Raz sets out to clarify how he purports to use the concept of an exclusionary reason by employing an informative distinction between conforming with a reason simply by acting in accordance with its content and complying with a reason by way of treating the relevant consideration as what makes one's action worthy of being performed. With this distinction in mind, Raz proceeds to label exclusionary reasons as negative second-order reasons the distinctive mark of which is that they count against *complying* (rather than just conforming) with other reasons to act in particular ways. It is the latter association that lends definitive support to the psychological role of exclusion.

Consequently, it is possible to argue that whereas the only thing that happens from a strictly metaphysical point of view is that the fact that a legal norm exists is or provides a first-order, content-independent reason to act as the norm stipulates, there is a another level at which an agent is required *not to treat* (or, equivalently, *not to comply with*) competing first-order reasons as bearing on the question of whether to act in conformity with a legal norm. This second level is not meant to qualify what it is for a legal fact *to be* a reason for action, but rather what it is for an agent to *treat a legal fact as a reason for action*. To treat

[32] Raz (1985: 10).
[33] Raz (1999b: 144).

a legal fact as a reason to φ is simply to treat it as an exclusionary reason which further entails that one must not treat other facts as reasons for not φ-ing.

On this approach, it is easy to see how pre-emption can be understood as Raz's preferred specification of the evaluative role of legal facts. What marks the evaluative dimension of pre-emption is precisely the property of *irrationality* attached to agents who fail to appreciate the exclusionary force of legal reasons. In the present context, the rationality of being guided by legal rules is supposed to be evidenced by the fact that law-conforming agents are more likely to conform with reasons that apply to them independently of the legal authority's say-so by treating a legal fact as an exclusionary reason – namely, *by not treating other non-legal facts as reasons not to act in conformity with a legal norm.*[34] Consequently, a positivist like Raz could claim that legal facts perform their evaluative role in the sense that treating them as (exclusionary) reasons for action constitutes an instance of rational behaviour.

At the opposite end of the jurisprudential spectrum, rationality gives way to moral standards of appraisal that fit better with the pivotal role antipositivist philosophers accord to morality broadly construed. As noted earlier, there are at least two ways in which an antipositivist can explain what it is to treat a legal fact as a reason for action. In other words, there are two ways in which an agent can be portrayed as being evaluatively reflected in her law-conforming behaviour on a broadly antipositivist conception of acting for legal reasons. The first and perhaps most prominent way is virtue-ethical in spirit, as it features law-abidance as the primary evaluative property. John Finnis attempts to locate a solution to the problem of 'how an obligation-imposing law provides a reason for action which would not exist independently of that law'[35] in the idea that a correct way to identify 'the law-abiding subject's practical reasoning'[36] is to reason as follows:

A. For the sake of the common good, we need to be law-abiding.
B. But where φ is stipulated by law as obligatory, the *only* way to be law-abiding is to do φ.
C. Therefore, we need [it is obligatory for us] to do φ where φ has been legally stipulated to be obligatory.[37]

On this broadly natural law-inspired conception, legal facts perform an evaluative function to the extent that they serve as standards for the attribution of the virtue of law-abidance. Crucially, law-abidance as a virtue does not amount to

[34] Raz's own distinction between mere conformity and compliance with reasons counts in favour of this reparsing of exclusionary reasons as a rational property which agents can be possessed of if they choose not to act on competing first-order reasons. In this vein, exclusionary reasons – as opposed to the first-order reasons they purport to protect – are such that they can only be complied with (not conformed) precisely because their function becomes apparent as soon as the agent acts in recognition of the value involved in authoritative guidance.

[35] Finnis (2011: 314).

[36] ibid 315.

[37] ibid 316.

a disposition to obey the law *qua* law regardless of its moral merits. As William Edmundson explains: 'The law-abiding regard the law as invariably a reason for action, but they are not generally disposed to obey regardless of their own assessments of the moral and rational merits.'[38]

According to a more deontological approach, the normative impact of treating legal facts as reasons for action need not involve the attribution of a monadic thick evaluative property to agents. The same evaluative task can be carried out in relational terms, in the sense that agents who treat their legal obligations as generating reasons for action are considered as morally praiseworthy by their fellow citizens. I must confess that I lack sufficient textual evidence for positioning Greenberg's account of legal bindingness within the thick–thin spectrum of moral evaluation. That said, there are occasions in his writings where he talks about our 'abiding concern'[39] with law, remarking that 'the way in which the law is supposed to generate an obligation for a person to act is not by giving the person extremely strong prudential reasons, in particular by threatening that person with sanctions'.[40] He contrasts this legally improper way of ensuring bindingness with what he calls the *legally proper* way of giving agents reasons for action. Part of what makes this reason-giving legally proper is that these reasons are not merely prudential reasons for action.

According to Greenberg's account, properly generated legal obligations are those that are morally binding, all things considered. In that sense, we are allowed to assume that what it is for an agent to treat a legal fact as a reason for action must be similar to what it is for the same agent to treat a moral fact, that is, a fact about her duty to act as morality requires, as a reason for action. Consequently, it would make sense to attribute to Greenberg the view that treating one's binding legal obligations as reasons for action serves as a standard of moral praise in much the same way that acting in recognition of one's moral obligations makes a person morally praiseworthy.

C. The Explanatory Role of Legal Facts

For a complete view of what it is for a legal fact to operate as a *Nexus* reason, we need to fix one more parameter. What we have seen so far is that both Raz's and Greenberg's theories of law are robust enough to allow legal facts to operate as reasons for action and be evaluatively relevant. What remains is a positive answer to the question of whether legal facts can also serve as normative explanations of law-conforming behaviour. In this regard, I shall argue that both positivist and non-positivist *Nexus* variants of the metric approach have a strongly similar conception of how normative explanations of law-conforming

[38] Edmundson (2006: 3).
[39] Greenberg (2014: 1341).
[40] Greenberg (2011: 83).

behaviour are to be modelled. I shall argue that whereas both positivist and non-positivist simulations of the *Nexus* model are committed to a subsumptive model of normative explanation, they differ with respect to how they define the counterfactual 'tenacity' of legal facts. The common yet not expressly voiced idea is that there is an informative analogy between legal and 'nomic' facts with respect to their explanatory function. This is precisely the reason why I will favour the term 'subsumptive' for the model of explanation I will impute to positivist and antipositivist theories of law that implicitly treat legal facts *as if* they were a non-natural subclass, so to speak, of nomic facts.

The analogy I aim to put forward between the explanatory function of legal and nomic facts is purely methodological in its aspiration and it is not meant to be an argument in favour of a global treatment of universally quantified facts. Moreover, the ambition of this analogy is moderated by the fact that it is notoriously difficult to single out a metaphysically neutral definition of nomic facts precisely because there is an unabated controversy with regard to their status as necessary, contingent (regularity-based) or dispositional facts.[41] Hopefully, nothing of crucial importance depends on taking sides in this debate. What is important is that on either competing conception, nomic facts are taken to have independent explanatory force such that atomic facts can be subsumed under them in an informative way.

The term 'subsumption' is broad enough to include under its scope both sides of the analogy I am employing with a view to describing the way in which normative explanations in law are commonly understood. Following a broad-brush approach, all varieties of subsumptive explanation converge in their treatment of universal facts of some sort: to explain an atomic fact *is just* to show how it falls under some universal fact. The latter fact can be about a law of nature, a normative principle or a nomic generalisation of an inexact science. Varieties of subsumptive explanation are common in both scientific and normative domains.[42] After all, it would be reasonable to assume that there is a conceptual affinity in appeals to the countable instance of the noun 'law' in legal (or para-legal) and scientific contexts alike. More precisely, the idea is that insofar as legal facts are universal in the sense that they are multiply exemplifiable

[41] Lange (2009: 194–95).

[42] Mark Schroeder informatively associates representatives of the British moral rationalist movement of the eighteenth century like Ralph Cudworth, Samuel Clarke and Richard Price with what he describes as the standard model of normative explanation. In Schroeder's reconstructive definition of the subsumptive model of normative explanation: 'The explanation that *X* ought to do *A* because *P* follows the *Standard Model* just in case it works because there is (1) some further action *B* such that *X* ought to do *B* and (2) not just because P and (3) P explains why doing *A* is a *way* for *X* to do *B*' (Schroeder 2005: 11). Schroeder takes the example of promise-making as a typical candidate for normative subsumption. The idea is that facts about promises are not independently reason-giving, but rather trigger the instantiation of an antecedent, general moral obligation to keep promises. In Schroeder's own analytic words, '[i]t is not *qua* showing up for lunch at Plato's Diner that an action is ever right or wrong or something I ought to do. It is only because it is an instance of keeping a promise, which is something that I independently ought to do, that I ought to do it' (at 13).

by atomic or singular legal facts about what one is legally obligated to do in a particular circumstance, it follows that instances of law-conforming behaviour can be normatively explained by reference to an obtaining general legal fact.

This 'nomological' model of normative explanation can be further adjusted to one's jurisprudential allegiances such that both for a positivist and an anti-positivist, legal facts can be likened to the nomic generalisations of the inexact sciences, thus being capable of supporting a basic set of counterfactual conditionals. The counterfactual stability of legal facts is commonly articulated in terms of a 'general efficacy' condition on legal systems. The latter term can be understood in dispositional terms such that the norms constituting the content of the law of a legal system at a particular time are such that they are normally obeyed. Based on this construal, a legal fact can enjoy the status of a quasi-nomic, explanatory generalisation so long as it can exhibit a sufficient degree of invariance under counterfactual perturbations.[43] This scope of invariance may include platitudes to the effect that a legal norm would still have been complied with even if law subjects do not actually attach any moral value to it. The latter counterfactual can be supported by a legal fact for as long as it remains conceptually consistent with what is conceptually entailed by one's jurisprudential theory.

Joseph Raz's specification of the efficacy of legal norms involves a shift of focus from the practices of law-enforcing institutions to the practices of law-applying institutions. In his words:

> [E]fficacy … is relevant only insofar as it affects the practices of the law-applying institutions. If, for example, the courts consistently refuse to act on a law, that law is not part of the legal system the courts operate, despite the fact that it was lawfully enacted and was never repealed … According to this approach, then, the existence of the law is logically related to the practice of the law-applying organs.[44]

Raz proceeds to associate this conception of efficacy in application with what he takes to be the proper type of counterfactual supported by facts about the existence of legal norms. The definition he stands up for serves to mitigate the demandingness of general efficacy by focusing on the counterfactual attitude of recognition of the validity of a legal norm by the courts. He notes that:

> The condition of a law's membership in a legal system is, however, a counterfactual: if presented with the appropriate case the courts would act on the law.[45] This may

[43] Philosophers like Hans Kelsen have gone a step further by arguing that the efficacy of laws may affect their validity. In his words, '[a] general legal norm is regarded as valid only if the human behaviour that is regulated by it actually conforms with it, at least to some degree. A norm that is not obeyed by anybody anywhere, in other words a norm that is not effective at least to some degree, is not regarded as a valid legal norm. A minimum of effectiveness is a condition of validity' (Kelsen 1967: 11).

[44] Raz (1971: 803–04).

[45] At a later point, Raz introduces a probabilistic criterion that can be authentically determined by the law-applying institutions of a given system. According to this criterion, a legal system and

> be true even though they are never-or seldom-presented with the appropriate case. Prosecutions in criminal cases may seldom be made, and civil cases may always be settled out of court in a way contrary to the law. Therefore a law may be valid even though it is largely inefficacious.[46]

On a broadly natural law approach, the counterfactual that legal facts are supposed to be successful at supporting is more likely to be generic by virtue of its content. Again, there are two ways to frame this counterfactual condition of stability. Assuming the correctness of the weak natural law thesis – that is, necessarily anything that does not exhibit a particular kind of normative feature (for example, serving as a rational standard for conduct) is either not law or is defective *qua* law – it is possible to determine the content of the relevant counterfactual by appeal to what distinguishes an alegal entity from something that is law but is defective as such. Hence, the counterfactual stability line can be drawn along the intersection of these two instances such that a legal norm remains efficacious and thus explanatorily potent if it is *constitutionally* capable of serving as a rational standard for conduct, even if it fails to non-defectively realise its capacity.[47]

Appeals to constitutional capability can be made intelligible by a common idea permeating both the strong and weak versions of natural law theory, according to which something is constitutionally incapable if its composition, content or configuration is such that it cannot even count as eligible for performing the function of rational guidance. On the natural law construal of legality, a legal fact can enjoy the status of a nomic generalisation insofar as it is capable of supporting the above counterfactual, which entails that even if it is somehow *defective*, it can still preserve its explanatory potency. On the contrary, would-be legal facts which, given a specified set of criteria, are *constitutionally incapable* of providing rational guidance – think of morally odious laws or extremely vague or irreversibly contradictory laws – will fall short of qualifying for legal facts and thus will fail to explain their instances in any informative way.

In a slightly different manner, antipositivist philosophers that deviate from the natural law canon are more likely to shift their focus from the constitutional capability of legal norms to serve as standards of rational conduct to the capacity of legal obligations to be morally binding all things considered. This is precisely the line followed by Greenberg when he claims that the actions of legal institutions are supposed to make the moral situation better by ensuring that the legal obligations they create provide decisive reasons for action. He makes this point explicit by combining two claims about the nature of legal systems.

consequently its norms remain efficacious 'if a certain ratio of cases of obedience to its laws to the total number of opportunities to obey them obtains' (Raz 1980: 203).

[46] Raz (1971: 804).

[47] For the purposes of formulating a natural law condition of counterfactual stability, I am relying heavily on Mark Murphy's account of constitutional capability. For the latter notion, see Murphy (2013).

The first claim is already familiar: it states that legal systems are supposed to ensure that the actions of legal institutions generate legal obligations that are morally binding (the Bindingness Hypothesis). The second claim is that 'it is part of the nature of law that a legal system is supposed to change our moral obligations in order to improve our moral situation – not, of course, that legal systems always improve our moral situation, but that they are defective as legal systems to the extent that they do not'.[48] The combination of these two claims results in the view that a legal system is not merely supposed to produce binding legal obligations, but to do so in a way that improves the moral situation.

With this combined claim in place, we may proceed to formulate a condition of counterfactual stability for legal facts that does not depend on a general efficacy clause, but rather invokes the bindingness of legal facts as the basic criterion of counterfactual tenacity. In other words, the idea is that legal facts will be capable of explaining atomic instances of law-conforming behaviour to the extent that, *despite their violation and partly because of their violability*, they remain morally binding in what Greenberg calls the *legally proper way*.[49] In much the same way as the explanatory status of moral principles is not affected by their actual violation, general legal obligations do not lose their explanatory potency simply because they are violated in practice. So long as they are binding in a way that makes the moral situation better, they retain their capacity to serve as normative explanations of actual conduct.

[48] Greenberg (2014: 1294).

[49] In a footnote to 'The Moral Impact Theory of Law', Greenberg acknowledges the strong connection between the notion of the legally proper way of changing the moral profile and the improvement of the moral situation. He notes that 'it is part of the Moral Impact Theory that the legal institutions that are relevant for its purposes – the ones that generate those moral obligations that are legal obligations – are ones that are supposed to improve the moral situation ... this point is really an elaboration of the notion of the legally proper way of changing the moral profile ... That is, in order for a change in the moral profile to come about in the legally proper way, it must be the result of action by a legal institution that, by its nature, is supposed to improve the moral situation' (Greenberg 2014: 1324).

7

Two Levels of Disagreement about the Normativity of Law

THE PICTURE I have presented so far serves to showcase how positivist and antipositivist applications of the metric approach can converge in their espousal of the *Nexus* variant, namely the most robust version of how law can be a source of normative reasons for action. The crucial test for verifying a theory's affinity with the *Nexus* model is to test whether the facts it postulates as normatively relevant can perform the three distinct roles (influential, evaluative and explanatory) I have associated with the notion of normative relevance in a synchronised manner.

On the one hand, I argued that an authority-based theory of legal normativity like Joseph Raz's theory of reasons generated by a legal authority contains the necessary elements for being modelled as a *Nexus*-type theory. More precisely, I tried to show that three distinct features of his theory of law – namely, content-independence, pre-emption and efficacy – enable what Raz takes to be a fact about the existence of legal norms to mandate an action (the influential role), to make its actual treatment as a pre-emptive reason a standard of rational agency (the evaluative role) and to normatively explain instances of law-conforming behaviour (the explanatory role).

On the other hand, I have tried to apply a similar method with a view to testing whether Greenberg's moral impact theory of law is eligible to be associated with the *Nexus* variant of the metric approach. The findings have been equally encouraging, thanks to Greenberg's strong association of proper legal obligations with all things considered to be moral obligations. By analogy, the three features of his theory that inclined me to label him as a *Nexus* theorist are the generic grounding of legal reasons for action, the legally proper way of changing the moral profile and the Bindingness Hypothesis. By virtue of the first feature, it turns out that it is an essential function of legal facts to provide decisive reasons for action in the sense that their failing to be binding, all things considered, marks a failure of the legal system that produced them. Second, part of what it is to be a properly generated legal obligation is that it enables agents to act independently of the mere pressure of prudence, which further implies that their treating a legal fact as a reason for action can result in their being considered as morally praiseworthy. Finally, precisely because legal obligations are taken to be morally binding all things considered, they retain the same degree of 'recalcitrance' to the disturbing effect of their actual violations which makes them fit to serve as counterfactually stable general explanations.

In what follows, I would like to steer the discussion back to its original focus on the nature of theoretical disagreement about law. By way of a similar breakdown to the one I reserved for the concept of theoretical disagreement about the metaphysics of law in Chapter 4, I would like to explore the hypothesis that legal normativity, much like legal truth, can be an object of theoretical disagreement. More precisely, the idea I have in mind is that the site of theoretical disagreement about the normativity of law can be properly reconfigured if we allow its scope to be wide enough to host both first-order and second-order disputes. In this regard, I will suggest that a proper statement of the site of theoretical disagreement about legal normativity must unpack its object in a way that encounters the same challenges we encountered in the first part with regard to the metaphysics of law. To that effect, I would like defend the idea that the relevant kind of theoretical disagreement is about the *grounds of the normative facts concerning the way in which legal facts or whatever these are reducible to bear upon conduct*. In contrast to the previous question of what grounds legal facts, our present concern is with the grounds of normative facts about legal facts or, equivalently, what grounds the normativity of legal facts.

Before proceeding with a more detailed presentation of how this type of disagreement can bifurcate into first-order and second-order variants, I would like to unpack a bit further the rationale behind the level of abstraction I have chosen to use in describing the site of theoretical disagreement about the normativity of law. I have deliberately chosen not to specify the structure of facts about the normative relevance of legal facts precisely because according to the two-dimensional framework I developed in Chapter 5, action-direction is not the only way in which a fact can be normatively relevant. Consequently, it will matter for our purposes whether two competing theories of legal normativity converge in their metanormative views on the precise way in which legal facts can be normatively relevant. If, for instance, two theories converge in their espousal of the general principles of the *Nexus* model, their disagreement becomes ipso facto first-order as it turns out to relate to the grounds of one and the same type of normative fact, namely, the fact that a legal fact gives someone a reason to act in a particular way. By contrast, if two theories diverge with regard to their metanormative commitments, their disagreement can become intelligible as a second-order dispute about the way in which legal facts are normatively relevant.

With these caveats in mind, I intend to divide this analysis into two distinct steps. The first step will feature two metanormatively convergent theories of law, namely Joseph Raz's account of reasons generated by a legal authority and Mark Greenberg's account of binding legal obligations, as being engaged in a first-order dispute about the grounds of legal reasons for action. More precisely, I shall argue that these two theories can be meaningfully juxtaposed on the basis of a common, first-order normative controversy, namely the political relevance of legal reasons. The second step will feature Ronald Dworkin's account of the force of law and Scott Shapiro's argument about the inner rationality of law as instances of a partial deviation from the *Nexus* rationale.

In much the same way that the same two theories were presented as being engaged in a second-order dispute about the possibility of legal constitution, I shall argue that what makes their opposition to *Nexus*-type theories of legal normativity intelligible is their dissenting view on the *normative* relevance of legal facts rather than the political relevance of legal *Nexus reasons*. That said, I should caution against forming the impression that, for instance, Dworkin's account of reasons of integrity is purely metanormative in its aspiration. Besides the fact that Dworkin would abhor such a classification for reasons that are well known, the point is rather that his preponderantly first-order account of the *political* relevance of reasons of integrity can be meaningfully contrasted with *Nexus*-type theories *only* by way of questioning their metanormative assumptions about the way in which legal facts display their *normative* relevance.

I. FIRST-ORDER DISAGREEMENT ABOUT THE GROUNDS OF *NEXUS* FACTS

One type of episode of disagreement about legal normativity can transpire against a common metanormative background. Given the essential profiles of the theories I have chosen to juxtapose, it turned out that Joseph Raz's account of reasons given by a legal authority and Mark Greenberg's account of binding legal obligations seem to converge in their metanormative assumptions. As noted earlier, both theories fit nicely with the most robust variant of the metric approach to legal normativity. In both cases, legal facts can be modelled as providing reasons for action of the *Nexus* kind precisely because a legal fact is such that it can simultaneously provide *normative direction* and *depictively impact* an agent's evaluative profile by way of being *actually* treated as a reason for action. This is a more compact way of saying that a legal fact can simultaneously perform an influential, evaluative and explanatory role.

That said, their metanormative convergence ends there, as evidenced by the fact that the two theories are radically different both in their conception of the nature of legal facts and in their account of what grounds the reason-giving force of these facts. With regard to the former difference, I should note again that for Raz, legal facts are *descriptive* facts about the existence of legal norms, whereas for Greenberg, legal facts are *normative* facts about the obtaining of legal obligations, powers, privileges and immunities. This metaphysical differentiation is informatively inherited by their latter justificatory difference, namely the way in which the reason-giving force of legal facts is grounded.

It is the latter type of difference that constitutes a proper object of first-order theoretical disagreement about the normativity of law. More precisely, the hypothesis I want to explore is how a Razian positivist and a Greenbergian antipositivist can meaningfully disagree about what grounds the *normative* fact that a legal fact is a reason to act in a particular way. I shall name this type of normative fact a *Nexus* fact precisely because it is a fact about the way in which a legal fact is *robustly* reason-giving. It is important to notice that the grounds of this dispute are not interchangeable with another, metaphysical type of dispute, namely the question of what grounds legal facts themselves! As one may recall, the latter type of dispute is such that a proponent of the descriptive character of legal facts and a proponent of the normative character of legal facts can meaningfully disagree only at a higher level of abstraction, where the question at stake is about the nature of legal grounding – namely, about the question of whether the grounding (rather than the grounds) of legal facts is a brute fact or a fact made intelligible by recourse to conceptual or normative considerations. By contrast, regardless of what one takes to be the character of legal facts per se, we also need to answer the *first-order* question of what grounds another type of *non-legal, normative* fact, namely the fact that a legal fact (whether normative or descriptive) is a reason to act in a particular way!

In the light of this crucial clarification, I suggest returning to the stage the two familiar aliases, Gonzo and Froddo, as illustrative impersonations of a Razian positivist and a Greenbergian antipositivist respectively. For the sake of brevity, I will replace my repetitive use of the expression 'legal fact' with the variable *L* mainly because in the current context, it does not matter whether a legal fact is structured as a descriptive fact about the existence of legal norms or as a normative fact about the obtaining of a legal obligation. We may take the following exchange between them as an instance of the relevant first-order dispute I want to showcase:

(a) Gonzo: the fact that L is a reason for A to φ in C is grounded in the fact that A is more likely to conform to reasons that apply to her independently of the actions that brought about L by φ-ing in C.
(b) Froddo: the fact that L is a reason to φ in C is grounded in the fact that the actions that brought about L changed the morally relevant circumstances in a way that makes φ-ing in C the right thing to do.

This exemplary episode of disagreement between Gonzo (the Razian positivist) and Froddo (the Greenbergian antipositivist) is centred on the question of whether and how legal facts can change the content of our normative reasons. From Gonzo's perspective, legal facts, instead of changing our antecedent reasons, replace them with reasons provided by a legal authority on the grounds that acting on these new reasons increases the probability of conforming to our antecedent reasons that obtain independently of the actions of legal institutions. From Froddo's perspective, legal facts are the result of the right-making impact of actions of legal institutions in the sense that their obtaining in the legally proper way marks a distinctive change in the content of our antecedent moral reasons.

According to this picture, the Razian *Normal Justification Thesis*[1] and the Greenbergian *Legal Propriety Thesis*[2] present an informative contrast between two visions of law's political relevance. This contrast is identified by the prominence of the role of authority in the former account and its striking absence in the latter account. The Razian conception of authority is paradigmatically instrumental in the sense that exercises of legal authority do not purport to effect a substantive change in the moral landscape, but to facilitate our responsiveness to its antecedently valid requirements.[3] What is crucially important is that according to this positivistic picture, legal authority is supposed to correctly track reasons whose content can be specified without reference to the concept of authority. By contrast, Greenberg's antipositivist vision reserves no place for authority for the simple reason that based on this view, the normative impact of the actions of legal institutions is taken to be of the right-making rather than of the facilitative sort, which means that institutional actions are deemed capable of changing what is the right thing to do in much the same way as ordinary descriptive facts can make an antecedently morally indifferent action morally obligatory.

That said, there is a crucial ambiguity in the notion of tracking antecedent reasons which I believe has in part misguided Greenberg in his criticism of Raz's account of legal authority. In 'The Standard Picture and its Discontents',

[1] In Raz's own words, the Normal Justification Thesis asserts that 'the normal way to establish that a person has authority over another person involves showing that the alleged subject is likely better to comply with reasons which apply to him (other than the alleged authoritative directives) if he accepts the directives of the alleged authority as authoritatively binding and tries to follow them, rather than by trying to follow the reasons which apply to him directly' (Raz 1986: 53).

[2] I have deliberately chosen this linguistic innovation with a view to illustrating in a symmetric way the contrast between these two views.

[3] Stephen Darwall contends that meeting the Normal Justification Thesis (NJT) is neither necessary nor sufficient for establishing that some person or institution possesses legitimate authority. His main line of criticism invokes the claim that Raz's understanding of practical authority as the capacity to create pre-emptive reasons holds him hostage to the so-called *wrong kind of reasons* problem. Darwall proceeds to define a central instance of this problem by remarking that: 'In considering whether to believe some proposition *p*, for example, it is simply impossible to conclude one's deliberation in a belief that *p* by reflecting on the desirable consequences of believing *p*. That is a reason of the right kind for desiring to believe that *p*, but not for believing that *p*' (Darwall 2010: 264). Darwall believes that Raz is vulnerable to this argument because, as he takes it, Raz claims that authority can be normally justified by virtue of the desirable effects (conformity with antecedent reasons) of treating authoritative directives as pre-emptive reasons. As a result, Darwall argues that the desirability of pre-emptive reasoning is the wrong kind of reason to justify one's belief that A has genuine practical authority over B. The problem with Darwall's criticism is that Raz would be happy to accept this conclusion and still argue that it does not affect the justificatory relevance of NJT. The reason is that Darwall takes the NJT to be a cumulative ground *both* for ascriptions of practical authority and applications of pre-emptive reasoning. But as I also briefly commented in the main text, the NJT only regards the former, not the latter instance; it does not state that A has authority over B because B has a reason to desire the benefits of treating A's directives as pre-emptive reasons, but rather because B's acting as the directive commands is a proper means of leading B to comply with reasons that apply to her independently of A's say-so. This point is made by Raz himself in a reply to Darwall's criticism; see Raz (2010: 299). For a critical account of both positions, see Star and Delmas (2011).

Greenberg drives a wedge between two ways in which law can achieve bindingness. The first approach which he rejects is the *morality-on-law* direction of dependence, by virtue of which 'the law changes morality simply by creating legal obligations that were not previously moral obligations. Given an obligation to obey the law, the law tows morality behind it'.[4] By contrast, the second approach which Greenberg comes to adopt is the law-on-morality direction of dependence, by virtue of which the law changes morality by changing the circumstances that, in combination with the most fundamental moral truths, determine our moral obligations. Greenberg then proceeds to associate the former *morality-on-law* approach with the *Standard Picture*, namely, the broadly Razian way of directly constituting the content of the law through the issuing of authoritative pronouncements.

As Greenberg himself remarks, the crucial difference between these two approaches is that in the former case, bindingness is supposed to be achieved by virtue of a general obligation to obey the content of authoritative pronouncements, whereas in the latter case, there is no such general moral obligation. The source of Greenberg's misunderstanding becomes visible the moment he argues that, as long as someone subscribes to the *Standard Picture*, 'the only way in which bindingness can be reliably achieved is by arranging matters so that citizens have a moral obligation to obey legally authoritative pronouncements. Thus, SP makes central the question of under what conditions citizens have a moral obligation to obey legally authoritative pronouncements'.[5] Despite Greenberg's recognition of Raz's explicit rejection of the possibility of a general moral obligation to obey the law, he proceeds to argue that Raz nevertheless remains captive to the problem of achieving bindingness because his piecemeal account of authority-induced reasons for action is too weak to account for bindingness *as Greenberg understands it*. In this regard, he remarks that 'since legitimate authority will be piecemeal, there will not be a single question of whether an authority is legitimate, but a vast number of more specific questions. Raz's theory therefore makes it difficult to know when the government has authority over someone, and thus whether the government can ensure bindingness'.[6]

I believe that Greenberg's emphasis on his understanding of bindingness puts the epicentre of his disagreement with Raz in the wrong ballpark, mainly because he takes for granted the fact that overall bindingness is the only way in which law can be normative. It should be recalled that the Bindingness Hypothesis does not amount to the claim that the law is a source of reasons for action, but to the far more robust claim that for every legal obligation, there can be a moral obligation with the same content. But this is not a vision that a

[4] Greenberg (2011: 98).
[5] ibid 99.
[6] ibid 101.

positivist like Raz has to embrace in order to engage in an informative disagreement with an antipositivist like Greenberg. For Raz, the sources – that is, the grounds of legal normativity – are extra-legal in the sense that it will always be an open moral question whether in a particular circumstance, the law succeeds in providing normative guidance. For Raz, the obtaining of a legal fact does not *eo ipso* mark a change in the moral profile precisely because the way in which Raz envisages the normative impact of law involves no *legally induced changes* in the pre-existing moral profile. By contrast, according to Greenberg's account, the sources of legal normativity are distinctly legal in the sense that *whenever* a new legal fact exists, there should be a change in facts about what is the right thing to do because, in his view, the actions of legal institutions operate as right-making facts.

I hope that these clarifications can help our understanding of where precisely the source of disagreement between these two theorists should be located. Although Greenberg tends to elevate this disagreement to the metanormative level, I remain confident that the crux of his disagreement with Raz is purely first-order and hence *political*. Greenberg's attempt to relocate this disagreement to the metanormative side is evidenced by the fact that he attributes to Raz and more broadly to defenders of the *Standard Picture* a failure to understand how bindingness is supposed to work. But this is not a failure that Raz deserves to own, precisely because he rejects bindingness on *first-order* grounds, namely for the reason that the legitimacy of legal authority is manifested in a system's capacity to facilitate our response to antecedent reasons rather than in a system's capacity to constitute reasons.

II. SECOND-ORDER DISAGREEMENT ABOUT THE NORMATIVITY OF LEGAL FACTS

At first sight, it seems that given how I chose to frame the dispute between the two imaginary discussants Gonzo and Froddo, it is conceptually impossible for a plan positivist or a legal interpretivist to intelligibly participate in the current version of the dispute without rendering it merely verbal. On the one hand, I plan to demonstrate that an interpretivist like Dworkin would retort that the direct effect of legal facts consists in their imposing constraints on how government should treat its citizens rather than on how citizens themselves should act. This stance preserves the concept of an action-directing reason as a salient feature of legal normativity, but it directs its application to institutional rather than ordinary action. On the other hand, there is ample evidence that a plan positivist like Shapiro would be very suspicious of any association of legal facts with reason-giving of any sort, robust or institutional. The reason is that for Shapiro, facts about the existence of plans are normatively inert and only attitudinal facts about the *adoption* of plans by institutional actors within a legal system can exert a normative pressure of some sort.

As I intend to explain later on, Shapiro's account of legal normativity is very thin in the sense that the kind of normativity he attaches to legal activity is not associated with the relationship between the output of this activity, namely, plans and the guidance of conduct of ordinary citizens. The latter type of action-direction is, according to Shapiro, a dispositional matter precisely because he believes that citizens can be guided insofar as they are either morally or prudentially disposed either by themselves or through a system's mechanisms of enforcement to carry out the planning output of their government. The only type of normative constraint imposed by law regards the *authorisation* of legal officials to plan for others, and this type of constraint is *not* associated with facts about the existence of plans, but with *attitudinal facts* about the beliefs of legal officials in the efficacy of a plan, as well as their representation, sincere or not, of a legal system's master plan as morally legitimate. Consequently, the only normative constraint that these attitudinal (not strictly legal in Shapiro's qualified sense) facts impose regards the *consistency* of attitudes of commitment of legal officials vis-a-vis following a plan, filling it out, ensuring its consistency with other plans and refraining from reconsidering it without a compelling reason to do so.[7]

Fortunately, this is not a real impasse as it is perfectly possible to engage both theories in an intelligible dialogue with the *Nexus*-type theories analysed above, provided that we are willing to elevate their objections to a higher level of abstraction. In what follows, I will start with Dworkin's account of the force of law in the hope that I can demonstrate how his main concern about the normative demands of law can be recast as a metanormative objection to theories of legal normativity that relate the reason-giving force of legal facts to their capacity to guide citizens. In this regard, I shall argue that whereas Dworkin does not intend to disassociate the citizen's perspective from legal action-direction, he wishes to draw a distinction between the *institutional* reasons provided by legal facts *themselves* and the reasons for *action* provided by a general associative obligation to obey the law. In a further step, I shall elaborate upon Shapiro's invocation of the inner rationality of law with a view to exploring the nature of his objection to more robust accounts of legal normativity. The hypothesis that I will venture to defend is that Shapiro would reject the platitude that law is robustly action-directing on the grounds that 'legal' plans themselves are normatively relevant by virtue of their being *represented as* serving a moral aim. Attitudinal facts about the moral representation of plans by legal officials rationally constrain the ways in which they can exhibit or retract their commitment to following a plan.

[7] Shapiro (2011: 183).

A. How Can a Legal Interpretivist Disagree with a *Nexus* Theorist?

The reason why I have decided to put Dworkin's case first in the order of analysis is that the position of his account is contiguous with the occupants of the *Nexus* quadrant precisely because both share the belief that legal facts are action-directing in one way or another. It should be noted that Dworkin's references to the normativity of law are rather scattered across his voluminous work, such that it becomes interpretively challenging to attribute specific commitments to him. First off, Dworkin's encoded way of referring to the normativity of law features the expression 'the force of law' as its main leitmotiv. Our first acquaintance with this concept takes place in *Law's Empire*, where Dworkin illustratively divides the path to law's imperial realm into two main components: the grounds of law, which, as we already discussed, regard the grounds of legal facts, and the force of law,[8] which Dworkin defines as 'the relative power of any true proposition of law to justify coercion in different sorts of exceptional circumstances'.[9] Dworkin appeals to ordinary legal practice to justify this distinction, noting that: 'Our lawyers and citizens recognize a difference between the question what the law is and the question whether judges or any other official or citizen should enforce or obey the law.'[10] The same point is presented as being verified on theoretical grounds. In this regard, Dworkin supplements his phenomenological claim with the claim that 'conceptions of law, which are theories about the grounds of law, commit us to no particular or concrete claims about how citizens should behave or judges should decide cases'.[11]

In the light of this distinction between the grounds of law and the force of law, there are two parallel questions I would like to raise, one about the taxonomical evidence that Dworkin's comments provide for his inclusion in the same normative quadrant that features practices of thick evaluation and another about the nature of his hypothetical disagreement with *Nexus* theorists like Raz or Greenberg. As I intend to argue, answering the first taxonomical question makes our guess at the answer to the second question a much easier task. If it turns out that for Dworkin, legal facts – which in his case, as we may recall, are more specifically formulated as facts about the instantiation of principles of political morality – provide reasons for action whose normative impact is of the constitutive rather than of the depictive sort, the metanormative grounds of

[8] Dworkin locates the bond between these two components in the fact that the grounds of law are also part of what grounds the normative fact that law provides reasons for enforcement upon demand. In his words: 'These two parts must be mutually supportive. The attitude a full theory takes up on the question how far law is commanding, and when it may or should be set aside, must match the general justification it offers for law's coercive mandate, which in turn is drawn from its views about the controversial grounds of law' (Dworkin 1986: 110).

[9] ibid. In a similar vein, Dworkin intensifies connection between legal facts and reasons for enforcement when he remarks that 'in a flourishing legal system the fact of law provides a case for coercion that must stand unless some exceptional counterargument is available' (at 110).

[10] ibid 109.

[11] ibid 112.

his disagreement with *Nexus*-type treatments of legal facts will become readily comprehensible.

To see why this could be the case, we should recall that *Nexus* reasons differ from *practice-based* reasons[12] by virtue of the fact that whereas the former associate one's evaluation *qua* agent with their actual treatment as reasons, the latter enable one's evaluation by requiring only their counterfactual treatment as reasons. In section I in Chapter 5, I described this contrast as being between one's depiction as being responsive to reasons in what she does and one's constitution as being kind, generous or cruel by what she does. Consequently, if reasons of integrity, as I proposed calling them, are *practice-based* reasons, the grounds of Dworkin's hypothetical dispute with a *Nexus* theorist must include reference to the fact that the normative impact of legal facts is constitutive rather than depictive. This is a metanormative rather than first-order argument precisely because it locates the relevant disagreement in what makes the 'practice' quadrant a more hospitable habitat for legal facts than the *Nexus* quadrant.[13]

As already evidenced by the textual references I provided above, Dworkin clearly associates the normative force of 'true legal propositions' or, in more precise language, of legal facts with their capacity to justify the enforcement of a claim of right or obligation on demand. Dworkin repeats this same point in his latest work when he remarks that 'legal rights [and their correlative duties] are those that people are entitled to enforce on demand, without further legislative intervention, in adjudicative institutions that direct the executive power of sheriff or police'.[14] This association between legal facts and reasons for enforcement on demand is accompanied by a distinction between the institutional reasons for enforcement provided by legal facts and the reasons for action provided by the fact about the obtaining of a political obligation, namely, a general moral obligation to obey the law.[15] Dworkin frames this distinction as being between the problem of the legitimacy of coercive power and the problem of political

[12] By this very general term, I intend to cover a wide range of institutional or social facts that give rise to reasons for action. As we saw earlier, a large group of practice-based reasons are reasons provided by facts about the instantiation of thick evaluative properties (ie, the fact that φ-ing in C is generous is a reason to φ). Another category is legal reasons as Dworkin purports to understand them. There may be other types of practice-based reasons that could fit in this quadrant like promissory reasons or reasons to play by the rules of a game.

[13] It is a conceptual implication of the two-dimensional model I am defending here that the nature of disagreement between theories occupying different quadrants will always be metanormative, whereas disagreements between theories figuring in a common quadrant will always be instances of first-order normative disputes.

[14] Dworkin (2011: 406). An alternative formulation in the same work states that: 'Legal rights are political rights, but a special branch because they are properly enforceable on demand through adjudicative and coercive institutions without need for further legislation or other lawmaking activity' (at 407).

[15] By presenting this distinction as being between reasons for enforcement and reasons for action, I do not intend to convey the thought that the former are not also, strictly speaking, reasons for action. Perhaps a more precise but slightly more verbose formulation of this distinction would feature reasons for institutional action versus reasons for action *simpliciter*.

obligation. In this regard, he notes that the former problem 'rides on the back of another classical problem: that of political obligation. Do citizens have genuine moral obligations just in virtue of law? Does the fact that a legislature has enacted some requirement in itself give citizens a moral as well as a practical reason to obey?'[16] Dworkin is willing to assert that there is such a thing as a general moral obligation to obey the law, which he further unpacks as a kind of associative obligation. However, unlike Greenberg, he cautiously disassociates the question of political obligation from the question of legal normativity proper:

> These two issues – whether the state is morally legitimate, in the sense that it is justified in using force against its citizens, and whether the state's decisions impose genuine obligations on them – are not identical. No state should enforce all of a citizen's obligations. But though obligation is not a sufficient condition for coercion, it is close to a necessary one.[17]

What enables Dworkin to separate these two questions and associate only the former question of legitimate coercion with the subject matter of legal normativity is the contrast he implies between the facts that provide reasons for enforcement and the facts that provide reasons for conformity. By virtue of their more specific meaning as facts about the *instantiation of principles of political* morality, legal facts are facts that purport to guide a state's adjudicative and executive institutions in realising (that is, enforcing on demand) claims of right and duty that best justify both past instances of coercive enforcement and current announcements about the future use of force or the imposition of sanctions. This strong connection in Dworkin's account between legal facts and reasons of enforcement is explanatorily upstream of his account of how legal facts obtain.

As a short reminder, we may recall here that in stark contrast to Greenberg's antipositivist metaphysics, Dworkin does not endorse the view that the relationship between the actions of legal institutions and legal facts is analogous to the relationship between right-making facts and facts about rightness. His view is nonlinear in the sense that the actions of legal institutions which he individuates by reference to their coercive impact *trigger* the principles of political morality which are embodied by a particular political community. This triggering consists in enabling more abstract principles to be instantiated by more particular obligations and rights. Now, for Dworkin, a legal fact is precisely a fact about this triggering, namely a fact about the *instantiation* of principles of political morality by more specific obligations or rights. The nonlinearity of his account is manifested by the fact that this triggering is justified to the extent that the particular obligations and rights that follow from more abstract principles can, in their turn, justify past and hence also future instances of coercive enforcement.

[16] Dworkin (1986: 191).
[17] ibid.

According to this picture, the relations of triggering, instantiation and justification of coercion are trapped in a purportedly virtuous circle of normative interpretation. What matters for our present purposes is that, precisely by virtue of their mode of obtaining, legal facts of this kind are facts that are tailored to provide reasons in order to justify the coercive enforcement of obligations and rights on official demand.

Becoming aware of this background story allows us to tap deeper into Dworkin's peculiar treatment of legal reasons for action as a specific kind of reasons for institutional action. The reason why I chose to characterise his treatment as peculiar is that he wants to preserve on board a pair of views that are typically taken to be mutually inconsistent, namely the view that legal facts provide piecemeal, case-by-case reasons for action and the view that law achieves bindingness via a general moral obligation to obey the law. He aspires to achieve this by marshalling two different kinds of fact, only one of which is strictly legal. On the one hand, he asserts that facts about the instantiation of principles of political morality by obligations or rights provide institutional reasons for enforcement on demand. These are typically legal facts that perform this task. On the other hand, the fact that members of a community of principle have a general moral obligation to obey the collective political decisions of their community provides atomic reasons for action by way of subsumption. This latter fact is not a legal fact, but a more abstract, political fact. At this level, the morality of political association tracks the content of the law by requiring whatever the law requires at a particular instance.[18]

To answer the taxonomical question I posed earlier – namely, whether reasons of integrity fall within the quadrant of practice-based reasons – it does not suffice to show that these reasons are institutional in the sense that they are reasons for the performance of institutional actions of official enforcement. As we may recall, practice-based reasons are distinguished from *Nexus* reasons not by virtue of their normative salience, but by virtue of their normative impact, that is, their capacity to condition the evaluation of an agent by way of constitution rather than by way of depiction. This difference is evidenced by the way we answer the question of whether one is supposed to recognise a fact as a reason for action in order to be eligible for a positive evaluation of

[18] Given that the purpose of my exposition is not to challenge Dworkin's account of political legitimacy, I would like to confine my comments to a calculated guess about what could motivate this peculiar combination of views. I believe that Dworkin thinks that one is entitled to preserve both aspects of bindingness so long as one disassociates the concept of authority understood as the normative power to impose duties on others from the theory of what brings legal obligations and rights into existence. Whereas I am sympathetic to the possibility of this disassociation, I remain sceptical about its prospect insofar as one is willing to preserve authority as explanatorily relevant for obligations of the associative kind. Dworkin makes this connection when he says that '[a] community of principle … can claim the authority of a genuine associative community and can therefore claim moral legitimacy – that its collective decisions are matters of obligation and not bare power – in the name of fraternity' (Dworkin 1986: 214).

her conduct. If the answer is positive, the reasons at hand are of the *Nexus* sort. If the answer is negative, which means that it suffices that one's ideal counterpart could treat this fact as a reason for action, the reasons at hand are practice-based reasons. Fortunately, Dworkin is fairly clear on this point as he provides the necessary textual material for concluding that reasons of integrity are indeed practice-based reasons – that is, constitutively impactful. In this regard, he remarks that:

> The responsibilities a true community deploys are special and individualised and display a pervasive mutual concern that fits a plausible conception of equal concern. *These are not psychological conditions.* Though a group will rarely meet or long sustain them unless its members by and large actually feel some emotional bond with one another, the conditions do not themselves demand this. *The concern they require is an interpretive property of the group's practices of asserting and acknowledging responsibilities – these must be practices that people with the right level of concern would adopt – not a psychological property of some fixed number of the actual members.* So, contrary to the assumption that seemed to argue against assimilating political to associative obligations, associative communities can be larger and more anonymous than they could be if it were a necessary condition that each member love all others, or even that they know them or know who they are. (Emphasis added)[19]

From the above passage, we can safely assume that the evaluative property of displaying equal concern and respect for others can be attributed to both citizens and legal officials on counterfactual grounds. On the one hand, insofar as a citizen's action *could be* informed by her recognition that a general obligation to obey the laws of a community of principle is a reason to act as she does in a particular context, this person is *constituted by* her actual conduct as a person driven by equal levels of concern and respect for her fellow citizens. On the other hand, a legal official that *could* treat a fact about what instantiates a (set of) principle(s) of political morality as a reason to enforce a right on demand is also *constituted by* the performance of her role as someone who treats members of this community with equal concern and respect.

In the hope that I have managed to settle the taxonomical question, there remains the less perplexing question of how we are to make sense of a hypothetical episode of theoretical disagreement between a proponent of Dworkin's view and a positivist or antipositivist proponent of the *Nexus* view. To see how this episode of disagreement could transpire, let us suppose that Dworkin himself intervenes in the previous exchange between our by now familiar *Nexus* fans Gonzo, the Razian positivist, and Froddo, the Greenbergian antipositivist:

(a) Gonzo: the fact that L is a reason for A to φ in C is grounded in the fact that A is more likely to conform to reasons that apply to her independently of the actions that brought about L by φ-ing in C.

[19] ibid 201.

(b) Froddo: the fact that L is a reason to φ in C is grounded in the fact that the actions that brought about L changed the morally relevant circumstances in a way that makes φ-ing in C the right thing to do.

What would be Dworkin's hypothetical reaction to this dispute? Could he, for instance, remark that the fact that L is a reason to enforce the obligation to φ in C is grounded in the fact that φ's enforcement is consistent with the principles that informed its enforcement in similar past cases? I believe that the reason why this could not be the case is obvious. The dispute would become merely verbal, as evidenced by the fact that whereas both Gonzo and Froddo appear to disagree about what grounds the fact that there is a reason to φ in C, Dworkin appears to disagree by offering his grounds for *another* type of fact, namely the fact that there is a reason to enforce the obligation to φ in C. As I have taken the liberty of mentioning many times so far, this is exactly what the two-dimensional model of disagreement I am trying to defend should predict.

A Dworkinian interpretivist cannot simply enter this disagreement without qualifying the content of her objection in second-order terms. This can be achieved if we remodel the same episode of disagreement as an instance of a metanormative dispute about the kind of reasons that law gives. According to this alternative picture, Dworkin's critical reply would be that both Gonzo and Froddo share the fallacious thought that legal facts are normatively relevant by virtue of their providing direct reasons for civilian action and, consequently, their grounding regards the way in which official actions can permissibly change our moral circumstances. He would supplement this response with the claim that reasons of law are institutional reasons and, consequently, the question of grounding that should concern us is not what explains the way in which official action changes what we ought to do, but what explains the fact that government officials have the power to force us to do what we ought to do.

Dworkin's hypothetical metanormative objection sheds light on the qualitative difference of grounding explanations that feature the principle of integrity as their main element. It must be evident by now that appeals to inclusive[20]

[20] Dworkin introduces this term in his effort to distinguish between the grounding relevance of integrity in the context of the generation of legal rights and obligations, and its grounding relevance in the context of how these facts about legal content acquire the force of reasons for enforcement on demand. In this regard, he notes that integrity in the latter context is not always sufficient to ground the normative force of legal facts, as exceptional circumstances may require the inclusion of considerations of justice and fairness as trumping determinants of the outcome. Dworkin develops this idea by noting that: 'The adjudicative principle that governs our law enforces *inclusive* integrity: this requires a judge to take account of all the component virtues. He constructs his overall theory of the present law so that it reflects, so far as possible, coherent principles of political fairness, substantive justice, and procedural due process, and reflects these combined in the right relation' (Dworkin 1986: 405). Based on this supplementation of integrity with other principles or values, he concludes that: 'The principle of integrity in adjudication, therefore, does not necessarily have the last word about how the coercive power of the state should be used' (at 219). He invokes the Fugitive Slave Act case to describe an exceptional occasion where what determined *what the law was* before the American Civil War (namely pure integrity) failed to also give *normative force* to this law; see Dworkin (2011: 411).

integrity serve to answer a normative question that *Nexus*-type theories of legal normativity fail to see as prominent. If my hypothesis about the possibility of metajurisprudential disagreement is sound, I would dare to assert that at least part of what explains this discrepancy is a conflict between different metanormative visions about law. This is not to say that a shift of focus from the way in which government affects our obligations to the responsibilities of government towards us is not marked by a shift in substantive political views. This is more than an apposite assumption. My point is rather that on some occasions, our first-order political disagreement should be mediated by a more abstract reflection about the orientation we strive to give to our theories.

In the present case, it appears that it is at least possible that the shape that Dworkin's account of integrity would take would not be the same if it turned out that legal reasons should be such that our evaluation *qua* agents depends on their actual rather than counterfactual treatment as reasons for action. This would beg the question to suppose that this conclusion could be avoided by mere appeal to the principle of integrity. The reason for this is that the question of whether it matters for our evaluation *qua* agents if someone is actually responsive to legal reasons, rather than counterfactually appreciative of their force, is explanatorily downstream of the question of whether the government is entitled to enforce our response to legal reasons. The order of these two explanatory tasks serves a conceptual purpose. If we could suppose that our starting question should be about what grounds the entitlement to enforce one's response to reasons, the question of whether it matters if we actually treat those reasons as reasons is easily discarded as conceptually misguided. If the pressing question is whether the *enforcement* of our response to reasons is permissible, it only matters whether we *could* treat those same facts as reasons. This counterfactual remains normatively compelling, even if we do not actually treat these reasons as relevant, either because we are motivated by other considerations or because we decide to break the law.

Finally, we should notice that by adhering to the suggested order of explanation, we need not be led to this same exclusionary result. If we agreed that it matters whether we actually treat legal facts as reasons for action, we would not count as being conceptually confused if we proceeded to ask the further question of when our response to legal reasons may be enforced. For instance, one may argue that a kind of principled enforcement like the one Dworkin defends is permissible because, for some legal reasons *independent of* the reasons for enforcement, official coercion *actually* facilitates us to conform because we can become aware of the relevance of these independent legal reasons.[21]

[21] This is an adapted rendition of AJ Julius' Independence Principle of interpersonal coercion. According to this principle, coercion between two persons is wrongful if A does y, intends by y'ing to bring it about that B does x, and fails to believe with justification that, for some reasons R independent of her, her y'ing facilitates B's [doing x because B takes R as giving her sufficient reason to x]. See Julius (2013: 365).

B. How Can a Plan Positivist Disagree with a *Nexus* Theorist?

The second instance of metanormative divergence from the *Nexus* is pithily represented by Scott Shapiro's planning account of legal normativity. In what follows, I will be referring to his account as a thesis about the inner rationality of law, a term which Shapiro describes as the body of rational requirements applicable in a given legal system.[22] As I am about to argue, what strongly recommends the positioning of his theory within the quadrant occupied by the requirements of rationality broadly construed is the limiting or constraining rather than robustly response-directing character of requirements emanating from the master plan and the body of subplans comprising the content of a legal system. Shapiro is willing to acknowledge that his account of legal normativity is rather thin, claiming that '[t]he inner rationality of law, of course, is a limited *set of constraints* because the rational norms of planning only apply to those who accept plans' (emphasis added).[23] Moreover, his way of associating the normativity of law with the normativity of rational constraints is indicative of the way he implements the metric approach, in the sense that he presents the rational normativity of 'legal' plans as a token of weaker normativity in comparison to the directional normativity of moral facts. In his words:

> [T]he normativity of the master plan of a legal system is *of a very limited sort. While legal officials are rationally required to conform to their shared plan, it is also true that those who do not accept the law are not similarly bound.* Furthermore, the master plan of a legal system may be morally illegitimate and hence not capable of imposing a moral obligation on anyone to obey. (Emphasis added)[24]

[22] Shapiro attributes the ownership of this term to Michael Bratman, who in turn has adapted Lon Fuller's famous phrase 'the inner morality of law'. In fact, Bratman develops his argument about the inner rationality of law partly with a view to interpreting Shapiro's original view on planning normativity. Bratman invokes Shapiro's Moral Aim Thesis, which, as Bratman notes, provides 'a model of a kind of sociality that helps solve these characteristic [moral] problems and thereby transmits, in means-end fashion, the normative force of general reasons we have to solve those problems to the specific legal actions mandated by the relevant planning structures' (Bratman 2011: 81). Bratman interprets Shapiro as attributing a transmissive function to plan requirements enacted by law in the sense that a legal plan enables pre-legal normative reasons to promote a given state of affairs to transmit their normative force to reasons for acting on the means that this legal plan makes salient. Bratman describes this process in the following way: 'there are, independently of law, reasons to solve the cited problems ... Law, we are now supposing, is a means to solving those problems. Law requires certain forms of conduct. So the reasons for solving those problems are transmitted by law to reasons for that conduct' (at 82). Whereas I do find Bratman's interpretation plausible, I tend to disagree in relation to the role it assigns to legal facts or facts about plans as triggers or enablers of normative transmission. The reason for this is that according to the planning theory of law, law is not just a mediating device between moral problems independently defined and their solutions. Law emerges before the individuation of problems on independent grounds by *representing* a system's master plan as a *morally legitimate* way of tackling the problems associated with the circumstances of legality. In that sense, law is also implicated in the identification of moral problems by way of representing its master plan as a morally proper blueprint for solving a particular set of problems represented as morally relevant.

[23] Shapiro (2011: 183).

[24] Shapiro defines these circumstances as follows: 'The circumstances of legality obtain whenever a community has numerous and serious moral problems whose solutions are complex, contentious,

The model Shapiro employs to describe the normative function of the practice of legal officials strongly resembles the type of normative pressure involved in ordinary instrumental reasoning. Legal officials adopt a master plan as a very general means of rectifying the moral deficiencies associated with the circumstances of legality.[25] Law appears as the mechanism that can determine which specific goals and values the legal system ought to pursue and also settle the questions that arise with regard to the achievement of those goals and the realisation of those values. In this regard, Shapiro sees the emergence of law as an institutional response to what he refers to as the 'complexity and contentiousness of communal life'.[26] Tellingly, as Shapiro remarks, the type of solutions that law offers are equally complex, contentious and arbitrary, which is why the actions of legal institutions must be capable of effecting a certain degree of normative closure by way of enacting norms. For that reason, Shapiro partly individuates the activity of legal officials by reference to its capacity to settle questions about how to act, noting that: 'Legal institutions are not in the business of either offering advice or making requests. They do not present their rules as one more factor that subjects are supposed to consider when deciding what they should do. Rather, their task is to *settle* normative matters in their favour and claim the right to demand compliance.'[27]

That said, an ambiguity lingers with regard to the relationship between settling or action-direction provided by plans and the normativity of legal planning *qua* activity. On the one hand, Shapiro is willing to accept that there is clear evidence of normative pressure with regard to the activity of legal planning. In particular, he associates this normativity with the normativity of facts about the adoption of plans. According to Shapiro, the latter type of planning normativity depends on the existence of two attitudinal facts: (a) the fact that the legal officials *believe* that a given subplan is a means of serving the purposes set out in the legal system's master plan; and (b) the fact that legal officials *represent* the system's master plan as a morally legitimate solution for what has been identified as morally problematic or contentious in a given community. Consequently, the normative pattern that plays out bifurcates in two consecutive theses:

> *The Authorisation Thesis*
>
> The fact that the legal officials of *S* represent the master plan *M* of *S* as morally legitimate response to the circumstances of legality gives rise to a rational requirement to [intend to plan for others, if they accept *M*].

or arbitrary. In such instances, the benefits of planning will be great, but so will the costs and risks associated with nonlegal forms of ordering behaviour, such as improvisation, spontaneous ordering, private agreements, communal consensus, or personalised hierarchies. Indeed, the costs and risks of nonlegal planning may be so large as to be prohibitive. Communities who face such circumstances, therefore, have compelling reasons to reduce these associated costs and risks. And in order to do so, they will need the sophisticated technologies of social planning that only legal institutions provide' (ibid 170).

[25] ibid 213.

[26] ibid 309.

[27] ibid 201–02.

> *The Inner Rationality of Law Thesis*
> The fact that the legal officials of *S* believe that *P* is a means to implement the master plan *M* of *S* gives rise to a rational requirement to [intend to fulfil, monitor and re-adjust *P* if the legal officials of *S* represent *M* as morally legitimate].

What is interesting about these two theses is that the facts that appear as normatively relevant – in the sense that they give rise to some rational constraints – are not descriptive facts about the existence of plans ('legal' facts), but *attitudinal* facts about the mental states of a group of legal officials. This is not paradoxical, at least if we pay more attention to Shapiro's recurrent distinction between the two components of the ability to plan for others. Shapiro notes that 'while the *authorization to plan for others* merely depends on the mental states of legal officials, the ability to plan depends on the mental states of ordinary citizens as well' (emphasis added).[28] At the same time, it must be possible for a legal process of planning to instil a disposition in citizens to conform to the requirements emanating from this process. To this effect, Shapiro notes that: 'Legal authorities have the ability to plan for others … only if they are able to motivate their subjects to obey under normal conditions.'[29] This can either be achieved by way of voluntary compliance on the part of those citizens who consider the relevant legal activity as morally legitimate or by way of coercive enforcement for members of the community who can only be prudentially motivated to comply.

In the light of this distinction between the normative (authorisation) and the dispositive aspect of legal activity, it turns out that according to the planning theory of law, legal normativity primarily concerns a certain aspect of the activity of legal officials rather than the entirety of what they do or the behaviour of citizens. This is not to say that citizens cannot also adopt an attitude of approval towards the master plan of a legal system as well as the plans for its implementation. If they are committed for whatever reason, we could also say that they are subject to the same rational requirements of consistency that bind legal officials. But their commitment is totally contingent, whereas it is necessary that legal officials represent their system as morally legitimate. In that sense, the attitudes of ordinary citizens are not a constitutive element of the normative aspect of legal activity, even though they remain a very important aspect of the dispositive aspect of legal planning.

With these clarifications in place, we may tap into the details of the two theses I presented above. The first normative thesis makes a general claim about

[28] ibid 421. Shapiro codifies the same point as follows: 'the Planning Theory claims that a body has legal authority in a particular legal system when two conditions are met: (1) the system's master plan authorizes that body to plan for others, and (2) the members of the community normally heed all those who are so authorized. Legal authority will be possible, therefore, just in case it is possible for both of these conditions to obtain' (at 180).

[29] ibid 179.

what type of normative requirement flows from another metaphysical thesis that Shapiro calls the 'Moral Aim Thesis'. According to the latter thesis, 'the fundamental aim of legal activity is to remedy the moral deficiencies of the circumstances of legality'.[30] Shapiro takes law to be a formidable and necessary supplement to other less sophisticated mechanisms of social coordination, such as custom, tradition persuasion, peer pressure, consensus and promise. Shapiro is very careful to distinguish between the *representation* of legal activity's aim as moral and the attribution of a normative *function* to law as such. This is crucial for his broader task of vindicating exclusive positivism as the correct theory of law, precisely because it must remain conceptually clear that the degree to which a legal system actually succeeds in improving the moral situation has no effect on the individuation of the legal system as legal. Shapiro makes this point when he claims that 'to say that the law's mission is to address the moral defects of alternative forms of social ordering is not to claim that legal systems *always* succeed in their mission … What makes the law *the law* is that it has a moral aim, not that it satisfies that aim'.[31] He then tries to disassociate the possession of a moral aim by law from its functional attachment to it by noting that to say that the law has a moral aim is nothing more than to say that 'high-ranking officials *represent* the practice as having a moral aim or aims. Their avowals need not be sincere, but they must be made' (emphasis added).[32]

On this approach, the *Authorisation Thesis* merely states the normative consequences of the Moral Aim Thesis. What it says is that facts about the representation of law or, more precisely, facts about the representation of the master plan of a legal system as serving a moral aim are normatively relevant by virtue of their giving rise to a rational requirement of instrumental consistency. This rational requirement should be read as taking wide scope over a conditional featuring the acceptance of the system's master plan as its content. In this way, we can say that the rational requirement to plan for others can be satisfied in two normatively asymmetrical ways. One way is for the group of high-ranking legal officials to abandon their commitment to representing this particular master plan as morally legitimate. The other way is for the same group to engage in the activity of producing plans that serve to guide the conduct of citizens.

To see why I have chosen to categorise this requirement as falling within the quadrant of general rational requirements, we need only observe that the way

[30] ibid 213.

[31] ibid 213–14.

[32] ibid 217. In this regard, if we want to be charitable about the plausibility of this distinction, the only avenue we can choose is the one I have also indicated with regard to the treatment of the property of legality *simpliciter*. In ch 4, I developed an argument about what the best understanding of Shapiro's talk of legality would be, noting that on the most charitable reading, legality is not a real property, but a second-order predicate that denotes the possession by planning organisations and plans of other real properties. In the same spirit, we could say that law does not really have the property of having a moral aim. On this charitable reading, to say that law has a moral aim is to say that law has the *property of being represented as having a moral aim* by high-ranking officials.

in which facts about the moral representation of a system's master plan become normatively salient is by *constraining* rather than directing our response. This is clearly evidenced by the fact that the only state of affairs that this type of requirement prohibits is the simultaneous preservation of a moral representation of the master plan and an akratic reaction towards the activity of planning for others. Beyond this negative prohibition, nothing about this requirement per se can provide decisive guidance as to how to steer a legal system.

Moving to the second thesis, it is fairly obvious that its function is ancillary to the foundational function of the rational requirement to plan for others. All it says is that there must be a rational pattern in realising the legal activity of planning for others. In this regard, it appears that the inner rationality of law consists in a set of rational requirements whose object is again a conditional rather than a particular response or course of action. This is a typical instance of a law-specific wide-scope principle of instrumental rationality, which by itself fails to provide robust guidance as to how to proceed, all things considered. The reason is that the above requirement can be satisfied in at least two ways that mark a distinct normative asymmetry. Necessarily, a legal official can satisfy this requirement either by intending to fulfil the plan or by ceasing to sincerely or pretentiously represent the system's master plan as morally legitimate. From the point of view of planning rationality *simpliciter*, the only normative constraint that obtains is that a legal official is necessary irrational if she persists in combining the following pair of attitudes: representing the system's master plan as morally legitimate *and* failing to intend to fulfil the plan that facilitates the implementation of the master plan.

The upshot of these interpretive remarks is that the normative aspect of legal activity is response-constraining rather than response-directing. This is not an outcome that should be regretted, mainly because it does not touch upon the dispositive aspect of legal activity that Shapiro emphatically associates with the guidance of both legal planners and ordinary citizens. This is another way to say that according to Shapiro's theory of law, the role reserved for normativity is limited in comparison to the space reserved for considerations of efficacy and trust between state officials.

That said, it is worth noting that Shapiro dedicates a considerable amount of space for detailing the way in which the legal activity of planning can also dispose the members of a community to abide by the requirements of legal plans. Shapiro's recognition of the guiding role of plans is expressed in a variety of argumentative modes. The most characteristic of these regards a set of recurring functional claims about plans like when, for instance, he remarks that '[t]here would be no point in making plans if we did not use them to guide our conduct'.[33] Other claims to the same effect are more metaphysical in nature.

[33] ibid 126. In the same spirit, Shapiro notes that 'shared plans are supposed to guide and coordinate behavior by resolving doubts and disagreements about how to act' (at 177).

This is evident in Shapiro's association between plans *qua* abstract propositional entities with norms, noting that the former are like the latter in the sense that they function 'as a guide for conduct and a standard for evaluation. In keeping with this characterization, plans too are norms. They are guides for conduct, insofar as their function is to pick out courses of action that are required, permitted, or authorized under certain circumstances'.[34]

What matters for the purposes of inducing citizens and legal officials alike to adhere to their role in the 'game of law' is the economy of motives. This requires a wise balance between internal and external motives, with an emphasis on enabling or encouraging citizens to be motivated to comply for reasons that are not merely prudential. As Shapiro notes: 'When members of the community consider legal authorities to be morally legitimate, encouraging compliant behaviour will be relatively straightforward. By designating a standard as *the* standard to be used to guide and evaluate conduct, their subjects will take themselves to have reasons to defer and, in the normal course, will obey.'[35]

In the hope that I have managed to delineate the limited scope of Shapiro's claim about the normativity of law, it is reasonable to ask how this theoretical claim can be juxtaposed with more robust claims. Again, the issue at stake has to do with the intelligibility of jurisprudential disputes between theories of legal normativity whose metanormative premises are radically different. In what follows, I will briefly pause the progress of my argument in order to measure the highest degree of affinity of Shapiro's theory with opposing theories of legal normativity. In a further step, I will try to show how Shapiro's Moral Aim Thesis can figure intelligibly in disputes about what grounds normative facts about the normative relevance of legal facts. As already noted, the idea I intend to put on the table is that the best terms in which a plan positivist like Shapiro can participate in this kind of dispute are metanormative rather than directly political.

Before coming up with a proposal, I would like to explain why, in a sense, Shapiro's account is closer to the *Nexus* theories of Raz and Greenberg than to Dworkin's theory of reasons of integrity. What both Shapiro's appeal to the inner rationality of law and the two *Nexus* accounts share is their understanding

[34] ibid 127. Expanding on this metaphysical statement, Shapiro explains that: 'While all plans are norms, not all norms are plans. The laws of logic and the principles of morality, for example, are norms but they are not usually considered plans. Plans are "positive" entities – they are created via adoption and sustained through *acceptance*. By contrast, logical and moral norms exist simply by virtue of their ultimate validity. They are not created by anyone. Plans are also typically partial norms that are supposed to be fleshed out over time, whereas it makes no sense to talk about incrementally developing the laws of logic or morality. Plans are also purposive entities. They are norms that are not only created, but are created *to be norms*' (at 128).

[35] ibid 180. In one sense, Shapiro seems to side with Mark Greenberg's position that the legally proper way of changing the moral situation is by providing citizens with reasons that are not merely prudential ones. However, despite appearances, this resemblance is only superficial in the sense that for Shapiro, the desirability of enabling citizens to be motivated by the law is a function of a legal system's efficacy, whereas for Greenberg, the same value is a function of a legal system's attaining its essential property of achieving bindingness.

of the normative impact of law as depictive. It should be recalled that normative impact is one of the two dimensions of normative relevance discussed in Chapter 5. To say that a fact's normative impact is depictive and not constitutive is to say that what matters for an agent's evaluation is whether she actually (instead of counterfactually) treats the relevant fact as reason-giving or, equivalently, the fact that serves as an explanation of one's actual conduct is also the fact serves a standard of evaluation. In the relevant position, I explained why both Raz and Greenberg would most probably favour this approach. The idea was that in both accounts, legal facts are viewed as indispensable items of one's practical deliberation about what to do. By indispensable, I mean that their capacity to serve as standards for evaluating instances of law-conforming or law-breaking behaviour is tied to whether they also figure in what explains one's actual conduct.

It is precisely in this respect that Shapiro's non-response-directing (ie, response-constraining) account and the two *Nexus* variants display their kinship. The depictive impact of carrying out plans is strongly evident in Shapiro's remarks about the function of plans as standards of evaluation:

> Regardless of who applies the plan, rationality requires that the plan adopter make sure that *someone* does. To adopt a plan and not use it, or use it incorrectly, is *irrational*. In other words, a planner is subject to criticism when she forgets that she adopted a certain plan, cannot figure out the content of the plan, does not bother to find out what the world is like, fails to use her beliefs to determine the application of the plan, uses these beliefs incorrectly, or simply does not carry out the plan that she believes applies. (Emphasis added)[36]

What Shapiro most probably means about the correct use of plans is what philosophers who want to affirm the normativity of wide-scope requirements of rationality refer to as the correct way of obviating the normative asymmetry between different ways of satisfying a wide-scope requirement.

To illustrate this case, we may take as an example the case of enkratic requirements. A typical instance of an enkratic requirement is the requirement to intend to act on one's normative beliefs. In more formal language, this is usually described in conditional terms, as in the following statement: one is rationally required to [intend to φ if she believes that she ought to φ]. Given the wide-scope character of this requirement, there are two ways in which someone may respond to it. One way is to acquire the intention to φ and an alternative way is to revise one's belief that she ought to φ. As we have already seen in previous examples, these two ways are not normatively equivalent. For instance, it may well be the case that there is overwhelming evidence that one's normative belief is correct. In that case, it would be normatively suboptimal to quit one's belief instead of acquiring the relevant intention. This kind of behaviour would amount to an empty exercise in rationalisation. On the other hand, it might

[36] ibid 127.

be the case that the content of one's normative belief is morally odious. In this case, it would be normatively infelicitous to intend to act on this belief instead of revising it in the light of reasons that demonstrate the wrongness of one's purported action.

The first step in solving this asymmetry problem is to take on board the idea that the fact that can *normatively explain* one's actual response *need not be identical with* the fact that serves to *constrain* one's behaviour. This is precisely the divergence we noticed earlier with regard to the way in which attitudinal facts display their normative salience. In this regard, whereas the fact that serves to constrain one's rational response is the fact that one believes that she ought to φ, the fact that serves to explain whether one's actual response is felicitous is a fact about the *overall reasons* that, depending on the context, either favour one's choosing to acquire an intention to φ or recommend the revision of one's normative belief. John Broome, for instance, refers to supplementary reasons[37] that count against failing to intend to φ as *basing prohibitions* and describes this kind of basing as *inferential*. As he notes:

> Rationality requires of you that you do *not* not believe you ought to *F* on the basis of your not intending to *F* ... This requirement is separate from Enkrasia; it rules out one particular way of satisfying Enkrasia. It is an example of a 'basing prohibition of rationality' ... Besides rational requirements such as Enkrasia, which are synchronic and require particular combinations of attitudes to obtain or not obtain at any time, there are also rational requirements that require some particular attitude, or lack of an attitude, not to be based on other particular attitudes or lacks. They are asymmetric, and they explain the asymmetry we have been exploring. (Emphasis added)[38]

Consequently, Broome proceeds to distinguish between the *inferential* role of reasons against satisfying the enkratic requirement by way of dropping one's normative belief from the *evidential* reasons that count against satisfying the enkratic requirement by acquiring an intention to act on one's normative belief. Whereas the former reasons are, so to speak, attitude-dependent, the latter are attitude-independent, in the sense that the moral wrongness of an action is a fact that holds independently of our beliefs. In a slightly different sense, Jonathan Way calls facts of both types (inferential and evidential) 'basing principles', noting that that are necessary supplements to the constraining function of wide-scope requirements. In his words:

> [T]he Wide-Scope view allows that rationality may involve more than mere compliance with a set of Wide-Scope requirements along the lines of those above. I will

[37] To be more precise, Broome avoids equating these asymmetric, response-guiding basing requirements with reasons, but this is more a result of his idiosyncratic treatment of 'oughts' as more basic than 'reasons'. Nothing of crucial importance depends on whether we adhere to Broome's terminology or not.

[38] Broome (2013: 132). Broome complements this claim with the remark that '[a] basing prohibition does not prohibit attitudes themselves. Without any irrationality, you might not believe you ought to F and at the same time not intend to F. Rationality prohibits you only from having the first of these attitudes on the basis of the second' (at 170).

> suggest that compliance with such requirements is at most a part of what it is to be rational. Being rational also involves forming, holding and revising attitudes for appropriate reasons. So Wide-Scope requirements must be supplemented with principles giving conditions under which attitudes are appropriately formed, held and revised. I will call such principles basing principles.[39]

Way's argument about the complementary role of basing principles brings us closer to my initial remark about the way in which facts about these basing principles or, as I would prefer to put it, facts about overall reasons figure in the *evaluation* of our actual responses to wide-scope requirements. As previously noted, the idea is that the nature of the normativity of wide-scope requirements makes them amenable to supplementation by 'narrow-scope' principles or reasons. In the present case, provided that facts about our normative beliefs cannot also normatively explain or rationalise our actual behaviour, it remains an open question how agents are supposed to be evaluatively reflected in their actual responses. The idea is that in the case of rationality, we get the following pattern: on the one hand, there is a 'benign', so to speak, *divergence* between the facts that constrain our attitudes and the facts that explain our particular way of satisfying this constraint and, on the other hand, there is a *convergence* between the facts that explain our actual responses as normatively felicitous and the facts that must be *actually* treated as reasons for a particular response in order for us to qualify as rational![40] In that sense, basing is a notion that purports to codify the way in which one's actual behaviour is subject to rational evaluation. If one's actual way of responding to a wide-scope requirement is properly based, it follows that she can be evaluated as rational precisely because she *actually treated a basing principle as a reason for responding in the way she did*.

Returning to our main case, we are in a better position to understand the affinity of Shapiro's account with the *depictive impact* of *Nexus* legal reasons. Whereas Shapiro's planning account of legal normativity is response-constraining rather than response-directing in the sense that *Nexus* theories are, both types of theory condition the evaluation of legal actors on their actual treatment of reasons in the ordinary sense. In other words, both theories treat as problematic any divergence between the facts that serve as standards for evaluating the rationality of planning agents and the facts that figure in the explanation of their actions. This is clearly evidenced by Shapiro's comment that 'an official who accepts her position within an authority structure will be rationally

[39] Way (2011: 230).

[40] Jonathan Way describes the same point in a slightly elliptical fashion when he remarks that 'there is a connection between rationality and the reasons *for which agents hold attitudes*. These reasons are simply the type of thing that can figure in a certain type of explanation: "Lindsay intends to leave because the game is starting", "Daniel believes he will pass because he believes he has a copy of the test", and so on. It is hard to see how it could be denied that reasons, in this sense, are relevant to rationality' (ibid, emphasis added).

criticizable if she disobeys her superiors, fails to flesh out their orders so that she may take the means necessary to satisfy their demands, adopts plans that are inconsistent with these orders, or reconsiders them *without a compelling reason to do so*' (emphasis added).[41]

It is for precisely these compelling reasons that a rational planner must actually treat as bearing upon her decision to satisfy a wide-scope planning requirement in one way or another if she is to count as rational.[42] What is crucially important is that these compelling reasons are not part of the body of wide-scope requirements that compose the content of a legal system! They are extra-legal considerations whose normative force is not inherited by planning requirements of the sort that Shapiro describes with respect to the authorisation to plan for others and the rational implementation of these plans. Nevertheless, they reserve a supplementary role in exactly the sense that Way and perhaps also Broome develop their respective notions of basing.[43]

In the remainder of this chapter, I will try to capitalise on my last remark that basing reasons are not constitutive of the normativity of wide-scope requirements in order to explore the way in which a wide-scope account like Shapiro's can figure in disagreements about the grounds of legal normativity. A natural explanation of my last remark that basing reasons are not part of an account of wide-scope normativity is that these basing reasons are not part of the *grounds* of normative facts about the obtaining of wide-scope requirements. This is precisely the sense in which defenders of the wide-scope approach try to extricate the normativity of rational requirements of coherence and consistency from the normativity of practical reasons.

It may be recalled that a type of argument I presented earlier with regard to the grounding of wide-scope requirements is constitutive. For instance, Michael Bratman has explored the possibility of grounding the normativity of wide-scope requirements of rationality in the fact that their obtaining is constitutive of the normative possibility of an intrinsically valuable type of agency, which in the relevant case is, according to Bratman, self-governance. In Bratman's

[41] Shapiro (2011: 183).

[42] Shapiro confirms the relevance of these normative reasons as basing principles that ultimately determine the proper way of satisfying a planning requirement when he claims that 'when judges disagree with one another about the relevance of some moral fact to the interpretation of a legal text, they cannot be disagreeing about the grounds of law. To understand the nature of these disagreements on the Planning Theory, we must recall an important feature of plans … When I plan to go to the movies to night, I am not planning to go *come what may*. I realize that there are compelling reasons that might arise that would force me to reconsider my decision, for example, I suddenly get sick, the movie theater increases the price of admission tenfold, my house catches fire, and so on. "Unless compelling reasons arise", therefore, is an implicit codicil that typically attaches to our plans and conditions their applicability' (ibid 303). It is worth emphasising that these compelling reasons are relevant for the normative guidance of plans, not for their existence or content.

[43] Way is explicit about his distinction between the normativity of wide-scope requirements and the normativity of basing principles, noting that: 'Wide-Scope requirements are not directly concerned with basing, and so need to be supplemented with independent basing principles. But then we can expect those principles to explain this type of asymmetry' (Way 2011: 231).

account, reasons of self-governance are directly grounded in the intrinsic value of this type of agency rather than in further reasons. This argumentative strategy enables Bratman to protect himself against the objection that the value of self-governance is transparent to the value of being responsive to reasons in general. That said, I do not intend to delve into this controversy, mainly because its settlement could only provide analogical support to Shapiro's view. However, what is important to note about this controversy is that *if* someone chooses to defend a wide-scope account of normativity, it is advisable that she fortifies her theory against the transparency objection just described.

Returning to Shapiro, there are grounds to believe both that he would choose to defend a wide-scope account of legal normativity and endorse a constitutive argument against the transparency objection. For the first belief, I believe that I have already adduced sufficient evidence in its support. For the second belief, I shall argue that Shapiro provides a preliminary account of this sort in his defence of the Moral Aim Thesis. First, he seems to be aware of the transparency objection in the technical sense that I have deployed here when he addresses an objection of triviality. More precisely, he refers to the worry a positivist could express with regard to the impossibility of attributing a moral aim to law that is simultaneously universal and non-trivial. As he describes it, some might argue that 'if we impute an end that is plausibly universal, such as coordinating social activity or guiding conduct, we end up with an empty truism. Of course, the law does those things, but so do games, religion, etiquette, and so on'.[44] This worry can be easily re-described as being about the transparency of legal requirements to the requirements emanating from the activity of other systems of value. In response to this worry, Shapiro's defence is characteristically constitutive:

> The Moral Aim Thesis, however, posits an end that is neither parochial nor empty. It is not parochial because it does not claim that the law is supposed to pursue any substantive end. It is agnostic, in other words, about which particular moral problems and opportunities the law should address. The law, we said, is a universal means, adapted to solve any kind of moral problem. But the aim the Planning Theory attributes to the law is not empty either, for it specifies one that most things do not pursue, namely, the rectification of the moral defects associated with the circumstances of legality. Any normative system coordinates social activity and guides action. But only a legal system is supposed to address those problems that less sophisticated methods of coordinating social activity and guiding action are unable to resolve.[45]

Without coming across as transgressing the limits of a charitable understanding, we could reparse this claim as the claim that the requirement to plans for others and the requirements to act consistently in one's implementation of a

[44] Shapiro (2011: 214).
[45] ibid.

legal system's master plan are important because they are constitutive of the normative possibility of an intrinsically valuable type of social coordination, namely the one that serves to rectify the moral deficiencies associated with the circumstances of legality. This reparsing can serve as a defence against the transparency objection in the sense that it shows that there is distinct moral value in the fact that a system *represents* itself as serving a moral purpose *irrespective of whether and how* it chooses to produce morally good outcomes.[46] As thin as it may be, this is an interpretation of Shapiro's invocation of the Moral Aim Thesis that is minimal enough to prevent his positivist project from becoming vulnerable to the objection that it flirts with collapsing into a covert natural law project. At the same time, of course, it is an interpretation that Shapiro himself makes evidentially salient when he remarks that:

> The kingdom is a kingdom because the king and his court represent it as having a moral mission. Members of the criminal syndicates we have been considering, by contrast, do not portray their threats as creating obligations and right for their victims. They drop the conceit that they are trying to solve the problems associated with the circumstances of legality – in fact, they realize that they *are* the problems of the circumstances of legality. It is that recognition, and their lack of shame about it, that make them mere criminals and not legal officials.[47]

[46] In a critical note on *Legality*, Arthur Ripstein expresses his doubts about the possibility of talking about the moral aim of law whilst associating its existence with the representations of legal officials. His suggestion is 'to resist the idea that law is an all-purpose tool for pursuing whatever planners *think of as* a moral aim in favor of the idea that it is the institutional solution to the problem of authority' (Ripstein 2012: 208). Furthermore, Ripstein believes that his identification of law as a solution to a moral problem about authority 'makes room for the possibility that questions about authority will be answered in morally odious ways, and that morally odious purposes will be pursued by putting people in charge of things and of other people. That is because it is possible to solve this moral problem-to genuinely solve it-in immoral ways. But it is it not merely planning to pursue what someone thinks is a moral aim that does the work here. For one thing, what the planner happens to think is not fundamental. Further, pursuing moral aims through planning does not make for a legal system unless officials are involved in the right way' (at 209). First off, I find it difficult to see how a moral problem can be genuinely solved in an immoral way, unless we further unpack this claim into the proposition that the moral problem about authority exhibits a wide-scope structure similar to that of the requirement of rationality such that there will be ways of genuinely satisfying this requirement in ways that are normatively suboptimal. Still I find it difficult to understand how Ripstein could regiment his point about authority in wide-scope terms. But, most importantly, I would dare to note that Ripstein seems to beg the question in a metaphysical sense. More precisely, he not only claims that what unifies the multitude of moral problems that Shapiro associates with the circumstances of legality is a problem about relations of authority between persons, but he also supposes that the solution to this moral problem about authority is another type of authority, namely legal authority understood as the official power to constitute roles and positions of interpersonal authority. The problem with this argument is not its content as such, which is perfectly defensible, but its force against Shapiro's claim that legal authority is just the authority of norms of instrumental rationality, which by its nature can be manifested only insofar as legal officials *represent* their plans as moral solutions. The former claim is a claim about the authority to constitute authority, whereas the latter claim is a claim about the authority to plan for others. From this perspective, adjudicating their opposition can be premised either on authority-independent reasons or on challenging an unpronounced premise that both views share.

[47] Shapiro (2011: 217).

The final step in this quest for a common ground of disagreement must feature Shapiro's planning account of normativity in some sort of adversarial encounter, with views hailing from different metanormative quadrants. To this effect, we may again raise the hypothetical exchange between Gonzo, the Razian positivist, and Froddo, the Greenbergian antipositivist. The reason for the recurring appearance of this example is that it presents an instance of intelligible first-order disagreement about the grounds of the reasons for action provided by the law. Against this background, it becomes more interesting to see how this episode of disagreement can be affected by the participation of an interlocutor who rejects from the very beginning the possibility that law itself is a source of reasons for action. This is precisely the case of a hypothetical interlocutor who happens to be a plan positivist. To refresh our recollection of this exchange, I shall repeat it for one last time:

(a) Gonzo: the fact that L is a reason for A to φ in C is grounded in the fact that A is more likely to conform to reasons that apply to her independently of the actions that brought about L by φ-ing in C.
(b) Froddo: the fact that L is a reason to φ in C is grounded in the fact that the actions that brought about L changed the morally relevant circumstances in a way that makes φ-ing in C the right thing to do.

How could a plan positivist interject in this dispute? She certainly cannot flatly proceed to offer her own grounds associated with the value of representing a system's master plan as morally legitimate precisely because these grounds cannot be offered as explanations of legal reason-giving! For a plan positivist, the only relevant normative facts that call for grounding are facts about one's authorisation to plan for others, as well as facts about implementing the master plan in a consistent way. As a result, the only plausible route available to a plan positivist directs her to a higher level of abstraction. What our hypothetical interjector could say in reaction to this exchange is that they pack too much content into the concept of legal normativity in the sense that they try to account for law's action-directing function in normative terms, whereas this task can be fully accounted for in dispositional terms. In other words, a plan positivist could object that the only strictly normative question about law that calls for grounding is about the constraints it imposes on the attitudes of legal planners and not about the all-things-considered justification of their way of satisfying these constraints. The latter task, the plan positivist would retort, is about the *efficacy* of law, not about the normativity of law.

According to this picture, the participation of the plan positivist in the dispute between a *Nexus* positivist and a *Nexus* antipositivist turns the latter first-order dispute into a second-order dispute. The object of disagreement is not directly about what grounds reason-giving facts about law, but rather about the type of normative facts about law that should be considered as amenable to grounding. Whereas both Gonzo and Froddo believe that the normativity of law is about the normative capacity of legal activity to guide people's actions, the plan positivist believes that the normativity of law is about the normative capacity of our representation of plans as morally legitimate to authorise and constrain a range of planning activities.[48]

[48] A similar type of objection on the part of a plan positivist could also be levelled against Dworkin's metanormative view. For instance, Shapiro could press against Dworkin's reasons-based model of state coercion by arguing that precisely because coercive enforcement is an aspect of the action-guiding function of law, it is not part of the normative aspect of legal activity, but rather is a part of its dispositive aspect. The main metanormative objection remains the same, namely that legal normativity should be distinguished from law's efficacy.

Bibliography

Abizadeh, A (2007) 'Cooperation, Pervasive Impact, and Coercion: On the Scope (Not Site) of Distributive Justice', *Philosophy & Public Affairs* 35: 318–58.

Assay, J (2014) 'Against Truth', *Erkenntnis* 79: 147–64.

Atria, F (2002) *On Law and Legal Reasoning* (Oxford: Hart Publishing).

Ayer, AJ (1946) *Language, Truth and Logic*, 2nd edn (London: Gollancz).

Baker, LR (2000) *Persons and Bodies: A Constitution View* (New York: Cambridge University Press).

Barker, S and Jago, M (2014) 'Monism and Material Constitution', *Pacific Philosophical Quarterly* 95: 189–204.

Bennett, K (2004) 'Spatio-temporal Coincidence and the Grounding Problem', *Philosophical Studies* 118: 339–71.

——. (2009) 'Composition, Colocation, and Metaontology' in D Chalmers, D Manley and R Wasserman (eds), *Metametaphysics: New Essays on the Foundations of Ontology* (Oxford University Press) 38–76.

——. (2011) 'Construction Area (No Hard Hat Required)', *Philosophical Studies* 154: 79–104.

Bennett, M (2011) 'Hart and Raz on the Non-instrumental Moral Value of the Rule of Law: A Reconsideration', *Law and Philosophy* 30: 603–35.

Bergmann, M and Brower, J (2006) 'A Theistic Argument against Platonism (and in Support of Truthmakers and Divine Simplicity)' in D Zimmerman (ed), *Oxford Studies in Metaphysics*, vol 2 (Oxford: Oxford University Press) 357–86.

Bertea, S (2009) *The Normative Claim of Law* (Oxford: Hart Publishing).

——. (2011) 'Law and Obligation: Outlines of a Kantian Argument' in S Bertea and G Pavlakos (eds), *New Essays on the Normativity of Law* (Oxford: Hart Publishing) 199–218.

Blackburn, S (1992) 'Through Thick and Thin', *Proceedings of the Aristotelian Society, Supplementary Volume* 66: 285–99.

Bratman, M (2009) 'Intention, Practical Rationality, and Self-Governance', *Ethics* 119: 411–43.

——. (2011) 'Reflections on Law, Normativity and Plans' in S Bertea and G Pavlakos (eds), *New Essays on the Normativity of Law* (Oxford: Hart Publishing) 73–85.

Broome, J (1999) 'Normative Requirements', *Ratio* 12: 398–419.

——. (2010) 'Rationality' in T O'Connor and C Sandis (eds), *A Companion to the Philosophy of Action* (Oxford: Wiley-Blackwell) 283–92.

——. (2013) *Rationality through Reasoning* (Oxford: Blackwell).

Brunero, J (2010) 'The Scope of Rational Requirements', *Philosophical Quarterly* 60: 28–49.

Burke, M (1994) 'Preserving the Principle of One Object to a Place: A Novel Account of the Relations among Objects, Sorts, Sortals, and Persistence Conditions', *Philosophy and Phenomenological Research* 54: 591–624.

Cameron, R (2008) 'Truthmakers and Modality', *Synthese* 164: 261–80.

——. (2010) 'Quantification, Naturalness and Ontology' in A Hazlett (ed), *New Waves in Metaphysics* (New York: Palgrave Macmillan) 8–26.

Campbell, T (1996) *The Legal Theory of Ethical Positivism* (Aldershot: Ashgate/Dartmouth).

——. (2004) *Prescriptive Legal Positivism: Law, Rights and Democracy* (London: UCL Press).

Carston, R (1996) 'Metalinguistic Negation and Echoic Use', *Journal of Pragmatics* 25: 309–30.

Chilovi, S and Pavlakos, G (2019) 'Law-Determination as Grounding: A Common Grounding Framework for Jurisprudence', *Legal Theory* 25: 53–76.

Chrisman, M (2012) 'The Meaning of "Ought"' in R Shafer-Landau (ed), *Oxford Studies in Metaethics*, vol 7 (Oxford: Oxford University Press) 304–32.

Coleman, J (1982) 'Negative and Positive Positivism', *Journal of Legal Studies* 11: 139–64.
——. (2007) 'Beyond the Separability Thesis: Moral Semantics and the Methodology of Jurisprudence', *Oxford Journal of Legal Studies* 27: 581–608.
Coleman, J and Simchen, O (2003) 'Law', *Legal Theory* 9: 1–41.
D'Almeida, L (2011) 'Legal Statements and Normative Language', *Law and Philosophy* 30: 167–99.
Dancy, J (1996) 'In Defense of Thick Concepts' in P French, T Uehling and H Wettstein (eds), *Midwest Studies in Philosophy XX: Moral Concepts* (Notre Dame: University of Notre Dame Press) 263–79.
——. (2000) *Practical Reality* (Oxford: Oxford University Press).
——. (2004) *Ethics without Principles* (Oxford: Oxford University Press).
Darwall, S (2010) 'Authority and Reasons: Exclusionary and Second-Personal', *Ethics* 120: 257–78.
Dasgupta, S (2016) 'Metaphysical Rationalism', *Noûs* 50: 379–418.
David, M (2009) 'Truth-Making and Correspondence' in EJ Lowe and A Rami (ed), *Truth and Truth-Making* (Stocksfield: Acumen) 137–57.
Delacroix, S (2009) 'You'd Better Be Committed: Legal Norms and Normativity', *American Journal of Jurisprudence* 54: 117–32.
DeRosset, L (2013) 'Grounding Explanations', *Philosophers' Imprint* 13: 1–26.
Dickson, J (2001) *Evaluation and Legal Theory* (Oxford: Hart Publishing)
——. (2004) 'Methodology in Jurisprudence: A Critical Survey', *Legal Theory* 10: 117–56.
Dworkin, R (1975) 'Hard Cases', *Harvard Law Review* 88: 1057–109.
——. (1986) *Law's Empire* (Cambridge, MA: Belknap Press).
——. (1996) 'Objectivity and Truth: You'd Better Believe it', *Philosophy & Public Affairs* 25: 87–139.
——. (1997) 'In Praise of Theory', *Arizona State Law Journal* 29: 353–76.
——. (2006) *Justice in Robes* (Cambridge, MA: Belknap Press).
——. (2011) *Justice for Hedgehogs* (Cambridge, MA: Harvard University Press).
Dyke, H (2008) *Metaphysics and the Representational Fallacy* (New York: Routledge).
Dyzenhaus, D (2000) 'Positivism's Stagnant Research Program', *Oxford Journal of Legal Studies* 20(4): 703–22.
Edmundson, W (2006) 'The Virtue of Law-Abidance', *Philosophers' Imprint* 6: 1–21.
Ehrenberg, K (2008) 'Archimedean Metaethics Defended', *Metaphilosophy* 39: 508–29.
——. (2013) 'Law's Authority is Not a Claim to Preemption' in W Waluchow and S Sciaraffa (eds), *Philosophical Foundations of the Nature of Law* (Oxford: Oxford University Press) 51–74.
Eklund, M (2006) 'Neo-Fregean Ontology', *Philosophical Perspectives* 20: 95–121.
Elstein, D and Hurka, T (2009) 'From Thick to Thin: Two Moral Reduction Plans', *Canadian Journal of Philosophy* 39: 515–36.
Essert, C (2012) 'A Dilemma for Protected Reasons', *Law and Philosophy* 31: 49–75.
——. (2013) 'Legal Obligation and Reasons', *Legal Theory* 19: 63–88.
Evnine, S (2009) 'Constitution and Qua Objects in the Ontology of Music', *British Journal of Aesthetics* 49: 203–17.
Fine, K (1982a) 'Acts, Events and Things' in W Leinfellner, E Kraemer and J Schank (eds), *Sprache und Ontologie: Akten des Sechsten Internationalen Wittgenstein-Symposiums* (Vienna: Hoelder-Pichler-Tempsky) 97–105.
——. (1982b) 'The Problem of Non-existents', *Topoi* 1: 97–140.
Finlay, S (2014) *Confusion of Tongues: A Theory of Normative Language* (Oxford: Oxford University Press).
Finlay, S and Schroeder, M. (2012) 'Reasons for Action: Internal vs External' in E Zalta (ed), *The Stanford Encyclopedia of Philosophy*, https://plato.stanford.edu/archives/fall2017/entries/reasons-internal-external.
Finnis, J (2011) *Natural Law and Natural Rights*, 2nd edn (Oxford: Oxford University Press).
Fuller, L (1969) *The Morality of Law* (New Haven: Yale University Press).
Greenberg, M (2004) 'How Facts Make Law', *Legal Theory* 10: 157–98.

——. (2011) 'The Standard Picture and its Discontents' in L Green and B Leiter (eds), *Oxford Studies in Philosophy of Law*, vol 1 (New York: Oxford University Press) 39–106.
——. (2014) 'The Moral Impact Theory of Law', *Yale Law Journal* 123: 1288–342.
——. (2017) 'The Moral Impact Theory, The Dependence View, and Natural Law' in G Duke and R George (eds), *The Cambridge Companion to Natural Law Jurisprudence* (Cambridge: Cambridge University Press) 275–313.
Hale, B and Wright, C (2001) *The Reason's Proper Study: Essays towards a Neo-Fregean Philosophy of Mathematics* (Oxford: Oxford University Press).
——. (2009) 'The Metaontology of Abstraction' in D Chalmers, D Manley and R Wasserman (eds), *Metametaphysics: New Essays on the Foundations of Ontology* (Oxford: Clarendon Press) 178–212.
Hart, HLA (1958) 'Legal and Moral Obligation' in A Melden (ed), *Essays in Moral Philosophy* (Seattle: University of Washington Press) 82–107.
——. (1982) *Essays on Bentham* (Oxford: Oxford University Press).
Heidemann, C (1997) *Die Norm als Tatsache: Zur Normentheorie Hans Kelsens* (Baden-Baden: Nomos).
Heil, J (2007) 'Précis of From an Ontological Point of View' in G Romano (ed), *Symposium on: From an Ontological Point of View by John Heil in SWIF Philosophy of Mind Review* 6: 11–21.
Heuer, U (2004) 'Reasons and Actions and Desires', *Philosophical Studies* 121: 43–63.
——. (2006) 'Explaining Reasons: Where Does This Buck Stop?', *Journal of Ethics & Social Philosophy* 1: 1–25.
——. (2012) 'Guided by Reasons: Raz on the Normative-Explanatory Nexus', *Jurisprudence* 2: 353–65.
Hieronymi, P (2005) 'The Wrong Kind of Reason', *Journal of Philosophy* 102: 437–57.
——. (2011) 'Reasons for Action', *Proceedings of the Aristotelian Society* 111: 407–27.
Hirsch, E (2005) 'Physical-Object Ontology, Verbal Disputes, and Common Sense', *Philosophy and Phenomenological Research* 70: 67–97.
Holton, R (1998) 'Positivism and the Internal Point of View', *Law and Philosophy* 17: 597–625.
Julius, AJ (2013) 'The Possibility of Exchange', *Politics, Philosophy & Economics* 12: 361–74.
——. (2017) 'Independent People' in S Kisilevsky and M Stone (eds), *Freedom and Force: Essays on Kant's Legal Philosophy* (Oxford: Hart Publishing) 91–110.
Kaplan, D (1969) 'Quantifying in' in D Davidson and J Hintikka (eds), *Words and Objections* (Dordrecht: Don Reidel) 206–42.
Kelsen, H (1967) *Pure Theory of Law*, M Knight (trans) (Berkeley: University of California Press).
Kim, J (1998) *Mind in a Physical World* (Cambridge, MA: MIT Press).
Kölbel, M (2004) 'Faultless Disagreement', *Proceedings of the Aristotelian Society* 104: 53–73.
Kolodny, N (2005) 'Why Be Rational?', *Mind* 114: 509–63.
Korsgaard, C (2008) *The Constitution of Agency: Essays on Practical Reason and Moral Psychology* (Oxford: Oxford University Press).
Koslicki, K (2004) 'Constitution and Similarity', *Philosophical Studies* 117: 327–64.
Kratzer, A (1981) 'The Notional Category of Modality' in HJ Eikmeyer and H Riser (eds), *Words, Worlds, and Contexts* (Berlin: Walter de Gruyter) 38–74.
Kristan, A and Vignolo, M (2018) 'Assessment Sensitivity in Legal Discourse', *Inquiry* 61: 394–421.
Lange, M (2009) *Laws and Lawmakers: Science, Metaphysics, and the Laws of Nature* (Oxford: Oxford University Press).
Leiter, B (2007) *Naturalizing Jurisprudence: Essays on American Legal Realism and Naturalism in Legal Philosophy* (Oxford: Oxford University Press).
——. (2009) 'Explaining Theoretical Disagreement', *University of Chicago Law Review* 76: 1215–50.
——. (2019) 'Theoretical Disagreements in Law: Another Look' in D Plunkett, S Shapiro and K Toh (eds), *Dimensions of Normativity: New Essays on Metaethics and Jurisprudence* (Oxford: Oxford University Press) 249–62.
Levinson, J (1980) 'What a Musical Work is', *Journal of Philosophy* 77: 5–28.

Lewis, D (2001) 'Truthmaking and Difference-Making', *Noûs* 35: 602–15.

Liggins, D (2011) 'Truthmakers and Dependence' in F Correia and B Schnieder (eds), *Grounding and Explanation* (Cambridge: Cambridge University Press) 254–71.

Lord, E (2014) 'The Coherent and the Rational', *Analytic Philosophy* 55: 151–75.

Lowe, EJ (2009) *More Kinds of Being: A Further Study of Individuation, Identity and the Logic of Sortal Terms* (Oxford: Wiley-Blackwell).

MacCormick, N (1985) 'A Moralistic Case for A-moralistic Law?', *Valparaiso University Law Review* 20: 1–41.

——. (1994) *Legal Reasoning and Legal Theory*, 2nd edn (Oxford: Oxford University Press).

Mantel, S (2014) 'No Reason for Identity: On the Relation between Motivating and Normative Reasons', *Philosophical Explorations* 17: 49–62.

Marcus, E (2006) 'Events, Sortals, and the Mind-Body Problem', *Synthese* 150: 99–129.

Markwick, P (2000) 'Law and Content-Independent Reasons', *Oxford Journal of Legal Studies* 20: 579–96.

McClennen, E (2004) 'The Rationality of Being Guided by Rules' in A Mele and P Rawling (eds), *The Oxford Handbook of Rationality* (Oxford: Oxford University Press) 222–39.

McDowell, J (1979) 'Virtue and Reason', *The Monist* 62: 331–50.

——. (1981) 'Non-cognitivism and Rule-Following' in SH Holtzman and CM Leich (eds), *Wittgenstein: To Follow a Rule* (London: Routledge & Kegan Paul) 141–62.

McPherson, T (2012) 'Unifying Moral Methodology', *Pacific Philosophical Quarterly* 9: 523–549.

Mellor, DH (2009) 'Truthmakers for What?' in H Dyke (ed), *From Truth to Reality: New Essays in Logic and Metaphysics* (New York: Routledge) 272–303.

Moore, M (2000) *Educating Oneself in Public: Critical Essays in Jurisprudence* (Oxford: Oxford University Press).

——. (2012) 'The Various Relations between Law and Morality in Contemporary Legal Philosophy', *Ratio Juris* 25: 435–71.

Morauta, J (2004) 'Three Separation Theses', *Law and Philosophy* 23: 111–35.

Murphy, M (2003) 'Natural Law Jurisprudence', *Legal Theory* 9: 241–67.

——. (2013) 'The Explanatory Role of the Weak Natural Law Thesis' in W Waluchow and S Sciaraffa (eds), *Philosophical Foundations of the Nature of Law* (Oxford: Oxford University Press, 2013) 3–21.

Nagel, T (2005) 'The Problem of Global Justice', *Philosophy and Public Affairs* 33: 113–47.

Perry, S (2009) 'Beyond the Distinction between Positivism and Non-positivism', *Ratio Juris* 22: 311–25.

——. (2013) 'Political Authority and Political Obligation' in L Green and B Leiter (eds), *Oxford Studies in Philosophy of Law*, vol 2 (Oxford: Oxford University Press) 1–74.

Plunkett, D (2012) 'A Positivist Route for Explaining How Facts Make Law', *Legal Theory* 18: 139–207.

——. (2013) 'Legal Positivism and the Moral Aim Thesis', *Oxford Journal of Legal Studies* 33: 563–605.

Plunkett, D and Sundell, T (2013) 'Dworkin's Interpetivism and the Pragmatics of Legal Disputes', *Legal Theory* 19: 242–81.

Postema, G (1986) *Bentham and the Common Law Tradition* (Oxford: Oxford University Press).

——. (1987) '"Protestant" Interpretation and Social Practices', *Law and Philosophy* 6: 283–319.

Quine, WVO (1948) 'On What There is', *Review of Metaphysics* 2: 21–38.

——. (1976) *The Ways of Paradox and Other Essays* (Cambridge, MA: Harvard University Press).

Rabinowicz, W and Rønnow-Rasmussen, T (2004) 'The Strike of the Demon: On Fitting Pro-attitudes and Value', *Ethics* 114: 391–423.

Rawls, J (2001) *Justice as Fairness: A Restatement* (Cambridge, MA: Harvard University Press).

Raz, J (1971) 'The Identity of Legal Systems', *California Law Review* 59: 795–815.

——. (1980) *The Concept of a Legal System: An Introduction to the Theory of the Legal System*, 2nd edn (Oxford: Clarendon Press).

——. (1981) 'The Purity of the Pure Theory', *Revue Internationale de Philosophie* 35, 441–459.

——. (1984) 'Hart on Moral Rights and Legal Duties', *Oxford Journal of Legal Studies* 4: 123–31.
——. (1985) 'Authority and Justification', *Philosophy & Public Affairs* 14: 3–29.
——. (1986) *The Morality of Freedom* (Oxford: Oxford University Press).
——. (1989) 'Facing Up: A Reply', *Southern California Law Review* 62: 1153–235.
——. (1994) *Ethics in the Public Domain: Essays in the Morality of Law and Politics* (Oxford: Oxford University Press).
——. (1998) 'Two Views of the Nature of the Theory of Law: A Partial Comparison', *Legal Theory* 4: 249–82.
——. (1999a) 'Intention in Interpretation' in R George (ed), *The Autonomy of Law: Essays on Legal Positivism* (Oxford: Oxford University Press) 249–86.
——. (1999b) *Practical Reason and Norms* (Oxford: Oxford University Press).
——. (2006) 'The Problem of Authority: Revisiting the Service Conception', *Minnesota Law Review* 90: 1003–44.
——. (2010) 'On Respect, Authority, and Neutrality: A Response', *Ethics* 120: 279–301.
——. (2011) *From Normativity to Responsibility* (Oxford: Oxford University Press).
——. (2012) *The Authority of Law: Essays on Law and Morality* (Oxford: Oxford University Press).
Ripstein, A (2004) 'Authority and Coercion', *Philosophy and Public Affairs* 32: 2–35.
——. (2012) 'Self-Certification and the Moral Aims of the Law', *Canadian Journal of Law and Jurisprudence* 25: 201–17.
Rodriguez-Blanco, V (2012) 'Social and Justified Legal Normativity: Unlocking the Mystery of the Relationship', *Ratio Juris* 25: 409–33.
——. (2014) *Law and Authority under the Guise of the Good* (Oxford: Hart Publishing)
Rodriguez-Pereyra, G (2005) 'Why Truthmakers?' in H Beebee and J Dodd (eds), *Truthmakers: The Contemporary Debate* (Oxford: Clarendon Press) 17–31.
Roversi, C (2011) 'On Constitutive Normativity' in S Bertea and G Pavlakos (eds), *New Essays on the Normativity of Law* (Oxford: Hart Publishing) 283–309.
Scanlon, T (1998) *What We Owe to Each Other* (Cambridge, MA: Harvard University Press).
——. (2008) *Moral Dimensions: Permissibility, Meaning, Blame* (Cambridge, MA: Belknap Press).
Schaffer, J (2003) 'Is There a Fundamental Level?', *Noûs* 37: 498–517.
——. (2008) 'Truthmaker Commitments', *Philosophical Studies* 141: 7–19.
——. (2009) 'On What Grounds What' in D Chalmers, D Manley and R Wasserman (eds), *Metametaphysics* (Oxford: Oxford University Press) 347–83.
Schmid, H (2000) *English Abstract Nouns as Conceptual Shells: From Corpus to Cognition* (Berlin: De Gruyter).
Schroeder, M (2005) 'Normative Explanations', *Journal of Ethics & Social Philosophy* 1: 1–27.
——. (2008) 'Having Reasons', *Philosophical Studies* 139: 57–71.
——. (2009) 'Means-End Coherence, Stringency, and Subjective Reasons', *Philosophical Studies* 143: 223–48.
——. (2010) 'Value and The Right Kind of Reason' in R Shafer-Landau (ed), *Oxford Studies in Metaethics*, vol 5 (Oxford: Oxford University Press) 25–55.
——. (2011) 'Ought, Agents, and Actions', *Philosophical Review* 120: 1–41.
Schueler, GF (2003) *Reasons and Purposes: Human Rationality and the Teleological Explanation of Action* (New York: Oxford University Press).
Sciaraffa, S (2009) 'On Content-Independent Reasons: It's Not in the Name', *Law and Philosophy* 28: 233–60.
Shapiro, S (2002) 'Law, Plans, and Practical Reason', *Legal Theory* 8: 387–441.
——. (2007) 'The Hart-Dworkin Debate: A Short Guide for the Perplexed' in A Ripstein (ed), *Ronald Dworkin* (Cambridge: Cambridge University Press) 22–55.
——. (2011) *Legality* (Cambridge, MA: Harvard University Press).
Shoemaker, D (2011) 'Attributability, Answerability, and Accountability: Toward a Wider Theory of Moral Responsibility', *Ethics* 121: 602–32.
Sider, T (2011) *Writing the Book of the World* (Oxford: Oxford University Press).

Silk, A (2013) 'Truth Conditions and the Meanings of Ethical Terms' in R Shafer-Landau (ed), *Oxford Studies in Metaethics*, vol 8 (Oxford: Oxford University Press) 195–222.
Simmonds, NE (2007) *Law as a Moral Idea* (Oxford: Oxford University Press).
Smith, B and Simon, J (2007) 'Truthmaker Explanations' in J Monnoyer (ed), *Metaphysics and Truthmakers* (Heusenstamm: Ontos Verlag) 79–98.
Smith, D (2010) 'Theoretical Disagreement and the Semantic Sting', *Oxford Journal of Legal Studies* 30: 635–61.
Soames, S (2003) 'Understanding Deflationism', *Philosophical Perspectives* 17: 369–83.
Sperber, D and Wilson, D (1981) 'Irony and the Use-Mention Distinction' in P Cole (ed), *Radical Pragmatics* (New York: Academic Press) 295–318.
Star, D and Delmas, C (2011) 'Three Conceptions of Practical Authority', *Jurisprudence* 2: 143–60.
Stone, M (2010) 'Positivism as Opposed to What? Law and the Moral Idea of Right', *Cardozo Legal Studies Research Paper* No 290, available at: http://ssrn.com/abstract=1554500.
Stavropoulos, N (2008) 'Interpretivist Theories of Law' in E Zalta (ed), *The Stanford Encyclopedia of Philosophy*, https://plato.stanford.edu/archives/fall2017/entries/reasons-internal-external.
Tappolet, C (2004) 'Through Thick and Thin: Good and its Determinates', *Dialectica* 58: 207–21.
Thomson, J (2008) *Normativity* (Chicago: Open Court).
Toh, K (2005) 'Hart's Expressivism and His Benthamite Project', *Legal Theory* 11: 75–123.
——. (2011) 'Legal Judgments as Plural Acceptances of Norms' in L Green and B Leiter (eds), *Oxford Studies in the Philosophy of Law*, vol 1 (Oxford: Oxford University Press) 107–37.
Trogdon, K (2013) 'An Introduction to Grounding' in M Hoeltje, B Schnieder and A Steinberg (eds), *Varieties of Dependence: Ontological Dependence, Grounding, Supervenience, Response-Dependence* (Munich: Philosophia Verlag) 97–122.
Väyrynen, P (2006) 'Resisting the Buck-Passing Account of Value' in R Shafer-Landau (ed), *Oxford Studies in Metaethics*, vol 1 (Oxford: Oxford University Press) 295–324.
——. (2011) 'A Wrong Turn to Reasons?' in M Brady (ed), *New Waves in Metaethics* (Basingstoke: Palgrave Macmillan) 185–207.
——. (2012) 'Thick Concepts: Where's Evaluation?' in R Shafer-Landau (ed), *Oxford Studies in Metaethics*, vol 7 (Oxford: Oxford University Press) 235–70.
Villa, V (2016) 'Deep Interpretive Disagreements and Theory of Legal Interpretation' in A Capone and F Poggi (eds), *Pragmatics and Law: Philosophical Perspectives* (New York: Springer) 89–120.
Waldron, J (1996) 'Kant's Legal Positivism', *Harvard Law Review* 109: 1535–66.
——. (2011) 'Normative (or Ethical) Positivism' in J Coleman (ed), *Hart's Postscript: Essays on the Postscript to 'The Concept of Law'* (Oxford: Oxford University Press) 410–34.
Way, J (2010) 'Defending the Wide-Scope Approach to Instrumental Reason', *Philosophical Studies* 147: 213–33.
——. (2011) 'The Symmetry of Rational Requirements', *Philosophical Studies* 155: 227–39.
Wedgwood, R (2006) 'The Meaning of "Ought"' in R Shafer-Landau (ed), *Oxford Studies in Metaethics*, vol 1 (Oxford: Oxford University Press) 127–60.
Wiggins, D (1967) *Identity and Spatio-temporal Continuity* (Oxford: Blackwell).
——. (1980) *Sameness and Substance* (Oxford: Blackwell).
Williams, B (1981) *Moral Luck* (Oxford: Oxford University Press).
——. (1985) *Ethics and the Limits of Philosophy* (Cambridge, MA: Harvard University Press).

Index

www.ingramcontent.com/pod-product-compliance
Ingram Content Group UK Ltd.
Pitfield, Milton Keynes, MK11 3LW, UK
UKHW020812290926
15470UKWH00003B/1109

9 781509 936502